U2

the complete

SONGS

U2

the complete

SONGS

_____

WISE PUBLICATIONS
LONDON • NEW YORK • PARIS • SYDNEY • COPENHAGEN • MADRID • TOKYO

Exclusive Distributors:
Music Sales Limited
8/9 Frith Street,
London W1D 3JB, England.
Music Sales Pty Limited
120 Rothschild Avenue,
Rosebery, NSW 2018,
Australia.

Order No. AM959541
ISBN 0-7119-7469-1
This book © Copyright 1999 by Wise Publications

Music arranged by Derek Jones and Jack Long
Music engraved by Paul Ewers Music Design
Design by Averill Design Associates - Dublin
Cover photography by Anton Corbijn (middle front and back), Rankin (spine)
Hugo McGuinness (top front) and Stèphane Sednaoui (bottom front)

Compiled by:
Debbie Williams, Alistair Norbury, Aislinn Meehan, James Sleigh,
Pete Evans, Jon Bunker, Candida Bottaci and Sharon Callaly.

Photographs used by kind permission:
Anton Corbijn, Kevin Davies, Colm Henry, James Mahon,
Hugo McGuinness/Amy Garvey, Rankin and Stephane Sednaoui.

Special thanks to:
U2, Principle Management and Bill Flanagan

contents

U2 have been so praised in the last twenty years, they have been the objects of so much acclaim and affection, that it might seem strange to suggest that they have not been given enough credit. But for all the honours directed toward them, U2's place as great songwriters has often been overshadowed by their bigger-than-life image as performers, as record-makers, as a world class rock band.

It's easy to understand why - all those other areas make a big bang. But U2's songwriting is the spine on which all the rest of their accomplishments are hung. Even their most ambitious record productions wouldn't mean much if the songs did not touch people's hearts. The spectacle of Zoo TV and Pop Mart would have been just a trip to the electronic circus if the words and music being projected were only part of the fireworks.

U2's concerts are celebrations, but they are celebrations that begin in intimacy. It is when you listen alone to *One* or *Running To Stand Still* or *Wake Up Dead Man* that the music gets under your skin and into your blood. You're lying on your bed in the dark, or you're driving a long distance, or you're on the street, isolated in your Walkman when the music really hits you, when the song finds the words you've felt but been unable to speak. The real soul connection is made one-to-one.

At its best, you feel that you've found in the music a voice like your own. It is not a voice you share with your family, your friends, the people you work with. It feels closer than that, and at the same time like it's coming from some place you've never seen. It feels like a secret. Sometimes you feel like you're the only one who really hears that song, like it was written just for you.

Then you go to a concert and - what a wonder -there are thousands of other people who are in on the secret. Thousands of other people have had the same private experience and feel the same way you do. That's why U2 concerts are so celebratory; it's the sound of twenty thousand people realizing at the same time that they are not alone. Bono has talked about that contradiction - he calls it putting private thoughts on a public address system. It's the most powerful, and probably the most valuable, thing a songwriter can do. It is the creation of a community.

U2 are a band in the true sense - four equals who grew up together and share their losses as well as their victories. They share writing credit on almost all their songs. That's fair enough - their songs would sound drastically different if any one of them were not there. Their early songs were written mostly out of jams - Bono, Edge, Adam, and Larry would get in a room and play until something good emerged. When they recognized a strong idea for a song they would follow it until its shape was revealed.

Those first songs, including *Stories For Boys*, *Out Of Control*, and *11 O'Clock Tick Tock* introduced U2 to the world. When *I Will Follow* began getting college radio play in the States, Edge said, "One good song will do more for your band than two years of gigs." With success the four musicians had the luxury of not living on top of each other, and they began to sometimes write separately or in teams. But even then, the songs were always brought back to the band to play with and shape (or leave alone if that was best for the song) and the credit was shared between the four of them.

It is fair to say that Bono writes most of U2's lyrics, but he does not write them all. Edge has come up with more of U2's signature riffs than any of the other three, but the other three have all written plenty. I've watched U2 compose and record. What surprised me was how they switched roles depending on who was feeling inspired. Listening to a playback, Larry came up with an idea for a new melody and sang it to Bono, who tried it on the track. When Edge left for the night, Edge took over writing lyrics. When Larry left the room, Edge sat down behind the drums and put down a beat for a demo. Adam picked up Edge's guitar and suggested some chords. The four members of U2 have been a band since they were schoolboys; they taught each other to write and play. It is almost impossible for an outsider to tell where one leaves off and the next begins. The songs truly come from all four of them.

What impressed me in watching how U2 write was their willingness to change direction in a moment and follow the music wherever it led them. They could be working on a song for days and have it just about done, when suddenly Adam would try a different bass lick, Larry would switch his drum beat around to go with it, Bono would get an idea for a new lyric and - fast

as that - they were gone, the almost finished song abandoned while U2 chased down a new one. I have never seen songwriters less worried about nailing a song down and being done with it. They seemed to delight in the creation itself, and not worry much about running out of ideas.

Bruce Springsteen once said that the first time he heard U2 playing in a club, he knew they'd fill arenas, because the songs were so big. Those early songs - *I Will Follow, Gloria* - were very personal but they were personal with their arms wide open. They were the sound of four young men crying out to be heard, to connect, to break through whatever limits they found around them. As their skill grew, the songs continued to reach out - *New Year's Day, Sunday Bloody Sunday* and *Pride* had big themes, big declarations, big ideas. But here is what sometimes gets missed; the more U2 reached out, the more they reached in. They went deep inside themselves to pull out of themselves ideas and emotions that all kinds of people would recognize.

In the mid-80s U2's friend, the musician T-Bone Burnett, asked if I had heard their latest songs. He said there was one called *I Still Haven't Found What I'm Looking For* which was like an Elvis Presley song. For T-Bone there could be no higher praise. He meant that U2 had written something so pure and honest and direct that people of all ages, from different backgrounds, would connect with it. (Get this: *I Still Haven't Found What I'm Looking For* began as a reggae song. But the band kept experimenting, letting the music play itself until it turned into what it was supposed to be.)

T-Bone pointed out that U2 shared with the Beatles a talent for making songs out of big, direct ideas - *Help, I Want To Hold Your Hand, Get Back, Don't Let Me Down* or *Rejoice, I Will Follow, Surrender, All I Want Is You*.

In the 1990s U2 re-invented their sound and image with *Achtung Baby*. But in fact, the new songs were a continuation of the themes that always drove the band - faith, loyalty, and betrayal between husbands and wives, parents and children, God and man. (When you feel like you completely know one of U2's love songs, sing it again with the thought that it may be about God. When you get used to one of their religious or political lyrics, give it a new spin by singing it as if it's about a lover. Odds are it will work just as well.)

The use of new technology in the recording studio can in the wrong hands disguise a lack of substance, but it inspired U2 to dig deeper in their writing. The glitz and flash and funny title with which *Achtung Baby* was presented to the world was to some degree a disguise for the band's deepest, most personal songs ever. From that point forward, U2's most revealing, even confessional statements often came wrapped in the most distracting sonic packages. Pick up your instrument, lay out this music, and sing *The Wanderer* or *The First Time* without a net. Those songs are as direct and sturdy as a Hank Williams tune.

The death of Bono's mother when he was a teenager has inspired U2's songs from *I Will Follow* forward (Larry's mother died in the early days of the band, too - it is one of the bonds U2's music is built on, as it was for Lennon and McCartney) but he never laid it out as bare as in Pop's *Mofo*. Strip away the aural camouflage and that song stands as naked and powerful as anything the group has ever written.

Like the Rolling Stones and the Who, U2 do not inspire a lot of covers - their songs seem definitively fixed in their own records. In the 90s the singers who tackled U2's compositions were usually women. The jazz vocalist Cassandra Wilson cut a haunting *Love Is Blindness*. Cher made *I Still Haven't Found What I'm Looking For* into an *I Did It My Way* - style anthem of show-biz brass. Tina Turner belted out the James Bond theme *Goldeneye* and the great Annie Ross found the sad heart in *Conversation On A Barstool*. Most rock songwriting still suffers from the disease of machoism; U2 should be proud that women can find their voices in U2 songs as easily as men can.

But of course, a well-written song is one in which anyone can find a voice. And while recordings and live shows allow us to participate as an audience, songbooks invite us to become singers and players ourselves. It is how songs lived for thousands of years - before there were recordings, before there were rock bands, before there were superstars.

Bono, Edge, Adam and Larry built these songs strong enough to pass along. Take them and use them. They're your songs, too.

introduction

TON CORBIJN

Bill Flanagan

Bill Flanagan wrote the book U2 at the End of the World

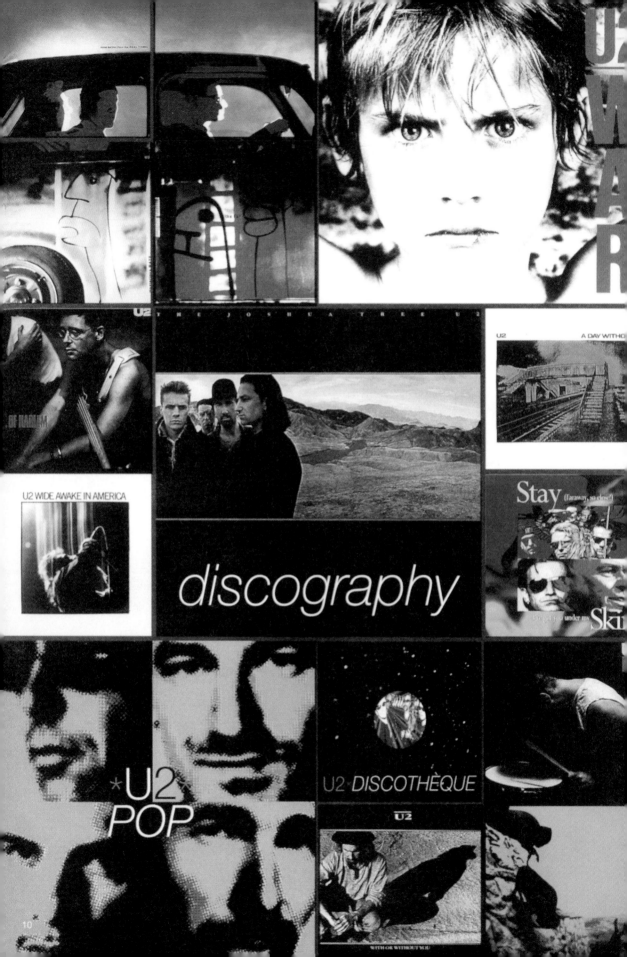

discography

U2
POP

U2·DISCOTHÈQUE

ALBUMS

BOY
I Will Follow/Twilight/An Cat Dubh/Into the Heart/Out of Control/Stories for Boys/ The Ocean/A Day Without Me
Another Time, Another Place/Electric Co./Shadows and Tall Trees
release date 17.11.80
producer Steve Lillywhite

OCTOBER
Gloria/I Fall Down/I Threw a Brick Through a Window Rejoice /Fire/Tomorrow/October/With a Shout/Stranger in a Strange Land/Scarlet/Is That All?
release date 13.10.81
producer Steve Lillywhite

WAR
Sunday Bloody Sunday/Seconds/New Year's Day/Like A Song/Drowning Man/The Refugee/Two Hearts Beat as One/Red Light/Surrender/40
release date 28.2.83
producer Steve Lillywhite

THE UNFORGETTABLE FIRE
A Sort of Homecoming/Pride/Wire/The Unforgettable Fire/Promenade /4th of July /Bad/Indian Summer Sky Elvis Presley and America/MLK
release date 1.10.84
producers Brian Eno/Daniel Lanois

THE JOSHUA TREE
Where the Streets Have No Name/I Still Haven't Found What I'm Looking For/With or Without You/Bullet the Blue Sky/ Running To Stand Still/Red Hill Mining Town In God's Country/Trip Through Your Wires/One Tree Hill Exit/Mothers Of The Disappeared
release date 9.3.87
producers Brian Eno/ Daniel Lanois

RATTLE AND HUM
Helter Skelter/Van Dieman's Land/Desire/Hawkmoon 269 All Along the Watchtower/I Still Haven't Found What I'm Looking For/(Freedom for My People)/Silver and Gold Pride/Angel of Harlem/Love Rescue Me/When Love Comes To Town/Heartland /God Part II/(The Star Spangled Banner)/Bullet The Blue Sky/All I Want Is You
release date 10.10.88
producer Jimmy Iovine

ACHTUNG BABY
Zoo Station/Even Better Than The Real Thing /One/Until The End Of The World/Who's Gonna Ride Your Wild Horses So Cruel/The Fly/ Mysterious Ways/Trying To Throw Your Arms Around The World/Ultra Violet (Light My Way) Acrobat/Love Is Blindness
*release date*18.11.91
producers Brian Eno/Daniel Lanois

ZOOROPA
Zooropa/Babyface/Numb/Lemon/Stay (Faraway, So Close!)/Daddy's Gonna Pay For Your Crashed Car/Some Days Are Better Than Others/The First Time/Dirty Day The Wanderer
release date 5.7.93
producers Flood/Brian Eno/Edge

POP
Discotheque/Do you Feel Loved/Mofo/If God Will Send His Angels/Staring At The Sun/Last Night On Earth Gone/Miami/The Playboy Mansion/If You Wear That Velvet Dress/Please/Wake Up Dead Man
release date 3.3.97
producer Flood
additional production Howie B/Steve Osborne

THE BEST OF 1980-1990
Pride (In the name of love)/New Year's Day/With or Without You/I Still Haven't Found What I'm Looking For/Sunday Bloody Sunday/Bad/Where The Streets Have No Name I Will Follow/The Unforgettable Fire/Sweetest Thing (Single Mix)/Desire/When Love Comes To Town/Angel Of Harlem/All I Want Is You
THE B-SIDES
The Three Sunrises/Spanish Eyes/Sweetest Thing/Love Comes Tumbling/Bass Trap/Dancing Barefoot/ Everlasting Love/Unchained Melody/Walk To The Water/ Luminous Times (Hold On To Love)/Hallelujah Here She Comes Silver and Gold/Endless Deep/A Room At The Heartbreak Hotel/Trash, Trampoline and the Party Girl
release date 2.11.98

MINI-ALBUMS

UNDER A BLOOD RED SKY
Gloria/11 O'Clock Tick Tock/I Will Follow/Party Girl Sunday Bloody Sunday/The Electric Co./New Year's Day/"40"
release date 11.83
producer Jimmy Iovine

WIDE AWAKE IN AMERICA
Bad/A Sort of Homcoming/Three Sunrises/Love Comes Tumbling
release date 6.83
producers Brian Eno/Tony Visconti

SINGLES

U23
Out of Control/Stories for Boys/Boy-Girl
release date 9.79
producers Chas de Whalley/U2

ANOTHER DAY
Another Day/Twilight
release date 2.80
producer Chas de Whalley

11 O'CLOCK TICK
11 O'Clock Tick Tock/Touch
release date 5.80
producer Martin Hannet

A DAY WITHOUT ME
A Day Without Me/Things to Make and Do
release date 8.80
producer Steve Lillywhite

I WILL FOLLOW
I Will Follow/Boy-Girl
release date 10.80
producer Steve Lillywhite

FIRE
Fire/J.Swallo
release date 6.81
producer Steve Lillywhite

GLORIA
Gloria/I Will Follow (Live)
release date 10.81
producer Steve Lillywhite

A CELEBRATION
Celebration/Trampoline/Party Girl
release date 3.82
producer Steve Lillywhite

NEW YEAR'S DAY
New Year's Day/Treasure
release date 1.83
producer Steve Lillywhite
NEW YEARS DAY - 5 track EP doublepack
New Years Day/Treasure/Fire/I Threw A Brick Through A Window(Live)/A Day Without Me (Live)
release date 1.83
producer Steve Lillywhite

TWO HEARTS BEAT AS ONE
Two Hearts Beat As One/Endless Deep
release date 3.83
producer Steve Lillywhite
TWO HEARTS BEAT AS ONE - 12"
Two Hearts Beat As One/New Years Day
Two Hearts (US remix)
release date 3.83
producer Steve Lillywhite
TWO HEARTS BEAT AS ONE - EP doublepack
Two Hearts Beat As One/Endless Deep/New Year's Day(US remix)/Two Hearts Beat As One (US remix)
release date 3.83
producer Steve Lillywhite

PRIDE (In the Name of Love)
Pride/Boomerang
release date 9.84
producers B. Eno/D. Lanois/T. Visconti
PRIDE (In the Name of Love) - 12"
Pride/Boomerang II /4th of July
release date 9.84
producers B. Eno/D. Lanois/T. Visconti
PRIDE (In the Name of Love)- EP doublepack
Pride/4th of July/Sunday Bloody Sunday/Love Comes Tumbling/60 Seconds In Kingdom Come

SINGLES
release date 9.84
producers Brian Eno/Daniel Lanois

THE UNFORGETTABLE FIRE
The Unforgettable Fire/A Sort Of Homecoming (live)
release date 4.85
producers B. Eno/D. Lanois/T. Visconti
THE UNFORGETTABLE FIRE - 12"
The Unforgettable Fire/The Three Sunrises/Love Comes Tumbling/Bass Trap
release date 4.85
producers B. Eno/D. Lanois/T. Visconti
THE UNFORGETTABLE FIRE - EP doublepack
The Unforgettable Fire/Love Comes Tumbling/60 Seconds in Kingdom Come
release date 4.85
producers B. Eno/D. Lanois/T. Visconti

WITH OR WITHOUT YOU
With Or Without You/Luminous Times/Walk To the Water
release date 3.87
producers Daniel Lanois/Brian Eno
mixed by Steve Lillywhite
WITH OR WITHOUT YOU - 12"
With Or Without You/Luminous Times/Walk To the Water
release date 3.87
producers Daniel Lanois/Brian Eno
mixed by Steve Lillywhite

I STILL HAVEN'T FOUND WHAT I'M LOOKING FOR
I Still Haven't Found What I'm Looking For/Spanish Eyes Deep In the Heart
release date 5.87
producers Daniel Lanois/Brian Eno
I STILL HAVEN'T FOUND WHAT I'M LOOKING FOR -12"
I Still Haven't Found What I'm Looking For/Spanish Eyes/Deep In the Heart
release date 5.87
producers Daniel Lanois/Brian Eno

WHERE THE STREETS HAVE NO NAME
Where the Streets Have No Name/Silver And Gold Sweetest Thing
release date 8.87
producers Daniel Lanois/Brian Eno
mixed by Steve Lillywhite
WHERE THE STREETS HAVE NO NAME - 12"
Where the Streets Have No Name/Silver And Gold Sweetest Thing/Race against Time
release date 8.84
producers Daniel Lanois/Brian Eno
mixed by Steve Lillywhite

IN GOD'S COUNTRY *(US Release Only)*
In God's Country/Bullet the Blue Sky/Running to Stand Still
release date 11.87
producers Daniel Lanois/Brian Eno

ONE TREE HILL *(NEW ZEALAND release only)*
One Tree Hill/Bullet the Blue Sky/Running to Stand Still
release date 11.87
producers Daniel Lanois/Brian Eno

DESIRE
Desire/Hallelujah (Here She Comes)
release date 9.88
producer Jimmy Iovine
DESIRE -12"
Desire/Hallelujah (Here She Comes)/Desire (Hollywood mix)
release date 9.88
producers Daniel Lanois/Brian Eno

ANGEL OF HARLEM
Angel Of Harlem/A Room At The Heartbreak Hotel
release date 12.88
producer Jimmy Iovine
ANGEL OF HARLEM -12"
Angel Of Harlem/Love Rescue Me (live)
release date 12.88
producer Jimmy Iovine

WHEN LOVE COMES TO TOWN
When Love Comes To Town/Dancing Barefoot - 7"
WHEN LOVE COMES TO TOWN
When Love Comes To Town/Dancing Barefoot/When Love Comes To Town (Live from the Kingdom mix)/God Part II (Hard Metal Dance Mix) - 12"/CD
release date 4.89
producer Jimmy Iovine

ALL I WANT IS YOU
All I Want Is You/Unchained Melody - 7"
release date 6.89
producer Jimmy Iovine
ALL I WANT IS YOU
All I Want Is You/Unchained Melody/Everlasting Love
- 12"/CD
release date 6.89
producer Jimmy Iovine

THE FLY
The Fly/Alex Decends into Hell for a Bottle of Milk
Korova 1- 7"
release date 11.91
producer Daniel Lanois
THE FLY
The Fly/Alex Decends into Hell for a Bottle of Milk/
The Lounge Fly Mix -12"/CD
release date 11.91
producer Daniel Lanois
producer Paul Barrett *(B Side only)*

MYSTERIOUS WAYS
Mysterious Ways/Mysterious Ways (solar plexus magic
hour remix) - 7"
release date 2.12.91
producers Daniel Lanois/Brian Eno
MYSTERIOUS WAYS
Mysterious Ways/Mysterious Ways *(x 2 mixes)* - 12"
release date 2.12.91
producers Daniel Lanois/Brian Eno
MYSTERIOUS WAYS
Mysterious Ways/Mysterious Ways *(x4 mixes)* - CD
release date 2.12.91
producers Daniel Lanois/Brian Eno

ONE
One/Lady With The Spinning Head - 7"
release date 24.2. 92
producers Daniel Lanois/Brian Eno
ONE
One/Lady With The Spinning Head/Satellite of Love
Night And Day -12"/CD
release date 24.2. 92
producers Daniel Lanois/Brian Eno
producer Paul Barrett *(B Side only)*

EVEN BETTER THAN THE REAL THING
EVEN BETTER THAN THE REAL THING
Even Better Than The Real Thing/Salome/Where Did It
All Go Wrong/Lady With The Spinning Head -7"/12"/CD
producers Steve Lillywhite/Brian Eno/Daniel Lanois
release date 6.92
EVEN BETTER THAN THE REAL THING
(x4 mixes) - 12"
producers Steve Lillywhite/Brian Eno/Daniel Lanois
release date 6.92
EVEN BETTER THAN THE REAL THING
(x5 mixes) - CD
producers Steve Lillywhite/Brian Eno/Daniel Lanois
release date 6.92

WHO'S GONNA RIDE YOUR WILD HORSES
Who's Gonna Ride Your Wild Horses(Temple Bar Edit)
Paint It Black - 7"
release date 23.11.92
producers Steve Lillywhite/Brian Eno/Daniel Lanois
Paul Barrett
WHO'S GONNA RIDE YOUR WILD HORSES
Who's Gonna Ride Your Wild Horses(TB remix & edit)
Paint It Black/Fortunate Son - 12"/CD
producers Steve Lillywhite/Brian Eno/Daniel Lanois
Paul Barrett *(B Side only)*
release date 23.11.92

LEMON
LEMON - US only release
Lemon (Bad Yard Club)/(Version Dub)
(Momo's reprise)/(Perfecto Mix)/(Jeep Mix) - 12"
release date 9.93
producer Flood/Eno/Edge

STAY (Faraway, So Close!)
Stay/I've Got You Under My Skin - 7"
release date 22.11.93
producer Flood/Eno/Edge & P Ramone (Under my skin)
STAY (Faraway, So Close!)
Stay/I've Got You Under My Skin
Lemon (Bad Yard Mix)/Lemon (Perfecto Mix) - 12"
release date 22.11.93

producer Flood/Eno/Edge & P Ramone (Under my Skin)
STAY (Faraway, So Close!) The Live Format- UK CD
Stay/Slow Dancing/Bullet The Blue Sky (Live)/Love
Is Blindness (Live)
release date 22.11.93
producer Flood/Eno/Edge & P Ramone (Under my Skin)
STAY (Faraway, So Close!)
Stay/I've Got You Under My Skin/Bullet The Blue
Sky/Lemon (Bad Yard Edit)/Love Is Blindness - CD 5"
release date 22.11.93
producer Flood/Eno/Edge & P Ramone (Under my Skin)

HOLD ME, THRILL ME, KISS ME, KILL ME.
HOLD ME, THRILL ME, KISS ME, KILL ME.
Hold Me, Thrill Me, Kiss Me, Kill Me, Themes From
Batman Forever - CD/Cass single/Red Vinyl 7' Ltd
Edition
release date 5.6.95
producers Nelloe Hooper, Bono & Edge

DISCOTHÈQUE
DISCOTHÈQUE
Discothèque /Holy Joe - Cass/CD
release date 3.2.97
producer Flood
DISCOTHÈQUE
Discothèque *(x 4 mixes)* - CD
release date 3.2.97
producer Flood

STARING AT THE SUN
STARING AT THE SUN
Staring at the Sun/North and South of the River
Your Blue Room - Cass/CD single
release date 7.4.97
producer Flood

LAST NIGHT ON EARTH
LAST NIGHT ON EARTH
Last Night on Earth/Pop Muzik/Happiness is a Warm
Gun - CD single
release date 21.7.97
producer Flood
LAST NIGHT ON EARTH
Last Night on Earth/Numb/Happiness is a Warm
Gun/Pop Muzik - CD single
release date 21.7.97
producer Flood

PLEASE
PLEASE
Please/Dirty Day (Junk Day)/Dirty Day (Bitter Kiss)
I'm Not Your Baby - CD single
release date 22.9.97
producer Flood
PLEASE
Please/Where the Streets Have No Name/With or
Without You/Staring at the Sun - CD single
release date 22.9.97
producer Flood

IF GOD WILL SEND HIS ANGELS
IF GOD WILL SEND HIS ANGELS
If God Will Send His Angels/Slow Dancing/Two
Shots of Happy, One Shot of Sad/Sunday Bloody
Sunday (Live from Sarajevo) - CD
release date 8.12.97
producer Flood

MOFO
MOFO
Mofo (Phunk Phorce Mix)/(Mother's Mix)/If God Will
Send His Angels (The Grand Jury Mix) - CD
release date 8.12.97
producer Flood

SWEETEST THING
SWEETEST THING
Sweetest Thing/Twilight (Live from Red Rocks)/An
Cath Dubh (Live from Red Rocks) - CD
release date 10.98
producers Steve Lillywhite/Brian Eno/Daniel Lanois
SWEETEST THING
Sweetest Thing/Stories for Boys (Live from Boston)
Out of Control (Live from Boston) - CD
release date 10.98
producers Steve Lillywhite/Brian Eno/Daniel Lanois

ANTON CORBIJN

videography

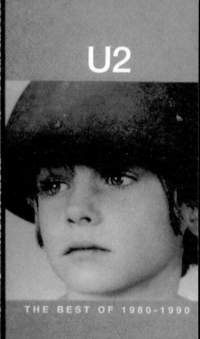

UNDER A BLOOD RED SKY
released 1983

Surrender
Seconds
Sunday Bloody Sunday
October
New Year's Day
I Threw A Brick
A Day Without Me
Gloria
Party Girl
11 O'Clock Tick Tock
I Will Follow
40

production associate Malcolm Gerrie
director Gavin Taylor
producers Rick Wurpel/Doug Stewart
executive producer for U2 at Red Rocks Associates:
Paul McGuinness

THE UNFORGETTABLE FIRE
released 1985

THE UNFORGETTABLE FIRE
director Meiret Avis
producer James Morris/Michael Hamlyn

BAD
director Barry Devlin
producer James Morris

PRIDE (In The Name Of Love)
director Donald Cammell
producer James Morris

A SORT OF HOMECOMING
director Barry Devlin
producer James Morris

THE MAKING OF THE UNFORGETTABLE FIRE
Documentary *(Including two versions of Pride)*
director Barry Devlin
producer James Morris/Michael Hamlyn

U2 RATTLE & HUM
released 1988

Helter Skelter
Van Diemen's Land
Desire
Exit
Gloria
I Still Haven't Found What I'm Looking For
Silver & Gold
Angel Of Harlem
All Along The Watchtower
In God's Country
When Love Comes To Town
Heartland
Bad
Where The Streets Have No Name
MLK
With Or Without You
Bullet The Blue Sky
Running To Stand Still
Sunday Bloody Sunday
Pride (In The Name Of Love)
All I Want Is You

Paramount Pictures *A Phil Joanou film*
director Phil Joanou
producer Michael Hamlyn
executive producer Paul McGuinness
music producer Jimmy Iovine

ACHTUNG BABY
THE VIDEOS, THE CAMEOS AND A WHOLE LOT OF
INTERFERENCE FROM ZOO TV
released 1992

Interference

EVEN BETTER THAN THE REAL THING
director Kevin Godley
Producer Iain Brown for MediaLab at The Mill

Interference

MYSTERIOUS WAYS
director Stephane Sednaoui
producer Phillippe Dupuis-Mendel *Bandits Productions*

ONE *(Version 1)*
director Anton Corbijn
producer Richard Bell *State*

THE FLY
director Ritchie Smyth/Jon Klein
producer Ned O'Hanlon/Juliet Naylor *Dreamchaser
Productions*

Interference

EVEN BETTER THAN THE REAL THING *(Dance Mix)*
director Ritchie Smyth
editor Juniper Calder
producer Ned O'Hanlon *Dreamchaser Productions*

ONE *(Version 2)*
director Mark Pellington
editor Bob Gleason
producer Carina Rubin *Woo Art International*

EVEN BETTER THAN THE REAL THING
director Armando Gallo and Kampah
designer Kampah
producer Armando Gallo *Pittard Sullivan Design*

ONE (Version 3)
director Phil Joanou
producer Ned O'Hanlon *Dreamchaser Productions*

UNTIL THE END OF THE WORLD
director Ned O'Hanlon *Dreamchaser Productions*

NUMB
released 1993

Numb
director Kevin Godley
producer Iain Brown
Numb (Video Remix)
created by Emergency Broadcast Network
Love Is Blindness
director/camera/editor Matt Mahurin
producer Trish Govoni

U2 ZOO TV LIVE FROM SYDNEY
Released 1994

Zoo Station
The Fly
Even Better Than The Real Thing
Mysterious Ways
One
Unchained Melody
Until The End Of The World
New Year's Day
Numb
Angel Of Harlem
Stay (Faraway, So Close!)
Satellite Of Love
Dirty Day
Bullet The Blue Sky
Running To Stand Still
Where The Streets Have No Name
Pride (In The Name Of Love)
Daddy's Gonna Pay For Your Crashed Car
Lemon
With Or Without You
Love Is Blindness
Can't Help Falling In Love

director David Mallet
producer Ned O'Hanlon, Rocky Oldham
executive producer Paul McGuinness

U2 POPMART LIVE FROM MEXICO CITY
released 1998

Pop Musik
Mofo
I Will Follow
Gone
Even Better Than The Real Thing

Last Night On Earth
Until The End Of The World
New Year's Day
Pride (In The Name Of Love)
I Still Haven't Found What I'm Looking For
All I Want Is You
Desire
Staring At The Sun
Sunday Bloody Sunday
Bullet The Blue Sky
Please
Where The Streets Have No Name
Discothèque
If You Wear That Velvet Dress
With Or Without You
Hold Me, Thrill Me, Kiss Me, Kill Me
Mysterious Ways
One
Wake Up Dead Man

director David Mallet
producer Ned O'Hanlon
executive producer Paul McGuinness
associate producer Sheila Roche

U2 THE BEST OF 1980-1990
released 1999

PRIDE (In The Name Of Love)
director Donald Cammell
producer James Morris *Windmill Lane*

NEW YEAR'S DAY
director Meiret Avis
producer James Morris

WITH OR WITHOUT YOU
director Meiret Avis
producer Michael Hamlyn & Paul Spencer

I STILL HAVEN'T FOUND WHAT I'M LOOKING FOR
director Barry Devlin
producer Anne-Louise Kelly

SUNDAY BLOODY SUNDAY
From Live At Red Rocks
director Gavin Taylor
producer Malcolm Gerrie, Rick Wurpel, Paul McGuinness

BAD
director Barry Devlin
producer James Morris *Windmill Lane*

WHERE THE STREETS HAVE NO NAME
director Meiert Avis
producer Michael Hamlyn, Ben Dossett

I WILL FOLLOW

THE UNFORGETTABLE FIRE
director Meiret Avis
producer James Morris and Michael Hamlyn

SWEETEST THING
director Kevin Godley
producer Ned O'Hanlon and Richard Holling

DESIRE
director Richard Lowenstein
producer Michael Hamlyn and Juliet Naylor

WHEN LOVE COMES TO TOWN
director Phil Joanou
producer Michael Hamlyn

ANGEL OF HARLEM
director Richard Lowenstein
producer Michael Hamlyn and Iain Brown

ALL I WANT IS YOU
director Meiert Avis
producer Ned O'Hanlon and Ben Dosset

ONE TREE HILL
From a previously unreleased cut of Rattle & Hum
director Phil Joanou
producer Michael Hamlyn

live dates

IRISH TOURS 1976-79

1976	MOUNT TEMPLE SCHOOL DUBLIN
1976	ST FINTAN'S SCHOOL DUBLIN
1976-77	OTHER HYPE GIGS
1978	OUR TIMES UNKNOWN
3/16/78	PROJECT ARTS CENTRE DUBLIN
3/17/78	HARP LAGER CONTEST LIMERICK
3/20/78	COMMUNITY CENTRE HOWTH
4/78	McGONAGLES DUBLIN
5/25/78	PROJECT ARTS CENTRE DUBLIN
7/31/78	McGONAGLES DUBLIN
	LIBERTY HALL DUBLIN
8/78	ARCADIA CORK
9/09/78	TOP HAT BALLROOM DUBLIN
9/18/78	PROJECT ARTS CENTRE DUBLIN
10/78	ARCADIA BALLROOM CORK
10/01/78	KEYSTONE STUDIOS DUBLIN
12/78	STARDUST DUBLIN
1/03/79	McGONAGLES DUBLIN
2/03/79	McGONAGLES DUBLIN
2/03/79	TRINITY BUTTERY DUBLIN
2/17/79	PROJECTS ARTS CENTRE DUBLIN
5/79	DANDELION CAR PARK DUBLIN
5/79	TRINITY COLLEGE DUBLIN
6/07/79	McGONAGLES DUBLIN
6/14/79	McGONAGLES DUBLIN
6/21/79	McGONAGLES DUBLIN
6/28/79	McGONAGLES DUBLIN
7/79	YOUTH CLUB HOWTH, DUBLIN
8/79	YOUTH CLUB HOWTH, DUBLIN
8/79	DANDELION CAR PARK DUBLIN
8/21/79	THE BAGGOT INN DUBLIN
9/79	PROJECT ARTS CENTRE DUBLIN
10/05/79	CORK OPERA HOUSE CORK

U2-3 LONDON CLUB TOUR 1979

12/01/79	MOONLIGHT CLUB WEST HAMPSTEAD
12/02/79	NASHVILLE ROOMS EARLS COURT
12/03/79	100 CLUB CLAPHAM
12/04/79	HOPE & ANCHOR ISLINGTON
12/05/79	ROCK GARDEN COVENT GARDEN
12/07/79	ELECTRIC BALLROOM CAMDEN
12/08/79	ELECTRIC BALLROOM CAMDEN
12/11/79	BRIDGE HOUSE CANNING TOWN
12/12/79	BRUNEL UNIVERSITY CAMDEN
12/14/79	DINGWALLS CAMDEN
12/15/79	WINDSOR CASTLE HARROW ROW

IRISH TOUR & LONDON DATE 1980

2/80	QUEEN'S UNIVERSITY BELFAST
2/03/80	BRIDGE HOUSE TULLAMORE
2/80	COUNTRY CLUB CORK
2/80	GARDEN OF EDEN CLUB TULLERMENY
2/26/80	NATIONAL STADIUM DUBLIN
3/19/80	ACKLAM HALL
	SENSE OF IRELAND FESTIVAL, LONDON

11 O'CLOCK TICK TOCK TOUR/UK & IRELAND

5/22/80	HOPE & ANCHOR LONDON
5/23/80	MOONLIGHT CLUB LONDON
5/24/80	UNIVERSITY SHEFFIELD
5/26/80	NEW REGENT BRIGHTON
5/27/80	ROCK GARDEN LONDON
5/28/80	TRINITY HALL BRISTOL
5/29/80	CEDAR BALLROOM BIRMINGHAM
5/30/80	NASHVILLE LONDON
5/31/80	POLYTECHNIC MANCHESTER
6/02/80	77 CLUB NUNEATON
6/03/80	BOAT CLUB NOTTINGHAM
6/04/80	BEACH CLUB MANCHESTER
6/05/80	FAN CLUB LEEDS
6/06/80	JB'S DUDLEY
6/07/80	MARQUEE CLUB LONDON
6/08/80	HALF MOON CLUB LONDON
7/10/80	CLARENDON HOTEL LONDON
7/11/80	HALF MOON CLUB LONDON
7/12/80	MOONLIGHT CLUB LONDON
7/80	MARQUEE CLUB LONDON
7/27/80	LEXLIP CASTLE FESTIVAL DUBLIN
7/28/80	DALYMOUNT FESTIVAL DUBLIN

THE BOY TOUR (1ST LEG) UK & EUROPE

9/06/80	GENERAL WOOLFE COVENTRY
9/07/80	LYCEUM BALLROOM LONDON
9/08/80	MARQUEE CLUB LONDON
9/09/80	BERKELEY BRISTOL
9/11/80	WELLINGTON CLUB HULL
9/12/80	TABOO CLUB SCARBOROUGH
9/13/80	QUEEN'S HALL LEEDS
9/15/80	MARQUEE CLUB LONDON
9/16/80	FIESTA SUITE PLYMOUTH
9/17/80	DEMELZAS PENZANCE
9/18/80	CIVIC HALL TOTNES
9/19/80	MARSHALL ROOMS STROUD
9/21/80	NAG'S HEAD WOLLASTON
9/22/80	MARQUEE CLUB LONDON
9/23/80	LIMIT CLUB SHEFFIELD
09/24/80	BOGART'S BIRMINGHAM
9/25/80	BRADY'S LIVERPOOL
9/26/80	EDAR BALLROOM BIRMINGHAM
9/27/80	POLYTECHNIC COVENTRY
9/29/80	MARQUEE LONDON
9/30/80	POLYTECHNIC BRIGHTON
10/02/80	FAN CLUB LEEDS
10/03/80	PORTERHOUSE RETFORD
10/04/80	SCHOOL OF ECONOMICS LONDON
10/05/80	HALF MOON CLUB LONDON
10/07/80	BOAT CLUB NOTTINGHAM
10/09/80	POLYTECHNIC MANCHESTER
10/11/80	KINGSTON POLYTECHNIC LONDON
10/15/80	THE MILKYWAY AMSTERDAM
10/16/80	VERA GRONINGEN
10/17/80	GIGANT APELDOORN
10/18/80	KLARICK BRUSSELS
10/19/80	LYCEUM BALLROOM LONDON
11/07/80	UNIVERSITY EXETER
11/08/80	UNIVERSITY SOUTHAMPTON
11/09/80	MOONLIGHT CLUB LONDON
11/11/80	KENT UNIVERSITY CANTERBURY
11/12/80	UNIVERSITY BRADFORD
11/13/80	LIMIT CLUB SHEFFIELD
11/14/80	TOWN HALL KIDDERMINSTER
11/15/80	POLYTECHNIC BRISTOL
11/18/80	UNIVERSITY REDDING
11/19/80	POLYTECHNIC WOLVERHAMPTON
11/20/80	POLYTECHNIC BLACKPOOL
11/21/80	NITE CLUB EDINBURGH
11/22/80	BRADY'S LIVERPOOL
11/24/80	POLYTECHNIC COVENTRY
11/26/80	MARQUEE CLUB LONDON
11/27/80	MARQUEE CLUB LONDON
11/28/80	ASTON UNIVERSITY BIRMINGHAM
11/29/80	KEELE UNIVERSITY STOKE
11/30/80	JENKINSON'S BRIGHTON
12/01/80	HAMMERSMITH ODEON LONDON
12/02/80	HAMMERSMITH PALAIS LONDON
12/03/80	BALTARD PAVILLION PARIS

THE BOY TOUR (2ND LEG) AMERICA & EUROPE

12/06/80	THE RITZ NEW YORK, NY
12/07/80	BAYOU CLUB WASHINGTON, DC
12/08/80	STAGE ONE BUFFALO, NY
12/09/80	EL MOCAMBO TORONTO, CANADA
12/11/80	MUDD CLUB NEW YORK, NY
12/12/80	MAIN EVENT PROVIDENCE, RI
12/13/80	PARADISE THEATER BOSTON. MA
12/14/80	TOAD'S PLACE NEW HAVEN, CT
12/15/80	BIJOU CAFE PHILADELPHIA, PA
12/17/80	ULSTER HALL BELFAST
12/18/80	LEISURELAND GALWAY
12/19/80	BAYMOUNT SLIGO
12/20/80	DOWNTOWN KAMPUS CORK
12/22/80	TV CLUB DUBLIN
01/24/81	STRATHCLYDE UNIVERSITY GLASGOW
01/25/81	VALENTINO'S CLUB EDINBURGH
01/26/81	UNIVERSITY YORK
01/27/81	POLYTECHNIC MANCHESTER
01/28/81	UNIVERSITY OF EAST ANGLIA NORWICH
01/29/81	IRON HORSE NORTHAMPTON
01/30/81	UNIVERSITY LOUGHBOROUGH
01/31/81	CITY HALL ST ALBANS
02/01/81	LYCEUM BALLROOM LONDON
02/09/81	UNDERGROUND STOCKHOLM
02/10/81	BEURSSCHOUWBURG BRUSSELS
02/11/81	PARADISO AMSTERDAM
02/12/81	PAARD VAN TROJE DEN HAGUE
02/13/81	DE LANTAARN ROTTERDAM
02/14/81	STADSSCHOUWBURG SITTARD
02/15/81	ONKEL PO'S CARNEGIE HALL HAMBURG
02/17/81	KANTKINO BERLIN
02/18/81	SUGAR SHACK MUNICH
02/19/81	SALLE DU FAUBURG GENEVA
02/20/81	ECOLE NATIONAL DES TRAVAUX PARIS
02/21/81	LE PALACE PARIS

THE BOY TOUR (3RD LEG) NORTH AMERICA

3/03/81	BAYOU CLUB WASHINGTON, DC (2 Shows)
3/04/81	BIJOU CAFE PHILADELPHIA, PA
3/05/81	JB SCOTT'S ALBANY, NY
3/06/81	PARADISE THEATER BOSTON, MA (2 Shows)
3/07/81	THE RITZ NEW YORK, NY
3/09/81	LE CLUB MONTREAL, QC
3/10/81	BARRYMORE'S OTTOWA, ON
3/11/81	MAPLE LEAF BALLROOM TORONTO, ON
3/14/81	GLOBE THEATER SAN DIEGO, CA
3/15/81	RESEDA COUNTRY CLUB RESEDA, CA
3/16/81	WOODSTOCK ANAHEIM, CA
3/18/81	COLLEGE AUDITORIUM SAN JOSE, CA
3/19/81	THE OLD WALDOR SAN FRANCISCO, CA
3/20/81	THE OLD WALDOR SAN FRANCISCO, CA
3/22/81	FOG HORN PORTLAND, OR
3/23/81	ASTOR PARK SEATTLE, WA
3/24/81	COMMODORE VANCOUVER, BC
3/26/81	NEW FACES CLUB SALT LAKE CITY
3/28/81	RAINBOW MUSIC HALL DENVER, CO
3/30/81	THE ROX LUBBOCK, TX
3/31/81	THE CLUB FOOT AUSTIN TX
4/01/81	CARDI'S HOUSTON TX
4/02/81	BIJOU DALLAS TX
4/03/81	QUICKSILVER'S OKLAHOMA CITY, OK
4/04/81	CAINES BALLROOM TULSA, OK
4/06/81	UPTOWN THEATER KANSAS CITY, MO
4/07/81	WASHINGTON U GRAHAM CHAPEL ST LOUIS, MO
4/09/81	UNCLE SAM'S MINNEAPOLIS, MN
4/10/81	FILMORES AMES, IA
4/11/81	UNIVERSITY OF CHICAGO INTERNATIONAL HOUSE CHICAGO, IL
4/12/81	PARK WEST CHICAGO, IL
4/14/81	MERLING'S MADISON, WI
4/15/81	PALM'S MILWAUKEE, WI
4/17/81	BOGART'S CLUB CINCINNATI, OH
4/18/81	HARPO'S DETROIT, MI
4/19/81	THE AGORA COLUMBUS, OH
4/20/81	THE AGORA CLEVELAND, OH
4/21/81	THE DECADE PITTSBURGH, PA
5/02/81	RATHSKELLER HALL UNIVERSITY OF FLORIDA, GAINSVILLE, FL
5/03/81	END ZONE TAMPA, FL
5/04/81	THE AGORA HALLENDALE, FL
5/06/81	THE AGORA ATLANTA, GA
5/08/81	OL' MAN RIVER'S NEW ORLEANS, LA
5/09/81	POET'S MEMPHIS, TN
5/11/81	RAINBOW MUSIC HALL DENVER, CO
5/13/81	SANTA MONICA CIVIC CENTER SANTA MONICA, CA
5/15/81	CALIFORNIA HALL SAN FRANCISCO, CA
5/19/81	RYERSON THEATER TORONTO, ON
5/20/81	RED CREEK ROCHESTER, NY
5/21/81	UNCLE SAM'S BUFFALO, NY
5/22/81	CITY LIMITS SYRACUSE, NY
5/23/81	JB SCOTT'S ALBANY, NY
5/24/81	CLUB CASINO HAMPTON BEACH, NH
5/25/81	CENTER STAGE PROVIDENCE, RI
5/27/81	TOAD'S PLACE NEW HAVEN, CT
5/28/81	THE METRO BOSTON, MA
5/29/81	PALLADIUM NEW YORK, NY
5/31/81	FAST LANE ASBURY PARK, NJ
6/04/81	UNIVERSITY SALFORD, UK
6/06/81	FRIARS CLUB AYLESBURY, UK
6/08/81	PINK POP FESTIVAL SPORTPARK, GELEEN, HOLLAND
6/09/81	HAMMERSMITH PALAIS LONDON, UK
8/16/81	SLANE CASTLE MEATH, IRELAND
8/23/81	PARIS CINEMA STUDIO LONDON, UK
8/24/81	GREENBELT ARTS & MUSIC FESTIVAL ODEL, ENGLAND
8/29/81	GATESHEAD FESITVAL GATESHEAD, UK
8/31/81	COASTERS EDINBURGH, UK

OCTOBER TOUR (IST LEG) EUROPE

10/01/81	UNIVERSITY OF EAST ANGLIA NORWICH
10/02/81	ROCK CITY NOTTINGHAM
10/03/81	SALFORD UNIVERSITY SALFORD
10/04/81	TIFFANY'S GLASGOW
10/06/81	WARWICK UNIVERSITY COVENTRY
10/07/81	POLYTECHNIC LEICESTER
10/08/81	LYCEUM SHEFFIELD
10/09/81	MAYFAIR NEWCASTLE
10/10/81	ROYAL COURT THEATRE LIVERPOOL
10/12/81	TOP RANK BRIGHTON

10/13/81	LOCARNO PORTSMOUTH	
10/14/81	TOP RANK CARDIFF	
10/16/81	KINGS HALL STOKE	
10/17/81	SPORTS CENTRE BRACKNELL	
10/18/81	LOCARNO BRISTOL	
10/19/81	LOCARNO BIRMINGHAM	
10/20/81	TIFFANY'S LEEDS	
10/21/81	PAVILLION HEMEL HEMPSTEAD	
10/24/81	BRIELPORT DEINZE	
10/25/81	ZAAL LUX HERENTHOUT	
10/26/81	ELYSEE MONMARTRE PARIS	
10/28/81	STADSGEHOORZAAL LEIDEN	
10/29/81	DE HARMONIE TILBURG	
10/30/81	PARADISO AMSTERDAM	
10/31/81	STOKVISHAL ARNHEM	
11/01/81	DE LANTAARN ROTTERDAM	
11/03/81	FABRIK HAMBURG	
11/04/81	METROPOL BERLIN	

OCTOBER TOUR (2ND LEG) NORTH AMERICA & EUROPE

11/13/81	JB SCOTT'S ALBANY
11/14/81	ORPHEUM THEATER BOSTON, MA
11/15/81	TOAD'S PLACE NEW HAVEN, CT
11/17/81	CENTER STAGE PROVIDENCE, RI
11/18/81	RIPLEY'S MUSIC HALL PHILADELPHIA, PA
11/20/81	THE RITZ NEW YORK, NY
11/21/81	THE RITZ NEW YORK, NY
11/22/81	THE RITZ NEW YORK, NY
11/24/81	HITSVILLE NORTH NIGHTCLUB PASSAIC, NJ
11/25/81	HITSVILLE SOUTH NIGHTCLUB ASBURY PARK, NJ
11/28/81	HOLLYWOOD PALLADIUM LA, CA
11/29/81	WARFIELD THEATER SAN FRANCISCO, CA
12/01/81	THE AGORA ATLANTA, GA
12/02/81	VANDERBILT UNIVERSITY NASHVILLE, TN
12/04/81	ROYAL OAK MUSIC THEATER DETROIT, MI
12/05/81	FOUNTAIN STREET CHURCH GRAND RAPIDS, MI
12/06/81	PARK WEST CHICAGO, IL
12/07/81	DOOLEY'S EAST LANSING, MI
12/08/81	THE AGORA CLEVELAND, OH
12/10/81	UNCLE SAM'S BUFFALO, NY
12/11/81	ONTARIO THEATER WASHINGTON, DC
12/12/81	STAGE WEST HARTFORD, CT
12/13/81	MALIBU DANCE CLUB LIDO BEACH, NY
12/20/81	LYCEUM BALLROOM LONDON
12/21/81	LYCEUM BALLROOM LONDON
1/23/82	LEISURELAND GALWAY
1/24/82	CITY HALL CORK
1/26/82	RDS HALL DUBLIN

OCTOBER TOUR (3RD LEG) AMERICA

2/11/82	SS PRESIDENT RIVERBOAT NEW ORLEANS, LA
2/13/82	OPRY HOUSE AUSTIN, TX
2/14/82	CARDI'S SAN ANTONIO, TX
2/15/82	CARDI'S HOUSTON, TX
2/16/82	CARDI'S DALLAS, TX
2/17/82	JAMMIES OKLAHOMA CITY, OK
2/19/82	NIGHT MOVES ST LOUIS, MO
2/21/82	FIRST AVENUE MINNEAPOLIS, MN
2/22/82	HEADLINERS MADISON, WI
2/23/82	UNIVERSITY OF ILLINOIS AUDITORIUM CHAMPAIGN, IL
2/25/82	UPTOWN THEATER KANSAS CITY, MO
2/27/82	RAINBOW MUSIC HALL DENVER, CO
2/28/82	COLORADO STATE UNIVERSITY LINCOLN, CO
3/03/82	LEE COUNTY ARENA FORT MEYERS, FL
3/04/82	CIVIC AUDITORIUM WEST PALM BEACH, FL
3/05/82	CURTIS HIXON HALL TAMPA, FL
3/06/82	LEON COUNTY ARENA TALAHASSEE, FL
3/10/82	UNIVERSITY OF TENNESSEE KNOXVILLE, TN
3/11/82	CIVIC CENTER ATLANTA, GA
3/12/82	NORTH HALL AUDITORIUM MEMPHIS, TN
3/12/82	MILLER'S CAVE MEMPHIS, TN
3/13/82	GARDEN'S LOUISVILLE, KY
3/14/82	CONVENTION CENTER INDIANAPOLIS, IN
3/16/82	UNIVERSITY OF MASSACHUSETTS BOWKER AUDITORIUM, AMHERST, MA
3/17/82	THE RITZ NEW YORK, NY

3/18/82	THE RITZ NEW YORK, NY
3/19/82	NASSAU COUNTY COMMUNITY COLLEGE BALLROOM GARDEN CITY, NY
3/20/82	ALUMNAE HALL BROWN UNIVERSITY PROVIDENCE, RI
3/21/82	NIGHTCLUB PHOENIX, AZ
3/25/82	COLISEUM PHOENIX, AZ
3/26/82	SAN DIEGO SPORTS ARENA SAN DIEGO, CA
3/27/82	LOS ANGELES SPORTS ARENA LA, CA
3/29/82	CIVIC CENTRE SAN FRANCISCO, CA
3/30/82	CIVIC CENTRE SAN FRANCISCO, CA

EUROPEAN DATES/FESTIVALS

5/14/82	T HEEM HATTEM HOLLAND
7/01/82	GROENOORDHALLEN LEIDEN, HOLLAND
7/02/82	FESTIVAL GROUNDS RASKILDE
7/03/82	FESTIVAL GROUNDS TORHOUT
7/04/82	FESTIVAL GROUNDS WERCHTER
7/18/82	PUCHESTOWN RACECOURSE DUBLIN
7/31/82	INTERNATIONAL STADIUM GATESHEAD
8/03/82	VILAR DE MOUROS PORTUGAL
8/07/82	RUISROCK FESTIVAL TURKU

PRE-WAR TOUR

12/01/82	TIFFANY'S GLASGOW
12/02/82	APOLLO THEATRE MANCHESTER
12/03/82	DE MONTFORT HALL LEICESTER
12/04/82	ODEON BIRMINGHAM
12/05/82	LYCEUM BALLROOM LONDON
12/06/82	HAMMERSMITH PALAIS LONDON
12/08/82	MUZIEKCENTRUM VREDENBURG UTRECHT
12/09/82	MARTINIHAL GRONINGEN
12/10/82	VOLKSBELANG MECHELEN
12/11/82	BREILPORT DEINZE
12/12/82	LIMBURGHAL GENK
12/14/82	FALKONER TEATRET COPENHAGEN
12/15/82	KONSERTHUSET STOCKHOLM
12/16/82	OSLO NORWAY
12/18/82	CITY HALL CORK
12/19/82	LEISURELAND GALWAY
12/20/82	MAYSFIELD LEISURE CENTRE BELFAST
12/22/82	SFX DUBLIN
12/23/82	SFX DUBLIN
12/24/82	SFX DUBLIN

THE WAR TOUR (1ST LEG) UNITED KINGDOM & EUROPE

2/26/83	CAIRD HALL DUNDEE
2/27/83	CAPITOL THEATRE ABERDEEN
2/28/83	EDINBURGH PLAYHOUSE EDINBURGH
3/01/83	CITY HALL NEWCASTLE
3/02/83	LANCASTER UNIVERSITY LANCASTER
3/03/83	ROYAL COURT THEATRE LIVERPOOL
3/04/83	VICTORIA HALL HANLEY
3/06/83	GUILDHALL PORTSMOUTH
3/07/83	COLSTON HALL BRISTOL
3/08/83	EXETER UNIVERSITY EXETER
3/09/83	ARTS CENTRE POOLE
3/10/83	ODEON BIRMINGHAM
3/11/83	ST DAVID'S HALL CARDIFF
3/13/83	TOP RANK BRIGHTON
3/14/83	HAMMERSMITH ODEON LONDON
3/15/83	GAUMONT THEATRE IPSWICH
3/17/83	CITY HALL SHEFFIELD
3/18/83	LEEDS UNIVERSITY LEEDS
3/19/83	APOLLO THEATRE MANCHESTER
3/20/83	ASSEMBLY ROOMS DERBY
3/21/83	HAMMERSMITH ODEON LONDON
3/22/83	HAMMERSMITH PALAIS LONDON
3/25/83	ROYAL COURT THEATRE LIVERPOOL
3/26/83	CITY HALL NEWCASTLE
3/27/83	ODEON BIRMINGHAM
3/28/83	ROYAL CENTRE NOTTINGHAM
3/29/83	HAMMERSMITH PALAIS LONDON
4/03/83	FESITVAL DE PRINTEMPS BOURGES

THE WAR TOUR (2ND LEG) NORTH AMERICA, EUROPEAN FESITVALS, JAPAN

4/23/83	KENAN STADIUM CHAPEL HILL, NC
4/24/83	CHRYSLER HALL NORFOLK, VA
4/25/83	RITCHIE COLISEUM COLLEGE PARK, MD
4/27/83	CAYHUGA COUNTY COMMUNITY COLLEGE GYM AUBURN, NY
4/28/83	ROCHESTER INSTITUTE OF TECHNOLOGY ICE RINK NY
4/29/83	STATE UNIVERSITY OF NEW YORK DEHLI, NY
4/30/83	BROWN UNIVERSITY PROVIDENCE, RI
5/01/83	STONY BROOK NY
5/03/83	FULTON THEATER PITTSBURGH, PA
5/05/83	ORPHEUM THEATER BOSTON, MA
5/06/83	ORPHEUM THEATER BOSTON, MA
5/07/83	STATE UNIVERSITY OF NEW YORK MAYFEST ALBANY, NY
5/08/83	TRINITY COLLEGE HARTFORD, CT
5/10/83	YALE UNIVERSITY WOOLSEY HALL, NEW HAVEN, CT
5/11/83	PALLADIUM NEW YORK, NY
5/12/83	CAPITOL THEATER PASSAIC, NJ
5/13/83	TOWER THEATER PHILADELPHIA, PA
5/14/83	TOWER THEATER PHILADELPHIA, PA
5/16/83	SHEA CENTER BUFFALO, NY
5/17/83	MASSEY HALL TORONTO, ON
5/19/83	MUSIC HALL CLEVELAND, OH
5/20/83	GRAND CIRCUS THEATER DETROIT, MI
5/21/83	ARAGON BALLROOM CHICAGO, IL
5/22/83	NORTHRUP AUDITORIUM MINNEAPOLIS, MN
5/25/83	QUEEN ELIZABETH THEATER VANCOUVER, BC
5/26/83	PARAMOUNT THEATER SEATTLE, WA
5/27/83	PARAMOUNT THEATER PORTLAND, OR
5/30/83	GLEN HELEN REGIONAL PARK THE US FESTIVAL DEVORE, CA
6/01/83	CIVIC AUDITORIUM SAN FRANCISCO, CA
6/03/83	SALT PALACE CONVENTION CENTER SALT LAKE CITY, UT
6/05/83	RED ROCKS AMPHITHEATER DENVER, CO
6/06/83	COLORADO STATE UNIVERSITY BOULDER, CO
6/07/83	WICHITA KS
6/08/83	MEMORIAL HALL KANSAS CITY, MO
6/09/83	THE BRADY THEATER TULSA, OK
6/10/83	LLOYD NOBLE CENTER NORMAN, OK
6/11/83	THE MEADOWS AUSTIN, TX
6/13/83	BRONCO BOWL DALLAS, TX
6/14/83	HOUSTON TX
6/17/83	LOS ANGELES SPORTS ARENA LA, CA
6/21/83	JAI ALAI FRONTON HALL ORLANDO, FL
6/22/83	CURTIS HIXON CENTER TAMPA, FL
6/23/83	SUNRISE MUSICALTHEATER MIAMI, FL
6/24/83	JACKSONVILLE FL
6/25/83	CIVIC CENTER ATLANTA, GA
6/27/83	COLISEUM NEW HAVEN, CT
6/28/83	THE CENTRUM WORCESTER, MA
6/29/83	PIER 84 NEW YORK, NY
7/02/83	FESTIVAL GROUNDS TORHOUT
7/03/83	FESTIVAL GROUNDS WERCHTER
8/14/83	PHOENIX PARK RACECOURSE A DAY AT THE RACES DUBLIN
8/20/83	LORELEY AMPHITHEATER ST GOARSHAUSEN
8/21/83	KALVOYA FESTIVAL OSLO
11/16/83	NBC ARENA HONOLULU, HI
11/22/83	FESTIVAL HALL OSAKA
11/23/83	SIMIN BUNKA CENTER NAGOYA
11/26/83	SUN PLAZA NAKANO TOKYO
11/27/83	SUN PLAZA NAKANO TOKYO
11/28/83	SUN PLAZA NAKANO TOKYO
11/29/83	SUN PLAZA NAKANO TOKYO
12/18/83	VICTORIA APOLLO THE BIG ONE LONDON

THE UNDER AUSTRALIAN SKIES TOUR • THE UNFORGETTABLE FIRE TOUR (1ST LEG) NZ, AUSTRALIA & EUROPE

8/29/84	TOWN HALL CHRISTCHURCH
8/31/84	SHOW BUILDING WELLINGTON
9/01/84	LOGAN CAMBELL CENTRE AUCKLAND
9/02/84	LOGAN CAMBELL CENTRE AUCKLAND
9/04/84	ENTERTAINMENT CENTRE SYDNEY
9/05/84	ENTERTAINMENT CENTRE SYDNEY
9/06/84	ENTERTAINMENT CENTRE SYDNEY
9/08/84	ENTERTAINMENT CENTRE SYDNEY
9/09/84	ENTERTAINMENT CENTRE SYDNEY
9/11/84	FESITVAL HALL BRISBANE, AUS
9/13/84	SPORTS & ENTERTAINMENT CENTRE MELBOURNE
9/14/84	SPORTS & ENTERTAINMENT CENTRE MELBOURNE

9/15/84	SPORTS & ENTERTAINMENT CENTRE MELBOURNE
9/17/84	SPORTS & ENTERTAINMENT CENTRE MELBOURNE
9/18/84	SPORTS & ENTERTAINMENT CENTRE MELBOURNE
9/20/84	APOLLO ENTERTAINMENT CENTRE ADELAIDE
9/21/84	APOLLO ENTERTAINMENT CENTRE ADELAIDE
9/23/84	ENTERTAINMENT CENTRE PERTH
9/24/84	ENTERTAINMENT CENTRE PERTH
10/18/84	ESPACE TONY GARNIER LYON
10/19/84	MARSEILLES STADIUM MARSEILLE
10/20/84	PALAIS DES SPORTS TOULOUSE
10/22/84	PATTINOIRE BORDEAUX
10/23/84	ST HERBLAIN NANTES
10/25/84	ESPACE BALLARD PARIS
10/27/84	VORST NATIONAAL BRUSSELS
10/28/84	VORST NATIONAAL BRUSSELS
10/30/84	SPORTSPALAIS AHOY ROTTERDAM
10/31/84	SPORTSPALAIS AHOY ROTTERDAM
11/02/84	BRIXTON ACADEMY LONDON
11/03/84	BRIXTON ACADEMY LONDON
11/05/84	EDINBURGH PLAYHOUSE EDINBURGH
11/06/84	BARROWLANDS GLASGOW
11/07/84	BARROWLANDS GLASGOW
11/09/84	APOLLO THEATRE MANCHESTER
11/10/84	APOLLO THEATRE MANCHESTER
11/12/84	NEC BIRMINGHAM
11/14/84	WEMBLEY ARENA LONDON
11/15/84	WEMBLEY ARENA LONDON
11/21/84	WESTFALENHALLE DORTMUND

THE UNFORGETTABLE, FIRE TOUR (2ND LEG) NORTH AMERICA

12/01/84	TOWER THEATER PHILADELPHIA, PA
12/02/84	CENTRUM WORCESTER, MA
12/03/84	RADIO CITY MUSIC HALL NY, NY
12/05/84	CONSTITUTION HALL WASHINGTON, DC
12/07/84	MASSEY HALL TORONTO, ON
12/08/84	FOX THEATER DETROIT, MI
12/09/84	MUSIC HALL CLEVELAND, OH
12/11/84	ARAGON BALLROOM CHICAGO, IL
12/15/84	CIVIC AUDITORIUM SAN FRANCISCO, CA
12/16/84	LONG BEACH ARENA LA, CA

THE UNFORGETTABLE FIRE TOUR (3RD LEG) EUROPE

1/23/85	DRAMMENSHALE DRAMMEN
1/25/85	ISSTADION STOCKHOLM
1/26/85	SCANDINAVIUM GOTHENBURG
1/28/85	CONGRESS CENTRE HAMBURG
1/29/85	STADHALLE OFFENBACH
1/31/85	SPORTHALLE KOLN
2/01/85	MUSENSAAL MANNHEIM
2/02/85	RUDI SEDLMAYERHALLE, MUNCHEN
2/04/85	PALAZETTO DELLO SPORT MILANO
2/05/85	TEATRO TENDA BOLOGNA
2/06/85	TEATRO TENDA BOLOGNA
2/08/85	HALENSTADION ZURICH
2/10/85	PALAIS DES OMNISPORTS DE PERCY PARIS

THE UNFORGETTABLE FIRE TOUR (4TH LEG) NORTH AMERICA

2/25/85	REUNION ARENA DALLAS, TX
2/26/85	FRANK ERWIN CENTER AUSTIN, TX
2/27/85	THE SUMMIT HOUSTON, TX
3/01/85	COMPTON TERRACE PHOENIX, AZ
3/02/85	LOS ANGELES SPORTS ARENA LA, CA
3/04/85	LOS ANGELES SPORTS ARENA LA, CA
3/05/85	LOS ANGELES SPORTS ARENA LA, CA
3/07/85	COW PALACE DALY CITY, CA
3/08/85	COW PALACE DALY CITY, CA
3/11/85	NEAL BLAISDELL CENTER ARENA HONOLULU, HI
3/17/85	McNICHOLS SPORTS ARENA DENVER, CO
3/19/85	MINNEAPOLIS AUDITORIUM MINNEAPOLIS, MN
3/21/85	UNIVERSITY OF ILLINOIS PAVILLION CHICAGO, IL
3/22/85	UNIVERSITY OF ILLINOIS PAVILLION CHICAGO, IL
3/23/85	JOE LOUIS ARENA DETROIT, MI
3/25/85	RICHFIELD COLISEUM CLEVELAND, OH
3/27/85	THE FORUM MONTREAL, QC

3/28/85	MAPLE LEAF GARDENS TORONTO, ON
3/30/85	CIVIC CENTER OTTAWA, ON
4/01/85	MADISON SQUARE GARDEN NEW YORK ,NY
4/02/85	CIVIC CENTER PROVIDENCE, RI
4/03/85	NASSAU VETERAN'S MEMORIAL COLISEUM, UNIONDALE, NY
4/08/85	CAPITOL CENTER LANDOVER, MD
4/09/85	CIVIC ARENA PITTSBUGH, PA
4/10/85	HAMPTON COLISEUM HAMPTON, VA
4/12/85	MEADOWLANDS EAST RUTHERFORD, NJ
4/14/85	MEADOWLANDS EAST RUTHERFORD, NJ
4/15/85	MEADOWLANDS EAST RUTHERFORD, NJ
4/16/85	CENTRUM, WORCESTER MA
4/18/85	CENTRUM, WORCESTER MA
4/19/85	CENTRUM, WORCESTER MA
4/20/85	CIVIC CENTER HARTFORD, CT
4/22/85	THE SPECTRUM PHILADELPHIA, PA
4/23/85	CIVIC CENTER HARTFORD, CT
4/24/85	THE SPECTRUM PHILADELPHIA, PA
4/27/85	THE SPECTRUM PHILADELPHIA, PA
4/29/85	THE OMNI ATLANTA, GA
4/30/85	JACKSONVILLE MEMORIAL COLISEUM JACKSONVILLE, FL
5/02/85	UNIVERSITY OF SOUTH FLORIDA SUN DOME TAMPA, FL
5/03/85	HOLLYWOOD SPORTATORIUM FORT LAUDERDALE, FL
5/04/85	HOLLYWOOD SPORTATORIUM FORT LAUDERDALE, FL

THE UNFORGETTABLE FIRE TOUR & EUROPEAN DATES AND FESTIVALS

5/25/85	NURENBURG RACECOURSE ADENAU /LOBLENZ
5/26/85	NECKARSTADION STUTTGART
5/27/85	FREIGELANDE HALLE MUNSTERLAND MUNSTER
6/01/85	ST JACOB'S FUSSBALSTADION BASEL
6/22/85	MILTON KEYNES BOWL MILTON KEYNES
6/28/85	CROKE PARK DUBLIN
6/29/85	CROKE PARK DUBLIN
7/06/85	FESTIVAL GROUNDS TORHOUT
7/07/85	FESTIVAL GROUNDS WERCHTER
7/13/85	LIVE AID WEMBLEY STADIUM, LONDON
7/25/85	LARK BY THE LEE FESTIVAL CORK
5/17/86	SELF AID CONCERT RDS, DUBLIN

AMNESTY INTERNATIONAL'S *CONSPIRACY OF HOPE* TOUR

6/04/86	COW PALACE SAN FRANCISCO, CA
6/06/86	THE FORUM INGLEWOOD, CA
6/08/86	McNICHOLS SPORTS ARENA DENVER, CO
6/11/86	THE OMNI ATLANTA, GA
6/13/86	ROSEMOUNT HORIZON CHICAGO, IL
6/15/86	GIANTS STADIUM EAST RUTHERFORD, NJ

THE JOSHUA TREE TOUR (1ST LEG) AMERICA

4/02/87	ARIZONA STATE UNIVERSITY ACTIVITY CENTER TEMPE, AZ
4/04/87	ARIZONA STATE UNIVERSITY ACTIVITY CENTER TEMPE, AZ
4/05/87	COMMUNITY CENTER TUCSON, AZ
4/07/87	THE SUMMIT HOUSTON, TX
4/08/87	THE SUMMIT HOUSTON, TX
4/08/87	LA CLUB HOUSTON, TX
4/10/87	PAN AMERICAN CENTER LAS CRUCES, NM
4/12/87	THOMAS & MACK ARENA LAS VEGAS, NV
4/13/87	SAN DIEGO SPORTS ARENA SAN DIEGO, CA
4/14/87	SAN DIEGO SPORTS ARENA SAN DIEGO, CA
4/17/87	LOS ANGELES SPORTS ARENA LA, CA
4/18/87	LOS ANGELES SPORTS ARENA LA, CA
4/20/87	LOS ANGELES SPORTS ARENA LA, CA
4/21/87	LOS ANGELES SPORTS ARENA LA, CA
4/22/87	LOS ANGELES SPORTS ARENA LA, CA
4/24/87	COW PALACE DALY CITY, CA
4/25/87	COW PALACE DALY CITY, CA
4/29/87	ROSEMOUNT HORIZON CHICAGO, IL
4/30/87	PONTIAC SILVERDOME DETROIT, MI
5/02/87	CENTRUM WORCESTER, MA
5/03/87	CENTRUM WORCESTER, MA
5/04/87	CENTRUM WORCESTER, MA

5/07/87	CIVIC CENTER HARTFORD, CT
5/08/87	CIVIC CENTER HARTFORD, CT
5/09/87	CIVIC CENTER HARTFORD, CT
5/11/87	MEADOWLANDS ARENA
5/12/87	MEADOWLANDS ARENA
5/13/87	MEADOWLANDS ARENA
5/15/87	MEADOWLANDS ARENA
5/16/87	MEADOWLANDS ARENA EAST RUTHERFORD, NJ

THE JOSHUA TREE TOUR (2ND LEG) EUROPE

5/27/87	STADIO FLAMINO ROME
5/29/87	STADIO COMUNALE BRAGLIA MODENA
5/30/87	STADIO COMUNALE BRAGLIA MODENA
6/02/87	WEMBLEY ARENA LONDON
6/03/87	NATIONAL EXHIBITION CENTRE BIRMINGHAM
6/06/87	ERIKSBERG SHIPYARD DOCKS GOTHENBURG
6/12/87	WEMBLEY STADIUM LONDON
6/13/87	WEMBLEY STADIUM LONDON
6/15/87	LE ZENITH PARIS, FRANCE
6/17/87	MUNGERDORFER STADION KOLN
6/21/87	ST JAKOB'S STADION BASEL
6/24/87	KINGS HALL BELFAST
6/27/87	CROKE PARK DUBLIN
6/28/87	CROKE PARK DUBLIN
7/01/87	ELLAND ROAD STADIUM LEEDS
7/04/87	HIPPODROME DE VINCENNES PARIS
7/08/87	VORST NATIONAAL BRUSSELS
7/10/87	FEYNOORD STADIUM ROTTERDAM
7/11/87	FEYNOORD STADIUM ROTTERDAM
7/15/87	ESTADIO SANTIAGO BERNABEU MADRID
7/18/87	ESPACE RICHTER MONTPELLIER
7/21/87	OLYMPIAHALLE MUNCHEN
7/22/87	OLYMPIAHALLE MUNCHEN
7/25/87	ARMS PARK CARDIFF
7/29/87	SCOTTISH EXHIBITION CENTRE
7/30/87	SCOTTISH EXHIBITION CENTRE GLASGOW
8/01/87	MURRAYFIELD STADIUM EDINBURGH
8/03/87	NATIONAL EXHIBITION CENTRE
8/04/87	NATIONAL EXHIBITION CENTRE BIRMINGHAM
8/08/87	PAIRC UI CHAOIMH CORK

THE JOSHUA TREE TOUR (3RD LEG) AMERICA

9/10/87	NASSAU COLISEUM UNIONDALE, NY
9/11/87	NASSAU COLISEUM UNIONDALE, NY
9/12/87	SPECTRUM ARENA PHILADELPHIA, PA
9/14/87	GIANTS STADIUM EAST RUTHERFORD, NJ
9/17/87	BOSTON GARDEN MA
9/18/87	BOSTON GARDEN MA
9/20/87	ROBERT F KENNEDY STADIUM WASHINGTON DC
9/22/87	SULLIVAN STADIUM BOSTON, MA
9/23/87	COLISEUM NEW HAVEN, CT
9/25/87	JFK STADIUM PHILADELPHIA, PA
9/28/87	MADISON SQUARE GARDEN
09/29/87	MADISON SQUARE GARDEN NEW YORK, NY
10/01/87	OLYMPIC STADIUM MONTREAL, QC
10/03/87	CANADIAN NATIONAL EXHIBITION STADIUM TORONTO, ON
10/06/87	MUNICIPAL STADIUM CLEVELAND, OH
10/07/87	MEMORIAL AUDITORIUM BUFFALO, NY
10/09/87	CARRIER DOME SYRACUSE, NY
10/11/87	SILVER STADIUM ROCHESTER, NY
10/13/87	THREE RIVERS STADIUM PITTSBURGH, PA
10/20/87	CARVER HAWKEYE ARENA, IOWA CITY, IA
10/22/87	UNIVERSITY ASSEMBLY HALL CHAMPAIGN, IL
10/23/87	RUPP ARENA LEXINGTON, KY
10/25/87	ST LOUIS ARENA ST LOUIS, MO
10/26/87	KEMPER ARENA KANSAS CITY, MO
10/28/87	ROSEMOUNT HORIZON
10/29/87	ROSEMOUNT HORIZON
10/30/87	ROSEMOUNT HORIZON ROSEMOUNT, IL
11/01/87	HOOSIER DOME INDIANAPOLIS, IN
11/03/87	CIVIC CENTER ST PAUL, MN
11/04/87	CIVIC CENTER ST PAUL, MN
11/07/87	McNICHOLS ARENA DENVER, CO
11/08/87	McNICHOLS ARENA DENVER, CO
11/11/87	JUSTIN HERMAN PLAZA SAN FRANCISCO, CA

11/12/87	BC PLACE STADIUM VANCOUVER, BC	
11/14/87	OAKLAND COLISEUM STADIUM	
11/15/87	OAKLAND COLISEUM STADIUM OAKLAND, CA	
11/17/87	LOS ANGELES MEMORIAL COLISEUM	
11/18/87	LOS ANGELES MEMORIAL COLISEUM LA. CA	
11/22/87	FRANK ERWIN CENTER AUSTIN, TX	
11/23/87	TARRANT COUNTY CONVENTION CENTER FORT WORTH, TX	
11/24/87	TARRANT COUNTY CONVENTION CENTER FORT WORTH, TX	
11/26/87	LOUISIANA STATE UNIVERSITY ASSEMBLY CENTER BATOB ROUGE, LA	
11/28/87	CHARLES M MURPHY ATHLETIC CENTER MURFREESBORO, TN	
12/03/87	ORANGE BOWL MIAMI, FL	
12/05/87	TAMPA STADIUM TAMPA, FL	
12/08/87	THE OMNI ATLANTA, GA	
12/09/87	THE OMNI ATLANTA, GA	
12/11/87	HAMPTON COLISEUM HAMPTON, VA	
12/12/87	HAMPTON COLISEUM HAMPTON, VA	
12/19/87	ARIZONA STATE UNIVERSITY SUN DEVIL STADIUM TEMPE, AZ	
12/20/87	ARIZONA STATE UNIVERSITY SUN DEVIL STADIUM TEMPE, AZ	

THE LOVETOWN TOUR (1ST LEG) NZ, AUSTRALIA & JAPAN

9/21/89	ENTERTAINMENT CENTER PERTH
9/22/89	ENTERTAINMENT CENTER PERTH
9/23/89	ENTERTAINMENT CENTER PERTH
9/27/89	ENTERTAINMENT CENTER SYDNEY
9/28/89	ENTERTAINMENT CENTER SYDNEY
09/29/89	ENTERTAINMENT CENTER SYDNEY
10/02/89	ENTERTAINMENT CENTER BRISBANE
10/03/89	ENTERTAINMENT CENTER BRISBANE
10/04/89	ENTERTAINMENT CENTER BRISBANE
10/07/89	NATIONAL TENNIS CENTER
10/08/89	NATIONAL TENNIS CENTER
10/09/89	NATIONAL TENNIS CENTER
10/12/89	NATIONAL TENNIS CENTER
10/13/89	NATIONAL TENNIS CENTER
10/14/89	NATIONAL TENNIS CENTER
10/16/89	NATIONAL TENNIS CENTER MELBOURNE
10/20/89	ENTERTAINMENT CENTER SYDNEY
10/21/89	ENTERTAINMENT CENTER SYDNEY
10/27/89	MEMORIAL DRIVE STADIUM ADELAIDE
10/28/89	MEMORIAL DRIVE STADIUM ADELAIDE
11/04/89	LANCASTER PARK CHRISTCHURCH
11/08/89	ATHLETIC PARK WELLINGTON
11/10/89	WESTERN SPRINGS STADIUM
11/11/89	WESTERN SPRINGS STADIUM AUCKLAND
11/17/89	ENTERTAINMENT CENTER SYDNEY
11/18/89	ENTERTAINMENT CENTER SYDNEY
11/19/89	ENTERTAINMENT CENTER SYDNEY
11/23/89	SPORTS ARENA YOHOHAMA
11/25/89	TOKYO DOME TOKYO
11/26/89	TOKYO DOME TOKYO
11/28/89	OSAKA CASTLE HALL OSAKA
11/29/89	OSAKA CASTLE HALL OSAKA
12/01/89	OSAKA CASTLE HALL OSAKA

THE LOVETOWN TOUR (2ND LEG) EUROPE

12/11/89	PALAIS OMNISPORTS DE BERCY PARIS
12/12/89	PALAIS OMNISPORTS DE BERCY PARIS
12/14/89	WESTFALENHALLE DORTMUND
12/15/89	WESTFALENHALLE DORTMUND
12/16/89	WESTFALENHALLE DORTMUND
12/18/89	RAI EUROPA HAL AMSTERDAM
12/26/89	POINT DEPOT DUBLIN
12/27/89	POINT DEPOT DUBLIN
12/30/89	POINT DEPOT DUBLIN
12/31/89	POINT DEPOT DUBLIN
1/05/90	SPORT PALEIS AHOY ROTTERDAM
1/06/90	SPORT PALEIS AHOY ROTTERDAM
1/09/90	SPORT PALEIS AHOY ROTTERDAM
1/10/90	SPORT PALEIS AHOY ROTTERDAM

ZOOTV TOUR (1ST LEG) NORTH AMERICA

2/29/92	LAKELAND CIVIC CENTER LAKELAND, FL
3/01/92	MIAMI ARENA MIAMI, FL
3/03/92	CHARLOTTE COLISEUM CHARLOTTE, NC
3/05/92	THE OMNI ATLANTA, GA
3/07/92	HAMPTON COLISEUM HAMPTON, VA

3/09/92	NASSAU COLISEUM UNIONDALE, NY
3/10/92T	HE SPECTRUM PHILADELPHIA, PA
3/12/92	CIVIC CENTER HARTFORD, CT
3/13/92	CENTRUM WORCESTER, MA
03/15/92	CIVIC CENTER PROVIDENCE, RI
03/17/92	BOSTON GARDEN BOSTON, MA
03/18/92	MEADOWLANDS ARENA EAST RUTHERFORD, NJ
03/20/92	MADISON SQUARE GARDEN NY, NY
3/21/92	KNICKERBOCKER ARENA ALBANY, NY
3/23/92	THE FORUM MONTREAL, QC
3/24/92	MAPLE LEAF GARDENS TORONTO, ON
3/26/92	RICHFIELD COLISEUM CLEVELAND, OH
3/27/92	PALACE OF AUBURN HILLS DETROIT, MI
3/30/92	TARGET CENTER MINNEAPOLIS, MN
3/31/92	ROSEMONT HORIZON ROSEMONT, IL
4/05/92	REUNION ARENA DALLAS, TX
4/06/92	THE SUMMIT HOUSTON, TX
4/07/92	FRANK ERWIN CENTER AUSTIN, TX
4/10/92	ASU ACTIVITY CENTER TEMPE, AZ
4/12/92	LOS ANGELES SPORTS ARENA
4/13/92	LOS ANGELES SPORTS ARENA LOS ANGELES, CA
4/15/92	SAN DIEGO SPORTS ARENA SAN DIEGO, CA
4/17/92	ARCO ARENA SACRAMENTO, CA
4/18/92	OAKLAND COLISEUM ARENA OAKLAND, CA
4/20/92	TACOMA DOME TACOMA, WA
4/21/92	TACOMA DOME TACOMA, WA
4/23/92	PACIFIC NATIONAL EXHIBITION COLISEUM VANCOUVER, BC

ZOOTV TOUR (2ND LEG) EUROPE

5/07/92	PALAIS OMNISPORTS DE BERCY PARIS
5/09/92	FLANDERS EXPO HALL GENT
5/11/92	ESPACE TONY GARNIER LYON
5/12/92	PATINOIRE DE MALLEY LAUSANNE
5/14/92	VELODROME ANOETA SAN SEBASTIAN
5/16/92	PALAU SANT JORDI BARCELONA
5/18/92	PALAU SANT JORDI BARCELONA
5/21/92	FORUM DI ASSAGO MILAN
5/22/92	FORUM DI ASSAGO MILAN
5/24/92	DONAU INSEL VIENNA
5/25/92	OLYMPIAHALLE MUNCHEN
5/27/92	HALLENSTADION ZURICH
5/29/92	FESTHALLE FRANKFURT
5/31/92	EARL'S COURT ARENA LONDON
6/01/92	NATIONAL EXHIBITION CENTRE BIRMINGHAM
6/04/92	WESTFALENHALLE DORTMUND
6/05/92	WESTFALENHALLE DORTMUND
6/08/92	SCANDINAVIUM GOTHENBURG
6/10/92	GLOBEN STOCKHOLM
6/11/92	GLOBEN STOCKHOLM
6/13/92	OSTSEEHALLE KIEL
6/15/92	AHOYHALLE ROTTERDAM
6/17/92	INDOOR SPORTS ARENA SHEFFIELD
6/18/92	SCOTTISH EXHIBITION CENTRE GLASGOW
6/19/92	G-MEX CENTER MANCHESTER

ZOOTV TOUR - OUTSIDE BROADCAST (3RD LEG) NORTH AMERICA

8/07/92	HERSHEY PARK STADIUM HERSHEY, PA
8/12/92	GIANTS STADIUM EAST RUTHERFORD, NJ
8/13/92	GIANTS STADIUM EAST RUTHERFORD, NJ
8/15/92	ROBERT F KENNEDY STADIUM
8/16/92	ROBERT F KENNEDY STADIUM WASHINGTON DC
8/18/92	SARATOGA RACEWAY SARATOGA SPRINGS, NY
8/20/92	FOXBORO STADIUM FOXBORO, MA
8/22/92	FOXBORO STADIUM FOXBORO, MA
8/23/92	FOXBORO STADIUM FOXBORO, MA
8/25/92	THREE RIVERS STADIUM PITTSBURGH, PA
8/27/92	OLYMPIC STADIUM MONTREAL, QC
8/29/92	YANKEE STADIUM NEW YORK, NY
8/30/92	YANKEE STADIUM NEW YORK, NY
9/02/92	VETERNS STADIUM PHILADELPHIA, PA
9/03/92	VETERNS STADIUM PHILADELPHIA, PA
9/05/92	CANADIAN NATIONAL EXHIBITION STADIUM TORONTO, ON
9/06/92	CANADIAN NATIONAL EXHIBITION STADIUM TORONTO, ON

9/09/92	PONTIAC SILVERDOME PONTIAC, MI
9/11/92	CYCLONE STADIUM AMES, IA
9/13/92	CAMP RANDALL STADIUM MADISON, WI
9/15/92	WORLD MUSIC AMPHITHEATER
9/16/92	WORLD MUSIC AMPHITHEATER
9/18/92	WORLD MUSIC AMPHITHEATER CHICAGO, IL
9/20/92	BUSCH MEMORIAL STADIUM ST LOUIS, MO
9/23/92	WILLIAMS BRICE STADIUM COLUMBIA, SC
9/25/92	GEORGIA DOME ATLANTA, GA
10/03/92	JOE ROBBIE STADIUM MIAMI, FL
10/07/92	LEGION FIELD BIRMINGHAM, AL
10/10/92	TAMPA STADIUM TAMPA, FL
10/14/92	HOUSTON ASTRODOME HOUSTON, TX
10/16/92	TEXAS STADIUM DALLAS, TX
10/18/92	ARROWHEAD STADIUM KANSAS CITY, MO
10/21/92	MILE HIGH STADIUM DENVER CO
10/24/92	SUN DEVILE STADIUM TEMPE, AZ
10/27/92	TEXAS SUN BOWL EL PASO, TX
10/30/92	DOGER STADIUM LA, CA
10/31/92	DOGER STADIUM LA, CA
11/03/92	BC PLACE STADIUM VANCOUVER, BC
11/04/92	BC PLACE STADIUM VANCOUVER, BC
11/07/92	OAKLAND COLISEUM STADIUM OAKLAND, CA
11/10/92	JACK MURPHY STADIUM SAN DIEGO, CA
11/12/92	SAM BOYD SILVER BOWL LAS VEGAS, NV
11/14/92	ANAHEIM STADIUM ANAHEIM, CA
11/21/92	PALACIO DE LOS DEPORTES
11/22/92	PALACIO DE LOS DEPORTES
11/24/92	PALACIO DE LOS DEPORTES
11/25/92	PALACIO DE LOS DEPORTES MEXICO CITY

ZOOTV TOUR ZOOROPA 93 EUROPE

5/09/93	FEYENOORD STADIUM ROTTERDAM
5/10/93	FEYENOORD STADIUM ROTTERDAM
5/11/93	FEYENOORD STADIUM ROTTERDAM
5/15/93	ESTADIO JOSE ALVALADE LISBON
5/19/93	ESTADIO CARLOS TARTIER OVIEDO
5/22/93	ESTADIO VICENTE CALDERON MADRID
5/26/93	STADE DE LA BEAUJOIRE NANTES
5/29/93	FESTIVAL GROUNDS WERCHTER
6/04/93	OLYMPIASTADION MUNCHEN
6/06/93	CANNSTATTER WASEN STUTTGART
6/09/93	WESERSTADION BREMAN
6/12/93	MUNGERSDORFSTADION KOLN
6/15/93	OLYMPIASTADION BERLIN
6/23/93	STADE DE LA MEINAU STRASBOURG
6/26/93	HIPPODROME DE VINCENNES PARIS
6/28/93	STADE DE LA PONTAISE LAUSANNE
6/30/93	ST JAKOBS STADION BASEL
7/02/93	STADIO BENTEGODI VERONA
7/03/93	STADIO BENTEGODI VERONA
7/06/93	STADIO FLAMINIO ROME
7/07/93	STADIO FLAMINIO ROME
7/09/93	STADIO SAN PAULO NAPLES
7/12/93	STADIO DELLE ALPI TURIN
7/14/93	STADE VELODROME MARSEILLE
7/17/93	STADIO COMUNALE BOLOGNA
7/18/93	STADIO COMUNALE BOLOGNA
7/23/93	NEP STADION BUDAPEST
7/27/93	GENTOFTE STADION COPENHAGEN
7/29/93	VALLE HOVIN STADION OSLO
7/31/93	STOCKHOLM STADION STOCKHOLM
8/03/93	GOFFERT PARK NIJMEGEN
8/07/93	CELTIC PARK GLASGOW
8/08/93	CELTIC PARK GLASGOW
8/11/93	WEMBLEY STADIUM LONDON
8/12/93	WEMBLEY STADIUM LONDON
8/14/93	ROUNDHAY PARK LEEDS
8/18/93	ARMS PARK CARDIFF
8/20/93	WEMBLEY STADIUM LONDON
8/21/93	WEMBLEY STADIUM LONDON
8/24/93	PAIRC UI CHAOIMH CORK
8/27/93	RDS ARENA DUBLIN
8/28/93	RDS ARENA DUBLIN

ZOOTV TOUR ZOOMERANG, NEW ZOOLAND, ZOOTV JAPAN

11/12/93	CRICKET GROUND MELBOURNE
11/13/93	CRICKET GROUND MELBOURNE
11/06/93	FOOTBALL PARK ADELAIDE
1/20/93	ANZ STADIUM BRISBANE
11/26/93	CRICKET GROUND SYDNEY
11/27/93	CRICKET GROUND SYDNEY

12/01/93	LANCASTER PARK CHRISTCHURCH
12/04/93	WESTERN SPRING STADIUM AUCKLAND
12/09/93	TOKYO DOME TOKYO
12/10/93	TOKYO DOME TOKYO

POPMART TOUR 97 (1ST LEG) NORTH AMERICA

4/25/97	SAM BOYD STADIUM LAS VEGAS, NV
4/28/97	JACK MURPHY STADIUM SAN DIEGO, CA
5/01/97	MILE HIGH STADIUM DENVER, CO
5/03/97	RICE STADIUM SALT LAKE CITY, UT
5/06/97	AUTZEN STADIUM EUGENE, OR
5/09/97	SUN DEVIL STADIUM PHOENIX, AZ
5/12/97	COTTON BOWL DALLAS, TX
5/14/97	LIBERTY BOWL MEMPHIS, TN
5/16/97	MEMORIAL STADIUM CELMSON, SC
5/19/97	ARROWHEAD STADIUM KANSAS CITY, MO
5/22/97	THREE RIVERS STADIUM PITTSBURGH, PA
5/24/97	OHIO STADIUM COLUMBUS, OH
5/26/97	RFK STADIUM WASHINGTON, DC
5/31/97	GIANTS STADIUM
6/01/97	GIANTS STADIUM
6/03/97	GIANTS STADIUM EAST RUTHERFORD, NJ
6/07/97	TIBETAN FREEDOM CONCERT DOWNING STADIUM, RANDALL'S ISLAND, NY
6/08/97	FRANKLIN FIELD PHILADELPHIA, PA
6/12/97	WINNIPEG STADIUM WINNIPEG, MB
6/14/97	COMMONWEALTH STADIUM EDMONTON, AB
6/18/97	OAKLAND STADIUM OAKLAND, CA
6/19/97	OAKLAND STADIUM OAKLAND, CA
6/21/97	LOS ANGELES MEMORIAL COLISEUM LOS ANGELES, CA
6/25/97	CAMP RANDALL STADIUM MADISON, WI
6/27/97	SOLDIER FIELD CHICAGO, IL
6/28/97	SOLDIER FIELD CHICAGO, IL
6/29/97	SOLDIER FIELD CHICAGO, IL
7/01/97	FOXBORO STADIUM FOXBORO, MA
7/02/97	FOXBORO STADIUM FOXBORO, MA

POPMART TOUR (2ND LEG) EUROPE

7/18/97	FEYENOORD STADION ROTTERDAM,
7/19/97	FEYENOORD STADION ROTTERDAM,
7/25/97	FESTIVAL GROUNDS WERCHTER
7/27/97	BUTZWELL HOF KOLN
7/29/97	FESTWEISE LEIPZIG
7/31/97	MALMARKT MANNHEIM
8/02/97	ULLEVI STADION GOTHENBURG
8/04/97	PARKEN STADIUM COPENHAGEN,
8/06/97	VALLEHOVIN OSLO
8/09/97	OLYMPIC STADIUM HELSINKI
8/12/97	HORSE TRACK WARSAW
8/14/97	STRAHOV STADIUM PRAGUE,
8/16/97	AIRFIELD WIENER NEUSTADT
8/18/97	ZEPPELINFELD NUREMBURG
8/20/97	EXPO HANNOVER
8/22/97	WEMBLEY STADIUM LONDON
8/23/97	WEMBLEY STADIUM LONDON
8/26/97	BOTANIC GARDENS BELFAST
8/28/97	ROUNDHAY PARK LEEDS
8/30/97	LANSDOWNE ROAD DUBLIN
8/31/97	LANSDOWNE ROAD DUBLIN
9/02/97	MURRAYFIELD EDINGBURGH
9/06/97	PARC DES PRINCES FRANCE
9/09/97	CALDERON MADRID
9/11/97	ESTADIO ALVALADE LISBON
9/13/97	ESTADI OLIMPIC DE MONTJUIE BARCELONA
9/15/97	ESPACE GRAMMONT MONPELLIER
9/18/97	AERPORTE DEL URBE ROME
9/20/97	FESTIVAL SITE REGGIO EMILIA
9/23/97	KOSEVO STADIUM SARAJEVO
9/26/97	KAFTATZOGLIO THESSALONIKI
9/30/97	RAMAT-GAN NATIONAL STADIUM TEL AVIV

POPMART TOUR (3RD LEG) NORTH AMERICA

10/26/97	SKYDOME TORONTO, ON
10/27/97	SKYDOME TORONTO, ON
10/29/97	METRODOME MINNEAPOLIS, MN
10/31/97	SILVERDOME DETROIT, MI
11/02/97	OLYMPIC STADIUM MONTREAL, QC
11/08/97	TRANSWORLD DOME ST LOUIS, MO
11/10/97	HOULIHANS STADIUM TAMPA, FL
11/12/97	MUNICIPAL STADIUM JACKSONVILLE, FL

11/14/97	PRO PLAYER STADIUM MIAMI, FL
11/21/97	SUPERDOME NEW ORLEANS, LA
11/23/97	ALAMODOME SAN ANTONIO, TX
11/26/97	GEORGIA DOME ATLANTA, GA
11/28/97	ASTRODOME USA HOUSTON, TX
12/02/97	AUTODROME MEXICO CITY
12/03/97	AUTODROME MEXICO CITY
12/09/97	BC PLACE STADIUM VANCOUVER, BC
12/12/97	KINGDOME SEATTLE, WA

POPMART TOUR (4TH LEG) SOUTH AMERICA

1/28/98	MARACANA RIO DE JANEIRO
1/30/98	MORUMBI SAO PAULO
1/31/98	MORUMBI SAO PAULO
2/05/98	ESTADIO RIVER PLATE BUENOS AIRES
2/06/98	ESTADIO RIVER PLATE BUENOS AIRES
2/10/98	ESTADIO NACIONAL SANTIAGO

POPMART TOUR (5TH LEG) AUSTRALIA, JAPAN & SOUTH AFRICA

2/17/98	BURSWOOD STADIUM PERTH
2/21/98	WAVERLY PARK MELBOURNE
2/25/98	ANZ PARK BRISBANE
2/27/98	FOOTBALL STADIUM SYDNEY
3/05/98	TOKYO DOME TOKYO
3/11/98	OSAKA DOME OSAKA
3/21/98	JOHANNESBURG STADIUM JOHANNESBURG

ANTON CORBIJN

chronology

1960

March 13 Adam Clayton born in Chinnor, Oxfordshire

May 10 Paul Hewson born in the Rotunda Hospital, Dublin

1961

August 8 David Evans born in Barking Maternity Hospital, East London

October 31 Larry Mullen Jr born in Artane, Dublin

1976

Autumn Under the name Feedback, Larry Mullen Jr, Dik and Dave Evans, Adam Clayton and Paul Hewson form a group following a note Larry pinned to their school noticeboard. They later change their name to The Hype

1978

March 17 Still in school, The Hype win £500 and some studio time at a talent contest in Limerick. Sponsors include CBS Records, whom they later record for

March 20 The Hype change their name to U2. Dik Evans leaves the band

April 28 Bill Graham writes first ever U2 interview in Hot Press under the heading *Yep! It's U2*

May 25 Paul McGuinness goes to see U2 live at a gig in Dublin's Project Arts Centre. He becomes their manager

September 9 U2 support the Stranglers at a gig in the Top Hat Ballroom, playing to 2,500 people

1979

May U2 play the first of six afternoon gigs at the Dandelion Market in Dublin.

September Their EP entitled *U2-3*, is released in Ireland only, on CBS Records and it tops the charts

December 8 Playing their first UK gigs, U2 are mis-billed at The Hope And Anchor pub in London as *V2*

1980

January 15 The group play live on the Late Late Show, Ireland's leading national chat show. They perform *Stories For Boys*. The following week they win 5 awards in the Hot Press readers poll

February 26 CBS Ireland release their second single *Another Day* which also peaks at No 1

March U2 play more dates in the UK. Soon after they sign a major international recording deal with Island Records

May 23 Island release the Martin Hannett-produced single *11 O'Clock Tick Tock* in Ireland and the UK

July U2 play to a 15,000 audience at an open-air festival Ireland with The Police and Squeeze

August The single *A Day Without Me* is released

October 15 The group play their first gig in mainland Europe in The Milkyway in Amsterdam

October 20 U2's debut album Boy, produced by Steve Lillywhite, is released in Ireland and the UK. It peaks at No 52 in the British charts

December 6 American gig at The Ritz in New York

1981

February 28 U2 appear on the BBC TV's, The Old Grey Whistle Test

March 3 The debut album *Boy* is released in the US and reaches No 63 in the chart

August 8 U2's first British hit single *Fire* enters the charts peaking at No 35

August 16 U2 play Slane Castle, Meath alongside Thin Lizzy and Hazel O'Connor

October 12 The groups second album *October* is released and enters the British charts at No.11

1982

January 26 U2 perform the first rock concert ever at Dublin's RDS Hall

April The single *A Celebration* goes to No 47 in the UK charts

August 8 U2 begin work on their third album *War* with Steve Lillywhite at Windmill Lane Studios, Dublin

1983

February In the UK chart *New Year's Day* hits No 10, while the album *War* reached No 12 in the US

February 28 In the UK *War* is released and goes to No 1

April 23 A two month American tour begins in North Carolina

June 5 U2 play at Red Rocks in Denver. The concert is recorded and later released on video. The live mini-album *Under A Blood Red Sky* is also released later and peaks at No 2 in the UK and No 28 in the US

August 14 U2 headline *A Day At The Races* concert in Dublin, supported by Eurythmics and Simple Minds

November 22 U2 play their debut gig in Japan at the Festival Hall, Osaka

December U2 are voted *Band of the Year* in the Rolling Stone writer's poll

1984

January 28 In the US chart *I Will Follow* climbs to No 81

May 7 U2 begin work on their fourth album *The Unforgettable Fire*, with producers Brian Eno and

Daniel Lanois at Slane Castle, Co. Meath

August Mother Records is established by U2 to introduce unsigned Irish acts

August 29 U2 play in New Zealand for the first time

September 29 In Britain *Pride (In The Name Of Love)* hits No 3

October 1 In the UK The Unforgettable Fire is released and charts at No 1 and No 12 in the US

November 25 Bono and Adam perform on Band Aid's *Do They Know It's Christmas*

December U2 begin their US leg of The Unforgettable Fire tour. *Pride (In The Name Of Love)* charts at No 33 in the US

1985

February Album sales for The Unforgettable Fire reach 1 million copies

April 1 U2 play a sell-out gig at Madison Square Garden in New York and Rolling Stone magazine names them Band Of The 80's

May The EP *Wide Awake In America* is released. The *Unforgettable Fire* makes No 6 in the UK

July 13 U2 play at the Live Aid concert Wembley Stadium, London. *Wide Awake In America* makes No 11 in UK charts

October In US charts *Wide Awake In America* reaches No 37

November Bono appears on the Little Steven organised *Sun City* single and video released in aid of Artists Against Apartheid

1986

January Irish group Clannad release *In A Lifetime* single featuring guest vocals from Bono. It reaches No 20 in the UK charts

February U2 win Best Band and Best Live Aid Performance in Rolling Stone's 1985 Reader's Poll

May 17 U2 headline Self Aid concert in Dublin along-side may other Irish artists to raise money for the unemployed

June 4 The *Conspiracy Of Hope* tour begins in aid of Amnesty International. U2 join Sting, Peter Gabriel, Joan Baez, Lou Reed and Bryan Adams on the bill

August U2 begin work on *The Joshua Tree* in Dublin with Brian Eno and Daniel Lanois. The Edge also records the film soundtrack album *Captive* which includes vocals from Sinead O'Connor

1987

March 9 The Joshua Tree is released and is the fastest selling record in UK history. *With Or Without You* reaches No 4 in the UK

March 27 The group film the music video for *Where The Streets Have No Name* in downtown LA

April 2 The Joshua Tree tour begins in the US

April 25 The album tops the US chart where it stays for 9 weeks

April 27 U2 appear on the cover of Time magazine, under the banner *U2: Rock's Hottest Ticket*. They are only the third rock band to do so

May 16 With Or Without You tops the US chart for three weeks becoming their first US No 1

May Album sales for The Joshua Tree reach 7 million

August 8 I Still Haven't Found What I'm Looking For tops the US charts

1988

February U2 begin work on the *Rattle And Hum* film with director Phil Joanou

March 2 U2 win 2 Grammy Awards for *Best Vocal Of The Year* for *I Still Haven't Found What I'm Looking For* and *Album Of The Year* for *The Joshua Tree*

October 8 Desire is released and becomes their first UK No 1

October 10 The Rattle And Hum album is released and reaches No 1 in the UK

October 27 The World Premiere of the *Rattle & Hum* movie takes place in Dublin

November 12 Rattle And Hum tops the US album chart

1989

February 13 U2 win Best International group at the BRIT Awards

February 22 U2 win two Grammy Awards for *Desire* and *Where The Streets Have No Name*

April When Love Comes To Town featuring BB King charts at No 6 in the UK and No 68 in the US

September 21 The *Lovetown* tour begins in Australia with BB King supporting

December 31 Final concert of U2's *Lovetown* tour, with BB King also on the bill, at Dublin's Point Depot. Bono announces the 500 million live radio listeners "We have to go away and dream it all up again"

1990

June Larry Mullen co-writes *Put 'Em Under Pressure*,

the official song for Ireland's World Cup soccer team

October U2 record Cole Porter's *Night & Day* for the album Red Hot + Blue to benefit AIDS education

November U2 begin recording *Achtung Baby* at Hansa Studios in Berlin

1991

November 18 Achtung Baby is released

1992

February 29 The *Zoo TV* arena tour begins in Florida, US

May 7 The European leg of the Zoo TV tour begins

June 13 Seven U2 albums appear in the UK Charts in one week

June 19 U2 play at the *Stop Sellafield* show in Manchester

August 1 The Outside Broadcast leg of Zoo TV begins in the US

November 21 U2 play Mexico for the first time

1993

January Larry & Adam perform a version of *One* with R.E.M.'s Michael Stipe and Mike Mills at the MTV 1993 Rock & Roll Inaugural Ball for the newly elected Bill Clinton

July 5 The album *Zooropa* is released

July 17 U2 link live to Sarajevo during their gig in Bologna, Italy

August 11 Salman Rushdie joins U2 on stage in Wembley Stadium, London

September 3 The Edge performs *Numb* solo at the MTV Awards in LA

November Bono records vocals for *I've Got You Under My Skin*, his duet with Frank Sinatra

December 10 The Zoo TV tour finishes in Tokyo, Japan

1994

March Zooropa wins a Grammy for *Best Alternative Album*

April Larry and Adam record with Nanci Griffith for her album *Flyer*

April 5 ZooTV *Live From Sydney* video is released

1995

February Bono and Edge write and record *North & South Of The River* with Irish songwriter Christy Moore

June 1 Hold Me, Thrill Me, Kiss Me, Kill Me is released and goes to No 2 in the UK, No 16 in the US and No 1 in Australia and Ireland. The track appears in the Batman Forever soundtrack

September 12 Bono, The Edge and Brian Eno perform *Miss Sarajevo* with Pavarotti at his annual concert in Modena, Italy

November 6 Passengers *Original Soundtracks 1* is released.

1996

January U2 start work on *Pop* in Dublin with producer Flood

May 1 Adam and Larry release their reworking of the *Mission Impossible* theme which reached the Top 10 in the US and UK amongst others

1997

February 11 Discotheque single released, charting at No 1 in over 13 countries

February 12 U2 announce the release of their new album *Pop* in the Greenwich Village K-Mart, New York

March 3 Pop album is released, entering the US charts at No 1

April 25 PopMart tour begins in Las Vegas

July 18 PopMart European tour begins in Rotterdam

September 23 U2 play Sarajevo

1998

May 19 U2 perform at concert held in Belfast in support of the Referendum for Peace in Northern Ireland

October 19 Sweetest Thing single is released. The single is a re-recorded version of the b-side to *Where The Streets Have No Name*, originally recorded in 1987

November 2 U2 *The Best Of 1980-1990* is released worldwide

November U2 *The Best Of 1980-1990* becomes the biggest selling greatest hits collection by any band in its first week of release on the Soundscan chart in the US

1999

January U2 begin work on new studio album in Dublin

February 16 Bono presents The Freddie Mercury Prize at the Brit Awards in London to Muhammad Ali, for his services to charity and Jubilee 2000 and high-lights the campaign to cancel third world debt

April 6 U2 perform live by satellite *Don't Take Your Guns To Town* at an all-star tribute to Johnny Cash in New York. Other guests include Sheryl Crow, Emmylou Harris, Willie Nelson and Kris Kristofferson

HUGO McGUINNESS

HUGO McGUINNESS

JAMES MAHON

ANTON CORBIJN

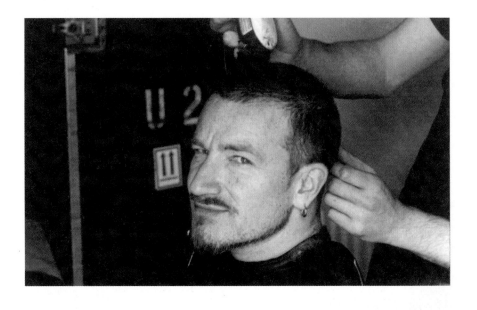

49

the lyrics

"40"

I waited patiently for the Lord.
He inclined and heard my cry.
He brought me up out of the pit
Out of the miry clay.

I will sing, sing a new song.
I will sing, sing a new song.
How long to sing this song?
How long to sing this song?
How long, how long, how long
How long to sing this song?

You set my feet upon a rock
And made my footsteps firm.
Many will see, many will see and hear.

I will sing, sing a new song.
I will sing, sing a new song
I will sing, sing a new song.
I will sing, sing a new song
How long to sing this song?
How long to sing this song?
How long to sing this song?
How long to sing this song?

11 O'CLOCK TICK TOCK

It's cold outside
It gets so hot in here
The boys and girls collide
To the music in my ear.

I hear the children crying
And I know it's time to go
I hear the children crying
Take me home.

A painted face
And I know we haven't long
We thought that we had the answers
It was the questions we had wrong.

I hear the children crying
And I know it's time to go
I hear the children crying
Take me home.

Say so, say so
Say so, say so.

A CELEBRATION

I gotta go!
I believe in a celebration
I believe we can be free.
I believe you can loose these chains
I believe you can dance with me, dance with me.
Shake! Shake!
Shake! Shake!

I believe in the Third World War
I believe in the atomic bomb.
I believe in the powers-that-be
But they won't overpower me.

And you can go there too,
And you can go, go, go, go!
Shake! Shake!
Shake! Shake!

And we don't have the time
And everything goes round and round
And we don't have the time
To watch the world go tumbling down.

I believe in the bells of Christchurch
Ringing for this land.
I believe in the cells of Mountjoy
There's an honest man.

And you can go there too, etc.

I believe in the walls of Jericho
I believe they're coming down.
I believe in this city's children
I believe the trumpet's sound.

And you can go there too, etc.

A DAY WITHOUT ME

Started a landslide in my ego
Looked from the outside to the world I left behind.
I'm dreaming, you're awake
If I was sleeping, what's at stake?

A day without me.

Whatever the feelings, I keep feeling
What are the feelings you left behind?

A day without me.

Started a landslide in my ego
Looked from the outside to the world I left behind.
In the world I left behind
Wipe their eyes and then let go
In the world I left behind
Shed a tear and let love go.

A ROOM AT THE HEARTBREAK HOTEL

From where I stand
I can see through you
From where you're sitting pretty one
I know it got to you.

I see the stars in your eyes
You say you want the truth but you need the lies
Like Judy Garland, like Valentino
You give your life for rock'n'roll.

Stand, we're on a landslide of love
You got everything you want
But what you need you give away
For primitive love and a ride on a mystery train
A primitive love.
A room at the heart, the heartbreak hotel.
A room at the heartbreak, heartbreak hotel.

You say it's love, it's not the money
You let them suck your life out like honey
Turning tricks you're on the street
Selling your kisses so bittersweet.

For primitive love and a ride on a mystery train
A primitive love
A room at the heartbreak, heartbreak hotel.

A SORT OF HOMECOMING

And you know it's time to go
Through the sleet and driving snow
Across the fields of mourning to a light that's in the distance.

And you hunger for the time
Time to heal, 'desire' time
And your earth moves beneath your own dream landscape.

On borderland we run.
I'll be there, I'll be there tonight
A high-road, a high-road out from here.

The city walls are all come down
The dust a smoke screen all around
See faces ploughed like fields that once
Gave no resistance.

And we live by the side of the road
On the side of a hill as the valleys explode
Dislocated, suffocated
The land grows weary of it's own.

O com-away, o com-away, o-com, o com-away, I say I
O com-away, o com-away, o-com, o com-away, I say I

Oh, oh on borderland we run
And still we run, we run and don't look back
I'll be there, I'll be there
Tonight, tonight

I'll be there tonight, I believe
I'll be there so high
I'll be there tonight, tonight.

Oh com-away, I say, o com-away, I say.

The wind will crack in winter time
This bomb-blast lightning waltz.
No spoken words, just a scream
Tonight we'll build a bridge across the sea and land
See the sky, the burning rain
She will die and live again tonight.

And your heart beats so slow
Through the rain and fallen snow
Across the fields of mourning to a light that's in the distance.
Oh, don't sorrow, no don't weep
For tonight at last I am coming home.
I am coming home.

ACROBAT

Don't believe what you hear, don't believe what you see
If you just close your eyes you can feel the enemy.
When I first met you girl, you had fire in your soul.
What happened t'your face of melting snow
Now it looks like this!
And you can swallow or you can spit
You can throw it up, or choke on it
And you can dream, so dream out loud
You know that your time is coming round
So don't let the bastards grind you down.

No, nothing makes sense, nothing seems to fit.
I know you'd hit out if you only knew who to hit.
And I'd join the movement
If there was one I could believe in
Yeah, I'd break bread and wine
If there was a church I could receive in.
'Cause I need it now.
To take the cup
To fill it up, to drink it slow.
I can't let you go.

And I must be an acrobat
To talk like this and act like that.
And you can dream, so dream out loud
And don't let the bastards grind you down.

What are we going to do now it's all been said?
No new ideas in the house, and every book's been read.

And I must be an acrobat
To talk like this and act like that.
And you can dream, so dream out loud
And you can find your own way out.
And you can build, and I can will
And you can call, I can't wait until
You can stash and you can seize
In dreams begin responsibilities
And I can love, and I can love
And I know that the tide is turning 'round
So don't let the bastards grind you down.

ALL I WANT IS YOU

You say you want diamonds on a ring of gold
You say you want your story to remain untold.
All the promises we make
From the cradle to the grave
When all I want is you.

You say you'll give me a highway with no-one on it
Treasure, just to look upon it
All the riches in the night.

You say you'll give me eyes in the moon of blindness
A river in a time of dryness
A harbour in the tempest.
All the promises we make, from the cradle to the grave
When all I need is you.

You say you want your love to work out right
To last with me through the night.

You say you want diamonds on a ring of gold
Your story to remain untold
Your love not to grow cold.
All the promises we break, from the cradle to the grave
When all I want is you.

AN CAT DUBH

Say goodnight
She waits for me to turn out the light
Really still
She waits to break my will.

Woah-oh
Yes, and I know the truth about you.
She cat.

And in the daylight
A blackbird makes a violent sight
And when she is done
She sleeps beside the one

Woah-oh-oh
Yes, and I know the truth about you
She cat.

Yes, and I know the truth about you
She cat.

ANGEL OF HARLEM

It was a cold and wet December day
When we touched the ground at J.F.K.
The snow was melting on the ground
On B.L.S. I heard the sound
(Of an angel).
New York like a Christmas tree
Tonight, this city belongs to me,
(Angel).

Soul love
Well this love won't let me go.
So long
Angel of Harlem.

Birdland on Fifty-Three
The street sounds like a symphony
We got John Coltrane and a love supreme
Miles and she's got to be an angel.
Lady Day got diamond eyes
She sees the truth behind the lies
(Angel).

Soul love
Well this love won't let me go.
So long
Angel of Harlem.

Blue light on the avenue
God knows they got to you
Empty glass, the lady sings
Eyes swollen like a bee-sting.

Blinded, you lost your way
In the side streets and the alleyways
Like a star exploding in the night
Filling up the city with broad daylight.

Angel in devil's shoes
Salvation in the blues
You never looked like an angel
Angel of Harlem.

ANOTHER DAY

Wake up, the dawn of another dull day.
Take up your dreams and on your way.
Oh, oh, oh.

Daylight, mother stands in the hall.
Last night, head against the wall.
Oh, oh, oh.

When night turns to day
And the children come out to play
Another day.

Stop, shout.
They come my way.
Oh, oh, oh, oh.

Boy, salute in a street uniform
Toy, soldier ripped and torn
Oh, oh, oh.

When night turns to day
And the children come out to play
Another day.

Stop, shout.
They come my way.
Oh, oh, oh, oh.

ANOTHER TIME, ANOTHER PLACE

Bright morning lights
Wipe the sleep
From another day's eye.
Turn away from the wall
And there's nothing at all.
Being naked and afraid
In the open space of my bed.

I'll be with you now
I'll be with you now
I'll be with you now
We lie on a cloud, we lie.

Just as I am
I awoke with a tear on my tongue
I awoke with a feeling of never before
In my sleep, I discovered the one
But she left with the morning sun.

I'll be with you now
I'll be with you now
I'll be with you now
We lie on a cloud, we lie.

Another time, another place
We lie.
Another time another place.
We lie.
Another time, another place
We lie.
Your time, your place.

BABYFACE

Catching your bright blue eyes in the freeze frame
I've seen them so many times
I feel like I must be your best friend.
You're looking fine, so fine
Dressed up like a lovely day.

Babyface, Babyface
Slow down child, let me untie your lace.
Babyface, Babyface
Cover girl with natural grace.
How could beauty be so kind
To an ordinary guy?

Comin' home late at night to turn you on
Checkin' out every frame,
I've got slow motion on my side.
Turnin' around and around
With the sound and colour under my control
Round and around, goin' down,
Dressed up like a lovely day.

Babyface, Babyface
Slow down child, let me untie your lace
Babyface, Babyface
Tinfoil hair all tied up in lace
Babyface, Babyface
Bitter-sweet girl, won't you give me a taste
How could beauty be so kind
To an ordinary guy?

Babyface, Babyface
Slow down child, let me untie your lace.
Babyface, Babyface
Open that door, let me unpack my case.
Babyface, Babyface
You're everywhere, child, you're all over the place.
Babyface, Babyface
You're comin' to me from outer space.
How could beauty be so kind
To an ordinary guy?

BAD

If you twist and turn away.
It you tear yourself in two again.
If I could, yes I would
If I could, I would let it go.
Surrender, dislocate.

If I could throw this lifeless life-line to the wind.
Leave this heart of clay, see you walk, walk away
Into the night, and through the rain
Into the half light and through the flame.

If I could, through myself, set your spirit free
I'd lead your heart away, see you break, break away
Into the light and to the day.

To let it go and so to find a way.
To let it go and so find a way.
I'm wide awake.
I'm wide awake, wide awake.
I'm not sleeping.

If you should ask, then maybe
They'd tell you what I would say
True colours fly in blue and black
Blue silken sky and burning flag.
Colours crash, collide in blood-shot eyes.

If I could, you know I would
If I could, I would let it go.

This desperation, dislocation
Separation, condemnation
Revelation, in temptation
Isolation, desolation
Let it go and so to find a way
To let it go and so to find a way
To let it go and so to find a way

I'm wide awake, I'm wide awake, wide awake
I'm not sleeping
Oh no, no, no.

BOOMERANG II

Soul wind blow
Soul wind blow
Soul wind blow
Blow by blow

Under her skin I feel her laughing
Under her nails a piece of me
Under her weight I feel weightless
Under her sheets a friend and enemy

Soul wind blow
Soul wind blow
Soul wind blow
Blow by blow
In the drift we come
In the drift we go...

Under her wings I feel I'm flying
Under her breath I hear my name
Under her spell I'm going under
Under her eyes...I disappear

Soul wind blow
Soul wind blow
Soul wind blow
Blow by blow
You blow me away, blow me away

In the drift we come
In the drift we go...
In the drift we come
In the drift we go...

Soul wind blow
Soul wind blow
Soul wind blow
Blow by blow

Under her roof I feel shelter
Under her hands I feel as clay
Under her weight I feel weightless
Under her clock time goes away

BOY/GIRL

Boy/Girl (girl)
Boy/Girl (girl)

When a boy meets a girl
Boy/Girl (girl)

Finding out
I'm finding out the things
That I've been talking about.
I'm finding out the things
That I've been missing out.
Finding all the things
That blow my mind
I sometimes fall behind.

You and I
We live on the big ship
And time sails by.
You make up
And I believe milady's lie.
The skinheads call it strawberries and cream
Sometimes I scream.

Boy/Girl (girl)
Boy/Girl (girl)

When a boy meets a girl
Boy/Girl (girl)

We go out
A picture or a disco or a roundabout
I walk you home,
I hold you there
You're giving out
I open doors so I can shut your face
Know your place.

Boy/Girl (girl)
Boy/Girl (girl)

When a boy meets a girl
Boy/Girl (girl)

You can take me in your hand
Stand back, leave me, come in.
Up and down and all around
Swinging sideways to the ground.

Boy/Girl (girl)
Boy/Girl (girl)
When a boy meets a girl

Boy/Girl (girl)
Boy/Girl (girl)
When a boy meets a girl

Boy/Girl (girl)
Boy/Girl (girl)
When a boy meets
When a boy meets
When a boy meets girl,

BULLET THE BLUE SKY

In the howlin' wind
Comes a stingin' rain
See it drivin' nails
Into the souls on the tree of pain.

From the firefly
A red orange glow
See the face of fear
Runnin' scared in the valley below.

Bullet the blue sky
Bullet the blue sky
Bullet the blue
Bullet the blue.

In the locust wind
Comes a rattle and hum.
Jacob wrestled the angel
And the angel was overcome.

You plant a demon seed
You raise a flower of fire.
We see them burnin' crosses
See the flames, higher and higher.

Woh, woh, bullet the blue sky
Bullet the blue sky
Bullet the blue
Bullet the blue.

Suit and tie comes up to me
His face red like a rose on a thorn bush
Like all the colours of a royal flush
And he's peelin' off those dollar bills
(Slappin' 'em down)
One hundred, two hundred.

And I can see those fighter planes
And I can see those fighter planes
Across the tin huts as children sleep
Through the alleys of a quiet city street.
Up the staircase to the first floor
We turn the key and slowly unlock the door
As a man breathes into his saxophone
And through the walls you hear the city groan.
Outside, is America
Outside, is America
America.

See across the field
See the sky ripped open
See the rain comin' through the gapin' wound
Howlin' the women and children
Who run into the arms
Of America.

DADDY'S GONNA PAY FOR YOUR CRASHED CAR

You're a precious stone, you're out on your own.
You know everyone in the world, but you feel alone.
Daddy won't let you weep, Daddy won't let you ache
Daddy gives you as much as you can take.
Aha, sha-la. Aha sha-la.
Daddy's gonna pay for your crashed car.

A little uptight, you're a baby's fist
Butterfly kisses up an' down your wrist.
When you see Daddy comin', you're lickin' your lips
Nails bitten down to the quick.

Aha, sha-la. Aha sha-la.
Daddy's gonna pay for your crashed car.
Daddy's gonna pay for your crashed car.

You've got a head full of traffic, you're a siren's song.
You cry for Mama, and Daddy's right along.
He gives you the keys to a flamin' car.
Daddy's with you wherever you are.

Daddy's a comfort, Daddy's your best friend
Daddy'll hold your hand right up to the end.

Aha, sha-la. Aha sha-la.
Daddy's gonna pay for your crashed car.
Daddy's gonna pay for your crashed car.

Sunday, Monday, Tuesday, Wednesday,
Thursday, Friday, Saturday's alright.

DEEP IN THE HEART

Angel, everything's gonna be alright.
Angel, everything's gonna work out tonight.

Thirteen years old
Sweet as a rose
Every petal of her wafer thin.

Love will make you blind
Creep up from behind
Get you jumping out of your skin
Angel, it's sink or swim.

Deep in the heart
Deep in the heart of this place.
Deep in the heart
Deep in the heart of this place.

Door is closed behind me now
The window is sealed to shut out the light.
Green as the leaves
And the cure for the nettle sting.
Do your homework it'll work out right.

Deep in the heart
Deep in the heart of this place.
Deep in the heart
Deep in the heart of this place.

The scent of cedar
I can still see her
You can't return to the place you never left.

Angel, we'll make it work out tonight
Angel, I wanna be home tonight.

Door is closed behind me now
The window's sealed, to shut out the light
Green as the leaves the cure for the nettle sting
Do your work and you'll work out right.

Deep in the heart
Deep in the heart of this place.
Deep in the heart
Deep in the heart of this place.

DESIRE

Lover, I'm off the streets
I'm gonna go where the bright lights
And the big city meet
With a red guitar, on fire
Desire.

She's the candle burnin' in my room
Yeah, I'm like the needle
The needle and spoon
Over the counter, with a shotgun
Pretty soon, everybody's got one
I'm in a fever, when I'm beside her
Desire
Desire.

And the fever, gettin' higher
Desire
Desire.
(Burning, burning).

She's the dollars
She's my protection
Yeah, she's the promise
In the year of election.
Sister I can't let you go
Like a preacher stealin' hearts at a travellin' show
For love or money, money, money... ?
And the fever, gettin' higher.
Desire.

DIRTY DAY

I don't know you, you don't know the half of it.
I had a starring role. I was the bad guy who walked out.
They say be careful where you aim
Because where you aim you might just hit.
You can hold onto something so tight
You've already lost it.
Dragging me down, that's not the way it used to be.
You can't even remember what I'm trying to forget.

It was a dirty day, dirty day.
Looking for explanations I don't even understand.
If you need someone to blame, throw a rock in the air,
you'll hit someone guilty.

From father to son, in one life has begun
A work that's never done, father to son.

(Love, it won't last kissin' time).
(Love, it won't last kissin' time).
(Love, it won't last kissin' time).

Get it right, there's no blood thicker than ink.
Hear what I say, nothing's as simple as you think.
Wake up, some things you can't get around
I'm in you, more so when they put me in the ground.

"The days, days, days run away like horses over the hill."

DISCOTHÈQUE

You can reach, but you can't grab it.
You can't hold it, control it
You can't bag it.

You can push, but you can't direct it
Circulate, regulate, oh no
You cannot connect it - *love*.

You know you're chewing bubble gum
You know what that is but you still want some.
You just can't get enough of that lovey-dovey stuff

You get confused, but you know it
Yeah, you hurt for it, work for it, love
You don't always show it - *love*.

Let go, let's go, discothèque.
Go, go, let go, discothèque.

Looking for the one
But you know you're somewhere else instead.
You want to be the song
The song that you hear in your head
Love, love, love, love.

It's not a trick, you can't learn it
It's the way that you don't pay that's okay
'Cause you can't earn it - *love*

You know you're chewing bubble gum
You know what that is
But you still want some
You just can't get enough of that lovey-dovey stuff

Let go, let's go, discothèque.
Go, go, go, go, discothèque.

Looking for the one
But you know you're somewhere else instead.
You want to be the song
The song that you hear in your head
Love, love, love.

But you take what you can get
'Cause it's all that you can find.
Oh you know there's something more
But tonight, tonight, tonight.
Boom cha, boom cha, discothèque.

DO YOU FEEL LOVED

Take these hands, they're good for nothing
You know these hands never worked a day
Take these boots they're going nowhere
You know these boots don't want to stray.

You got my head filled with songs
You got my shoelaces undone.
Take my shirt, go on, take it off me
You can tear it up if you can tie me down.

Do you feel loved?
Do you feel loved?
Do you feel loved?

Take the colours of my imagination
Take the scent hanging in the air
Take this tangle of a conversation
Turn it into your own prayer.
With my fingers as you want them
With my nails under your hide
With my teeth at your back
And my tongue to tell you the sweetest lies.

Do you feel loved?
Do you feel loved?
And it looks like the sun
But it feels like the rain, oh.

Love's a bully, pushing and shoving
In the belly of a woman.
Heavy rhythm taking over
To stick together a man and a woman
Stick together man and a woman
Stick together.

Do you feel loved?
Do you feel loved?

And it looks like the sun
But it feels like rain
And there's heat in the sun
To see us through the rain.

Do you feel loved?
Do you feel loved?
Do you feel loved?
Do you feel loved?

DROWNING MAN

Take my hand
You know I'll be there
If you can
I'll cross the sky for your love.
For I have promised
For to be with you tonight
And for the time that will come.

Take my hand
You know I'll be there
If you can
I'll cross the sky for your love.
And I understand
These winds and tides
This change of times
Won't drag you away.

Hold on, and hold on tightly.
Hold on, and don't let go of my love.
The storms will pass, it won't be long now.
This love will last, this love will last forever.

And take my hand, you know I'll be there.
If you can I'll cross the sky for your love.
Give you what I hold dear.

Hold on, hold on tightly.
Hold on, and hold on tightly.
Rise up, rise up with wings like eagles.
You run, you run.
You run and not grow weary.

Hold on, and hold on tightly.
Hold on, hold on tightly
This love, lasts forever.
Now this love lasts forever.

EVEN BETTER THAN THE REAL THING

Give me one more chance, and you'll be satisfied.
Give me two more chances, you won't be denied.
Well my heart is where it's always been
My head is somewhere in between
Give me one more chance, let me be your lover tonight.

(Check it out)
You're the real thing
Yeah the real thing
You're the real thing
Even better than the real thing.

Give me one last chance, and I'm gonna make you sing
Give me half a chance to ride on the waves that you bring
You're honey child to a swarm of bees
Gonna blow right through ya like a breeze
Give me one last dance, we'll slide down the surface of things

You're the real thing
Yeah the real thing
You're the real thing
Even better than the real thing.

We're free to fly the crimson sky
The sun won't melt our wings tonight.
Oh now, oh yeah, here she comes
Take me higher, take me higher
You take me higher, you take me higher.

You're the real thing
Yeah, you're the real thing.
You're the real thing
Even better than the real thing.
Even better than the real thing.
Even better than the real thing.

EXIT

You know he got the cure
But then he went astray
He used to stay awake
To drive the dreams he had away.
He wanted to believe
In the hands of love.

His head it felt heavy
As he came across the land
A dog started cryin'
Like a broken-hearted man
At the howling wind
At the howling wind.

He went deeper into black
Deeper into white.
He could see the stars shine
Like nails in the night.

He felt the healing
Healing, healing, healing hands of love
Like the stars shiny, shiny from above.

A hand in the pocket
Fingering the steel
The pistol weighed heavy
And his heart he could feel was beating
Beating, beating, beating,
Oh my love, oh my love
Oh my love, oh my love.

So hands that build
Can also pull down
The hands of love.

FIRE

Calling, calling the sun is burning black
Calling, calling, it's beating on my back
With a fire
With a fire.

Calling, calling, the moon is running red
Calling, calling, it's pulling me instead
With a fire, fire.

But there's a fire inside
And I'm falling over
There's a fire in me
When I call out
You built a fire, fire
I'm going home.

Calling, calling, the stars are falling down
Calling, calling, they knock me to the ground
With a fire, fire.

But there's a fire inside
And I'm falling over
There's a fire inside
When I call out
There's a fire inside
When I'm falling over
You built a fire, fire
I'm going home.

GLORIA

I try to sing this song
I, I try to stand up
But I can't find my feet.
I, I try to speak up
But only in you I'm complete.

Gloria
In te domine
Gloria
Exultate
Gloria
Gloria
Oh, Lord, loosen my lips.

I try to sing this song
I, I try to get in
But I can't find the door
The door is open
You're standing there, you let me in.

Gloria
In te domine
Gloria
Exultate
Oh, Lord, if I had anything, anything at all
I'd give it to you.

Gloria
In te domine
Gloria
Gloria.

GOD PART II

Don't believe the devil
I don't believe his book
But the truth is not the same
Without the lies he made up.
Don't believe in excess
Success is to give
Don't believe in riches
But you should see where I live.
I, I believe in love.

Don't believe in forced entry
Don't believe in rape
But every time she passes by
Wild thoughts escape.
Don't believe in Death Row
Skid row or the gangs.
Don't believe in the Uzi
It just went off in my hands.
I, I believe in love.

Don't believe in cocaine
Got a speedball in my head
I could cut and crack you open
Did you hear what I said?
Don't believe them when they tell me
There ain't no cure.
The rich stay healthy
The sick stay poor.
I, I believe in love.

Don't believe in Goldman
His type like a curse
Instant karma's gonna get him
If I don't get him first.
Don't believe that Rock 'n' Roll
Can really change the world
As it spins in revolution
Yeah, it spirals and turns.
I, I believe in love.

Don't believe in the sixties
The golden age of pop
You glorify the past
When the future dries up.
Heard a singer on the radio
Late last night
Says he's gonna kick the darkness
Till it bleeds daylight.
I, I believe in love.

Feel like I'm fallin'
I'm spinnin' on a wheel
It always stops beside a name
A presence I can feel.
I believe in love.
Stop!

GONE

You get to feel so guilty
Got so much for so little
The you find that feeling just won't go away.
You're holding on to every little thing so tightly
Till there's nothing left for you anyway.

Goodbye, you can keep this suit of lights
I'll be up with the sun
I'm not coming down
I'm not coming down
I'm not coming down.

You wanted to get somewhere so badly
You had to lose yourself along the way.
You changed your name
Well that's okay, it's necessary
And what you leave behind you don't miss anyway.

Goodbye, you can keep this suit of lights
I'll be up with the sun
I'm not coming down
I'm not coming down
I'm not coming down.

'Cause I'm already gone
Felt that way all along.
Closer to you every day
I didn't want it that much anyway.

You're taking steps that make you feel dizzy
Then you learn to like the way it feels.
You hurt yourself, you hurt your lover
Then you discover
What you thought was freedom is just greed.

Goodbye, and it's an emotional
Goodnight, I'll be up with the sun.
Are you still holding on?
I'm not coming down…
I'm not coming down
I'm not coming down.

HALLELUJAH HERE SHE COMES

I see you dressed to kill
I know I can't wait until
Hallelujah, here she comes
I see you dressed in black
I guess I'm not coming back.
Hallelujah, here she comes.
Born and raised on the wrong side of town
You get so high that you can't come down.

I see the road is rough
You know I'm not giving up
Hallelujah, here she comes
I know where the lady goes
I know she got rings on her toes
Hallelujah, here she comes.

Born and raised on the wrong side of town
You get so high that you can't come down.

I'm goin' higher, higher, higher on love.
Higher, higher, higher on love.
Higher, higher, higher on love.
Higher, higher, higher on love.
I'm gonna be there
When that light gonna shine.
I'm gonna be there
When her heart kindles next to mine.
I'm gonna be ...
Here she comes
Yeah, here she comes.

I see you dressed to kill
I know I can't wait until Hallelujah.
Here she comes
I see you dressed in black
I guess I'm not coming back.
Hallelujah... here she comes.

Born and raised on the wrong side of town
You get so high that you can't come down.

I'm gonna be there
Higher, higher on love
Gonna get higher
Higher, higher on love.

HAWKMOON 269

Like a desert needs rain
Like a town needs a name
I need your love.

Like a drifter needs a room
Hawkmoon
I need your love.
I need your love.

Like a rhythm unbroken
Like drums in the night
Like sweet soul music
Like sunlight
I need your love.

Like coming home
And you don't know where you've been
Like black coffee
Like nicotine
I need your love,
I need your love.

When the night has no end
And the day yet to begin
As the room spins around
I need your love
I need your love.

Like a Phoenix rising needs a holy tree
Like the sweet revenge
Of a bitter enemy
I need your love.

Like heat needs the sun
Like honey on her tongue
Like the muzzle of a gun
Like oxygen
I need your love,
I need your love.

When the night has no end
And the day yet to begin
As the room spins around
I need your love
I need your love.

Like thunder needs rain
Like a preacher needs pain
Like tongues of flame
Like a sweet stain
Need your love
I need your love.

Like a needle needs a vein
Like someone to blame
Like a thought unchained
Like a runaway train
Need your love,
I need your love.
Need your love
I need your love.

Like faith needs a doubt
Like a freeway out
Need your love.

Like powder needs a spark
Like lies need the dark
I need your love.

HEARTLAND

See the sunrise over her skin
Don't change it.
See the sunrise over her skin
Dawn changes everything, everything.
And the delta sun
Burns bright and violent.

Mississippi and the cotton wool heat
Sixty-six - a highway speaks
Of deserts dry
Of cool green valleys
Gold and silver veins
All the shining cities
In this heartland
In this heartland
In this heartland
Heaven knows
This is a heartland.
Heartland, our heartland.

See the sunrise over her skin
She feels like water in my hand
Freeway, like a river
Cuts through this land
Into the side of love
Like a burning spear
And the poison rain
Like dirty tears
Through the ghostranch hills
Death Valley waters
In the towers of steel
Belief goes on and on
In this heartland.
In this heartland
In this heartland.
Heaven knows
This is a heartland.

HOLD ME, THRILL ME, KISS ME, KILL ME

You don't know how you took it
You just know what you got
Oh lawdy, you been stealing from the thieves
And you got caught
In the headlights of a stretch car,
You're a star.

Dressing like your sister
Living like a tart
If they don't know what you're doin'
Babe it must be art,
You're a headache, in a suitcase
You're a star.

Oh, no, don't be shy
You don't have to go blind,
Hold me
Thrill me
Kiss me
Kill me.

You don't know how you got here
You just know you want out
Believing in yourself almost as much as you doubt,
You're a big smash
You wear it like a rash
Star.

Oh no, don't be shy
You need a crowd to cry,
Hold me
Thrill me
Kiss me
Kill me.

They want you to be Jesus
They'll got down on one knee
But they'll want their money back
If you're alive at thirty-three,
And you're turning tricks
With your crucifix.
You're a star, oh child

Of course you're not shy
You don't have to deny love,
Hold me
Thrill me
Kiss me
Kill me.

HOLY JOE

I, I'm a humble guy
No really, I try
You know it's hard sometimes
You, you're messed up too
But both of us are gonna get through
Working my way to get to you.

Come on, come one, come on, come on
Be good to me.
Come on, come one, come on, come on
Be good to me.
Come on, come one, come on, come on
Be good to me.
Here it comes, here it comes
Holy Joe.

Please, don't make me say please
To champagne and ice cream
It's not what I want
It's what I need
Devotion, a little appreciation
A little heavy rotation
Oh, looks good on me.
I'm having the best of anybody's life
Closer than ever to everybody's wife, yeah.

Come on, come one, come on, come on
Be good to me.
Come on, come one, come on, come on
Be good to me.
Here it comes, here it comes
Holy Joe.

Come on, come one, come on, come on
Be good to me.
Come on, come one, come on, come on
Be good to me.
Come on, come one, come on, come on
Be good to me.
Come on, come one, come on, come on
Be good to me.
Here it comes, here it comes
Holy Joe.
Here it comes, here it comes
Holy Joe.
Here it comes, here it comes
Holy Joe.

I FALL DOWN

Julie says, John I'm getting nowhere
I wrote this letter, hope to get someplace soon
I want to get up
When I wake up
But when I get up
I fall down.

Julie wake up, Julie tell the story
You wrote the letter, said you were gonna
Get there someday
Gonna walk in the sun
And the wind and the rain
Never look back again
Now you fall down
You're falling down
You fall down
You fall down.

You're falling down
You fall down
You fall down.

Julie say something, Julie say you're sorry
You're gonna get better, you better not
Leave me here anyway
I want to get up, when you wake up
But when I get up
I fall down
I'm falling down
I fall down
I broke myself.

I fall, I fall down
I'm falling down
I fall down...
When you fall
I fall with you
And when you're falling down
Is when I hit the ground.
I fall with you
I fall down.

I STILL HAVEN'T FOUND WHAT I'M LOOKING FOR

I have climbed the highest mountains
I have run through the fields
Only to be with you
Only to be with you.

I have run, I have crawled
I have scaled these city walls
These city walls
Only to be with you.

But I still haven't found
What I'm looking for.
But I still haven't found
What I'm looking for.

I have kissed honey lips
Felt the healing in her finger tips
It burned like fire
(I was) burning inside her.

I have spoke with the tongue of angels
I have held the hand of a devil
It was warm in the night
I was cold as a stone.

But I still haven't found
What I'm looking for.
But I still haven't found
What I'm looking for.

I believe in the Kingdom Come
Then all the colours will bleed into one
Bleed into one.
But yes, I'm still running.

You broke the bonds
And you loosed the chains
Carried the cross of my shame
Oh my shame, you know I believe it.

But I still haven't found
What I'm looking for.
But I still haven't found
What I'm looking for.

But I still haven't found
What I'm looking for.
But I still haven't found
What I'm looking for.

I THREW A BRICK THROUGH A WINDOW

I was talking, I was talking to myself
Somebody else talk, talk, talking.
I couldn't hear a word, a word he said.

He was my brother
I said there was no other way out of here
Be my brother
(Brother).
Got to get out, got to get out.

I was walking, I was walking into walls
And back again
I just keep walking
I walk up to a window to see myself
And my reflection, when I thought about it
My direction, going nowhere, going nowhere.

No-one, no-one is blinder
Than he who will not see.
No-one, no-one is blinder
Than me.

I was talking, I was talking in my sleep
I can't stop talk, talk, talking
I'm talking to you, it's up to you
Be my brother, there is no other way out of here
Be my brother
Got to get out, got to get out
Got to get out of here.

I WILL FOLLOW

I was on the outside when you said
You needed me
I was looking at myself
I was blind, I could not see.

A boy tries hard to be a man
His mother takes him by the hand
If he stops to think, he starts to cry
Oh why?

If you walk away, walk away
I walk away, walk away
I will follow.
If you walk away, walk away
I walk away, walk away
I will follow.
I will follow.

I was on the inside
When they pulled the four walls down
I was looking through the window
I was lost, I am found.

If you walk away, walk away
I walk away, walk away
I will follow.
If you walk away, walk away
I walk away, walk away
I will follow.
I will follow.

Your eyes make a circle
I see you when I go in there
Your eyes, your eyes
Your eyes, your eyes.

If you walk away, walk away
I walk away, walk away
I will follow.
If you walk away, walk away
I walk away, walk away
I will follow.
I will follow.

I'M NOT YOUR BABY

It's a beautiful day
Everything is goin' my way
Even the words are doing what I say
Oh babe, got to get away.
To be impossible
Isn't that difficult
In the city you're invisible
When you come from a small town.

Everything is alright
Everything is alright
I'm not your baby, please.

Tourist in a traffic jam
Babycham and handicam.
I'm not your mother, you're not my man.
I'm not your baby.
Don't treat me like I'm a trick
I won't treat you like you're a prick.
Don't need no doctor, I'm not ill.
I'm not your baby.
Everything is alright, etc.

Cut out the poetry
Let's hit the main artery
No time for a tourniquet
Let the colours all run out of me.
You've brought me all kinds of goods
Now my heart is so full up it hurts.
It's heavy as a shopping bag
Full of things I should give back.

Everything is alright
Everything is alright
I'm not your baby, please.

Not dizzy, just busy
Didn't drink nothing fizzy
No pills to feel easy
Don't know what got into me
Daylight a kinda robbery
The night is your geography
You're not white
You're pink and rosy
You could be right
But you're way above me.

I'm in recovery
A star of pornography.
I'm a tourist
There's a lot to see
You don't like the photographs of me
So, you've got a lot to say
You don't sleep around, but sometimes you stray
You don't believe
But oftentimes you pray for something
What is it babe?

Don't treat me like I'm a trick
I won't treat you like you're a prick.
Don't need no doctor, I'm not sick.
I'm not your baby.
Everything is alright
Everything is alright
I'm not your baby.

IF GOD WILL SEND HIS ANGELS

Nobody else here baby
No-one else here to blame
No-one to point the finger
It's just you and me and the rain.

Nobody made you do it
No one put words in your mouth.
Nobody here taking orders
When love took a train heading south.
It's the blind leading the blond
It's the stuff, it's the stuff of country songs.

Hey, if God will send his angels
And if God will send a sign
And if God will send his angels
Would everything be alright?

God's got his phone off the hook, babe
Would he even pick up if he could?
It's been a while since we saw that child
Hangin' round this neighbourhood.

See his mother dealing in a doorway
See Father Christmas with a begging bowl.
And Jesus' sister's eyes are a blister
The High Street never looked so low.

It's the blind leading the blond
It's the cops collecting for the cons.
So where is the hope and
Where is the faith and the love?
What's that you say to me
Does love light up your Christmas tree?
The next minute you're blowing a fuse
And the cartoon network turns into the news.

If God will send his angels
And if God will send a sign
Well if God will send his angels
Where do we go?
Where do we go?

Jesus never let me down
You know Jesus used to show me the score.
Then they put Jesus in show business
Now it's hard to get in the door.

It's the stuff, it's the stuff of country songs
But I guess it was something to go on.

Hey, if God will send his angels
I sure could use them here right now
Well, if God will send his angels...

Where do we go?
Where do we go?

IF YOU WEAR THAT VELVET DRESS

Tonight, the moon is playing tricks again
I'm feeling seasick again.
The whole world could just dissolve
Into a glass of water.

I've been good, 'cause I know you don't want me to.
Do you really want me to be blue as you?
It's her daylight that gets me through.

We've been here before
Last time you scratched at my door
The moon was naked and cold
I was like a two-year-old
Who just wanted more.

If you wear that velvet dress.
If you wear that velvet dress.

Tonight, the moon's drawn its curtains
It's a private show
No-one else gonna know
I'm wanting.

Sunlight, sunlight fills my room
It's sharp and it's clear
But nothing at all like the moon.

It's okay
The struggle for things not to say
I never listened to you anyway
And I got my own hands to pray.

But if you wear that velvet dress.
If you wear that velvet dress.

Tonight the moon is a mirror-ball
Light flickers from across the hall
Who'll catch the star when it falls.

If you wear that velvet dress.

IN GOD'S COUNTRY

Desert sky, dream beneath the desert sky.
The rivers run but soon run dry.
We need new dreams tonight.
Desert rose, dreamed I saw a desert rose
Dress torn in ribbons and bows
Like a siren she calls (to me).

Sleep comes like a drug in God's country
Sad eyes, crooked crosses, in God's country

Set me alight, we'll punch a hole right through the night.
Every day the dreamers die to see what's on the other side.
She is liberty, and she comes to rescue me.
Hope, faith, her vanity
The greatest gift is gold.

Sleep comes like a drug in God's country
Sad eyes, crooked crosses, in God's country

Naked flame, she stands with a naked flame
I stand with the sons of Cain
Burned by the fire of love
Burned by the fire of love.

INDIAN SUMMER SKY

In the ocean cuts ring deep, the sky.
Like there, I don't know why.
In the forest there's a clearing
I run there towards the light.
Sky, it's a blue sky.

In the earth the hole deep, deep, decide.
If I could I would.
Up for air to swim against the tide.
Hey, hey, hey.
Up towards the sky.
It's a blue sky.

To lose along the way the spark that set the flame
To flicker and to fade on this the longest day.

So wind go through to my heart.
So wind blow through my soul.
So wind go through to my heart.
So wind blow through my soul.
So wind go through to my heart.

You give yourself to this the longest day.
You give yourself, you give it all away.

Two rivers run too deep, the seasons change and so do I.
The light that strikes the tallest trees the light away for I.
The light away, up towards the sky.
It's a blue sky.

To lose along the way the spark that set the flame
To flicker and to fade on this the longest day.

So wind go through to my heart.
So wind blow through my soul.
So wind go through to my heart.
So wind blow through my soul.
So wind go through my heart.
So wind blow through my soul.
So wind go through to my heart.

You give yourself to this the longest day.
You give yourself, you give it all away.

INTO THE HEART

Into the heart of a child
I stay awhile
But I can go there.

Into the heart of a child
I can smile
I can't go there.

Into the heart, into the heart of a child
I can't go back
I can't stay awhile.
Into the heart.

Into the heart.

IS THAT ALL?

Oh to sing this song makes me angry
I'm not angry with you.
Is that all?
Is that all?
Is that all?

Oh to sing this song makes me happy
I'm not happy with you.
Oh to sing this song makes me dance.
Is that all?
Is that all?
Is that all?

Is that all?
Is that all?
Is that all?
Is that all you want from me?

LADY WITH THE SPINNING HEAD

Here she comes
Lady luck again
Figure of eight
Six and nine again.
I, I, I, my lady with the spinning head.

Whatever the deal
She won't let me down
Wherever I go
She's always hanging round.

Lady with the spinning head.
Lady with the spinning head.

She's been gone
But I knew she'd be back
She's got the rent
She put me in the black.
I, I need you lady with the spinning head.

Mean old man took away my car
those credit guys they've got the power
I'm on top
When she's around
She's the ticket
Out of town.

Lady with the spinning head.
Lady with the spinning head.
Lady with the spinning head.

LAST NIGHT ON EARTH

She feel the ground is giving way
But she thinks we're better off that way.
"The more you take, the less you feel
The less you know the more you believe
The more you have, the more it takes today".

You gotta give it away
You gotta give it away
You gotta give it away
Give it away
You gotta give it away
You gotta give it away

Well she don't care what it's worth
She's living like it's the last night on earth
The last night on earth.

She's not waiting on a saviour to come
She's at the bus stop
With the News Of The World
And the sun, sun, here it comes.
She's not waiting for anyone.

You gotta give it away
You gotta give it away
You gotta give it away
Give it away.
You gotta give it away
You gotta give it away

Well she don't care what it's worth
She's living like it's the last night on earth
The last night on earth.

Slipping away, slip, slide
Too many slipping away.
The world turns and we get dizzy
Slipping away.

She's living
She's living next week now.
You know she's gonna pay you back somehow.

She hasn't been to bed in a week
She'll be dead soon, then she'll sleep.

You gotta give it away
You gotta give it away
Give it away
You gotta give it away
You gotta give it away

She already knows it hurts
She's living like it the last night on earth
The last night on earth
Last night on earth
Last night.

LEMON

Lemon, see-through in the sunlight.
She wore lemon, see-through in the daylight.
She's gonna make you cry, she's gonna make you whisper
and moan.
When you're dry she draws water from a stone.
I feel like I'm slowly, slowly, slowly slippin' under.
I feel like I'm holding on to nothing.

She wore lemon to colour in the cold grey night.
She had heaven and she held on so tight.

A man makes a picture, a moving picture
through the light projected, he can see himself up close.
A man captures colour, a man likes to stare.
He turns his money into light to look for her.
And I feel like I'm drifting, drifting, drifting from the shore.
And I feel like I'm swimming out to her.

Midnight is where the day begins.
Midnight is where the day begins.
Lemon, see-through in the sunlight.

A man builds a city, with banks and cathedrals.
A man melts the sand so he can see the world outside.
A man makes a car, and builds a road to run (them) on.
A man dreams of leaving, but he always stays behind.

You're gonna meet her there
She's your destination
You gotta get to her
She's imagination

And these are the days when our work has come asunder.
And these are the days when we look for something other.

Midnight is where the day begins.
Midnight is where the day begins.
Midnight is where the day begins.
Midnight is where the day begins.

A man makes a picture, a moving picture;
Through light projected, he can see himself up close.
A man captures colour, a man likes to stare.
He turns his money into light to look for her.

Gotta meet her there
She's your destination
There's no sleeping there
She's imagination

She is the dreamer, she's imagination.
Through the light projected, he can see himself up close.

LIKE A SONG

Like a song I have to sing
I sing it for you.
Like the words I have to bring
I bring it for you.

And in leather, lace and chains we stake our claim.
Revolution once again
No I won't, I won't wear it on my sleeve.
I can see through this expression and you know I don't believe.
Too old to be told, exactly who are you?
Tonight, tomorrow's too late.

And we love to wear a badge, a uniform
And we love to fly a flag
But I won't let others live in hell
As we divide against each other
And we fight amongst ourselves
Too set in our ways to try to rearrange
Too right to be wrong, in this rebel song
Let the bells ring out
Let the bells ring out
Is there nothing left?
Is there, is there nothing?
Is there nothing left?
Is honesty what you want?

A generation without name, ripped and torn
Nothing to lose, nothing to gain
Nothing at all
And if you can't help yourself
Well take a look around you
When others need your time
You say it's time to go... it's your time.
Angry words won't stop the fight
Two wrongs won't make it right.
A new heart is what I need.
Oh, God make it bleed.
Is there nothing left?

LOVE COMES TUMBLING

Love don't need to find a way
You'll find your own way.
I forget that I can't stay
And so I say that all roads lead to where you are.
All roads lead to where you are.

The seed is split, the bed defiled
For you a virgin bride
Find yourself in someone else
Don't find yourself in me
I can't lift you up again
Love comes tumbling down again.

Love don't need to find a way
You'll find your own way
I forget that you can't stay
But I know that
All roads lead to where you are
All roads lead to where you are.

LOVE IS BLINDNESS

Love is blindness, I don't want to see
Won't you wrap the night around me?
Oh, my heart, love is blindness.

In a parked car, in a crowded street
You see your love made complete.
Thread is ripping, the knot is slipping
Love is blindness.

Love is clockworks and cold steel
Fingers too numb to feel.
Squeeze the handle, blow out the candle
Love is blindness.

Love is blindness, I don't want to see
Won't you wrap the night around me?
Oh, my love,
Blindness.

A little death without mourning
No call and no warning
Baby, a dangerous idea
That almost makes sense.

Love is drowning in a deep well
All the secrets, and no one to tell.
Take the money, honey...
Blindness.

Love is blindness, I don't want to see
Won't you wrap the night around me?
Oh, my love,
Blindness.

LOVE RESCUE ME
(with Bob Dylan)

Love rescue me
Come forth and speak to me
Raise me up
And don't let me fall.
No man is my enemy
My own hands imprison me.
Love rescue me.

Many strangers have I met
On the road to my regret
Many lost who seek to find themselves in me.
They ask me to reveal
The very thoughts they would conceal.
Love, rescue me.

And the sun in the sky
Makes a shadow of you and I
Stretching out as the sun sinks in the sea.
I'm here without a name
In the palace of my shame
I said, love, rescue me.

In the cold mirror of a glass
I see my reflection pass
I see the dark shades of what I used to be.
I see the purple of her eyes
The scarlet of my lies.
Love, rescue me.

Yeah, though I walk
In the valley of the shadow
Yet, I will fear no evil.
I have cursed thy rod and staff
They no longer comfort me.
Love, rescue me.

Sha la la la etc.
I said love, love, rescue me.

Yeah, I'm here without a name
In the palace of my shame
I said love, rescue me.

I've conquered my past
The future is here at last
I stand at the entrance to a new world I can see.
The ruins to the right of me
Will soon have lost sight of me.
Love, rescue me.

LUMINOUS TIMES

Hey sister love
Hey sister soul
Hey, only love
Can turn me 'round tonight.
Hey sister love
Save my soul
Save my soul

Hold on to love.
Hold on to love
Love won't let you go
Love won't let you go.
Hold onto love
See the sunshine in her song.

Hey sister love, hey sweet surrender

She comes like carnival
She is the big wheel
She turned my head around
She turned my head around
She is the speedway
She is the slipstream
She is coming 'round.

Hold on to love, hold on to love
Love won't let you go
Hold on to love, hold on to love
See the sunlight in her song
See the sunlight in her song.

She is the gun fire
She is the car crash
She is the avalanche
She is the thunder
She is the waves
And she pulls me under.

I love you 'cause I need to
Not because I need you
I love you 'cause I understand
That God has given me your hand
It holds me in a tiny fist
And still I need your kiss.

Hold on to love
Oh, see the sunlight in her song.
See the sunlight in her song, yeah!

MIAMI

Weather 'round here choppin' and changin'
Surgery in the air
Print shirts and southern accents
Cigars and big hair.

We got the wheels, petrol's cheap
We only went there for a week
Got the sun, got the sand
Got the batteries and the handicam.

Her eyes all swimming pool blue
Dumb-bells on the diving board
Baby's always attracted to
The things she's afraid of.

Big girl with a sweet tooth watches
Skinny girl in the photo shoot.
Freshmen, squeaky-clean she tastes of chlorine.
Miami, my mammy.

Love the movies, babe
Love to walk through movie sets
Get to shoot someone in the foot
Get to smoke some cigarettes.

No big deal, we know the score
Just back from the video store.
Got the car and the car chase.
What's he got inside that case?
I want a close-up of that face.
Here comes the car chase.

I bought two new suits
Miami
Pink and blue
Miami
I took a picture of you
My mammy
Getting hot in a photo booth
Miami.

I said you looked like a madonna.
You said maybe.
You said I wanna have your baby, baby.
We could make something beautiful
Something that wouldn't be a problem
We could make something beautiful
Something that wouldn't be a problem
Least not in Miami.

You know, some places are like your auntie
But there's no place like Miami
My mammy
Miami
My mammy.

MISS SARAJEVO

Is there a time for keeping your distance
A time to turn your eyes away.
Is there a time for keeping your head down
For getting on with your day.

Is there a time for kohl and lipstick
Is there time for cutting hair
Is there a time for high street shopping
To find the right dress to wear.

Here she comes, heads turn around
Here she comes, to take her crown.

Is there a time to run for cover
A time for kiss and tell.
A time for different colours
Different names you find hard to spell.

Is there a time for first communion
A time for East 17
Is there time to turn to Mecca
Is there time to be a beauty queen.

Here she comes, beauty plays the clown
Here she comes, surreal in her crown.

Dici che il fiume trova la via al mare
Che come il fiume giungerai a me
Oltre i confini e le terre assetate
L'amore giungerà, l'amore
E non so più pregare
E nell'amore non so più sperare
E quell'amore non so più aspettare.

Is there a time for tying ribbons
A time for Christmas trees.
Is there a time for laying tables
When the night is set to freeze.

MLK

Sleep, sleep tonight
And may your dreams be realised.
If the thunder cloud passes rain
So let it rain, rain down on he.
So let it be.
So let it be.

Sleep, sleep tonight
And may your dreams be realised.
If the thunder cloud passes rain
So let it rain, let it rain
Rain down on he.

MOFO

Lookin' for to save my, save my soul
Lookin' in the places where no flowers grow.
Lookin' for to fill that God-shaped hole
Mother, mother-suckin' rock an'roll.

Holy dunc, space junk comin' in for the splash
White dopes on punk staring into the flash.
Lookin' for the baby Jesus under the trash
Mother, mother-suckin' rock an' roll.
Mother. (scat singing)

Mother, am I still your son?
You know I've waited for so long
To hear you say so.

Mother, you left and made me someone.
Now I'm still a child, but no one tells me no.

Lookin' for a sound that's gonna drown out the world.
Lookin' for the father of my two little girls.
Got the swing, got the sway, got my straw in lemonade.
Still lookin' for the face I had before the world was made.
Mother, mother-suckin' rock an' roll

Soothe me, mother
Rule me, father
Move me, brother
Woo me, sister.

Soothe me, mother
Rule me, father
Show me, mother
Show me, mother.

Show me, mother
Show me, mother
Show me, mother
Show me, mother.

MOTHERS OF THE DISAPPEARED

Midnight, our sons and daughters
Were cut down and taken from us.
Hear their heartbeat
We hear their heartbeat.

In the wind we hear their laughter
In the rain we see their tears.
Hear their heartbeat, we hear their heartbeat.

Night hangs like a prisoner
Stretched over black and blue.
Hear their heartbeats
We hear their heartbeats.

In the trees our sons stand naked
Through the walls our daughter cry
See their tears in the rainfall.

MYSTERIOUS WAYS

Johnny, take a walk with your sister the moon
Let her pale light in, to fill up your room.
You've been living underground, eating from a can
You've been running away from what you don't understand.

She's slippy, you're sliding down.
She'll be there when you hit the ground.

It's alright, it's alright, it's alright.
She moves in mysterious ways.
It's alright, it's alright, it's alright.
She moves in mysterious ways, oh.

Johnny, take a dive with your sister in the rain
Let her talk about the things you can't explain.
To touch is to heal, to hurt is to steal.
If you want to kiss the sky, better learn how to kneel
On your knees, boy!

She's the wave, she turns the tide
She sees the man inside the child.

It's alright, it's alright, it's alright.
She moves in mysterious ways.
It's alright, it's alright, it's alright.
She moves in mysterious ways, yeah, oh, ah.

Lift my days, light up my nights, oh.

One day you'll look back, and you'll see
Where you were held now by this love.
While you could stand there,
You could move on this moment
Follow this feeling.

It's alright, it's alright, it's alright.
She moves in mysterious ways.
It's alright, it's alright, it's alright.
She moves in mysterious ways.

Move you, spirits move you
Move, spirits 'its move you, oh yeah.
Does it move you?
She moves with it.
Lift my days, and light up my nights, oh.

NEW YEAR'S DAY

All is quiet on New Year's Day.
A world in white gets underway.
I want to be with you, be with you night and day.
Nothing changes on New Year's Day.
On New Year's Day.

I... will be with you again.
I... will be with you again.

Under a blood-red sky
A crowd has gathered in black and white
Arms entwined, the chosen few
The newspaper says, says
Say it's true, it's true...
And we can break through
Though torn in two
We can be one.

I... I will begin again
I... I will begin again.

Oh, oh. Oh, oh. Oh, oh.
Oh, maybe the time is right.
Oh, maybe tonight.
I will be with you again.
I will be with you again.

And so we are told this is the golden age
And gold is the reason for the wars we wage
Though I want to be with you
Be with you night and day
Nothing changes
On New Year's Day
On New Year's Day
On New Year's Day

NUMB

Don't move, don't talk out-a time,
Don't think, don't worry, everything's just fine, just fine.
Don't grab, don't clutch, don't hope for too much,
Don't breathe, don't achieve, don't grieve without leave.
Don't check, just balance on the fence,
Don't answer, don't ask, don't try and make sense.
Don't whisper, don't talk, don't run if you can walk,
Don't cheat, compete, don't miss the one beat.

Don't travel by train, don't eat, don't spill
Don't piss in the drain, don't make a will.
Don't fill out any forms, don't compensate
Don't cover, don't crawl, don't come around late
Don't hover at the gate.
Don't take it on board, don't fall on your sword
Just play another chord if you feel you're getting bored.

I feel numb, I feel numb. Too much is not enough, hey.
Gimme some more, gimme some more
Of that love stuff
Too much is not enough.

Don't change your brand, don't listen to the band,
Don't gape, don't ape, don't change your shape.
Have another grape.

Too much is not enough
I feel numb
I feel numb
Gimme what you got
Gimme what I don't get
Gimme what you got
Too much is not enough
I feel numb

Don't plead, don't bridle, don't shackle, don't grind,
don't curve, don't swerve.
Lie, die, serve.
Don't theorise, realise, polarise,
Chance, dance, dismiss, apologise.

Don't spy, don't lie, don't try, imply
Detain, explain, start again.

I feel numb
Gimme some more
Gimme some more
Of that stuff love
Gimme some more
Too much is not enough
I feel numb

Don't triumph, don't coax, don't cling, don't hoax
Don't freak, peak, don't leak, don't speak.

Don't project, don't connect, protect, don't expect, suggest.
Don't project, don't connect, protect, don't expect, suggest.

Don't struggle, don't jerk, don't collar, don't work
Don't wish, don't fish, don't teach, don't reach.

Don't borrow, don't break, don't fence, don't steal
Don't pass, don't press, don't try, don't feel.

Don't touch, don't dive, don't suffer, don't rhyme
Don't fantasise, don't rise, don't lie.

Don't project, don't connect, protect, don't expect, suggest.
Don't project, don't connect, protect, don't expect, suggest.

OCTOBER

October and the trees are stripped bare
Of all they wear.
What do I care?

October and kingdoms rise
And kingdoms fall
But you go on
And on.

ONE

Is it getting better, or do you feel the same?
Will it make it easier on you, now you got someone to blame?
You say one love, one life, when it's one need in the night.
One love, we get to share it
Leaves you baby if you don't care for it.

Did I disappoint you or leave a bad taste in your mouth?
You act like you never had love and you want me to go without.
Well, it's too late tonight to drag the past out into the light.
We're one, but we're not the same.
We get to carry each other, carry each other... one

Have you come here for forgiveness,
Have you come to raise the dead
Have you come here to play Jesus to the lepers in your head
Did I ask too much, more than a lot
You gave me nothing, now it's all I got.
We're one, but we're not the same.
Well, we hurt each other, then we do it again.

You say love is a temple, love a higher law
Love is a temple, love the higher law.
You ask me to enter, but then you make me crawl
And I can't be holding on to what you got, when all you got is hurt.

One love, one blood, one life, you got to do what you should.
One life with each other: sisters, brothers.
One life, but we're not the same.
We get to carry each other, carry each other.
One, one.

ONE TREE HILL

We turn away to face the cold, enduring chill
As the day begs the night for mercy, love.

A sun so bright it leaves no shadows
Only scars carved into stone on the face of earth.

The moon is up and over One Tree Hill
We see the sun go down in your eyes.

You run like a river on to the sea
You run like a river runs to the sea.

And in the world, a heart of darkness, a fire-zone
Where poets speak their heart then bleed for it

Jara sang, his song a weapon in the hands of love.
You know his blood still cries from the ground.

It runs like a river runs to the sea.
It runs like a river to the sea.

I don't believe in painted roses or bleeding hearts
While bullets rape the night of the merciful.

I'll see you again when the stars fall from the sky
And the moon has turned red over One Tree Hill.

We run like a river runs to the sea
We run like a river to the sea.

And when it's rainin', rainin' hard
That's when the rain will break a heart.

Rainin', rainin' in your heart
Rainin' in your heart.
Rainin', rain into your heart
Rainin', rainin', rainin'
Rain into your heart.
Rainin', ooh, rain in your heart, yeah.
Feel it.

Oh great ocean
Oh great sea
Run to the ocean
Run to the sea.

OUT OF CONTROL

Monday morning
Eighteen years dawning
I said how long.
Say how long.

It was one dull morning
I woke the world with bawling
I was so sad
They were so glad.

I had the feeling it was out of control
I was of the opinion it was out of control.

Boys and girls to school
And girls they make children
Not like this one.

I had the feeling it was out of control
I was of the opinion it was out of control.

I was of the feeling it was out of control
I had the opinion it was out of control.

I fought fate
There's blood at the garden gate
The man said childhood
It's in his childhood

One day I'll die
The choice will not be mine
Will it be too late?
You can't fight fate.

I had the feeling it was out of control
I was of the opinion it was out of control.

PLEASE

So you never knew love
Until you crossed the line of grace.
And you never felt wanted
Till you'd someone slap your face.
So you never felt alive
Until you'd almost wasted away.

You had to win, you couldn't just pass
The smartest ass at the top of the class
Your flying colours, your family tree
And all your lessons in history.

Please, please, please
Get up off your knees.
Please, please, please, please, oh yeah.

And you never knew how low you'd stoop
To make that call
And you never knew what was on the ground
Till they made you crawl.
So you never knew that the heaven
You keep you stole.

Your Catholic blues, your convent shoes,
Your stick-on tattoos now they're making the news
Your holy war, your northern star
Your sermon on the mount from the boot of your car.

Please, please, please
Get up off your knees.
Please, please, please
Leave me out of this, please.

So love is hard
And love is tough
But love is not
What you're thinking of.

September, streets capsizing
Spilling over down the drains
Shard of glass, splinters like rain
But you could only feel your own pain.

October, talk getting nowhere.
November, December; remember
We just started again.

Please, please, please
Get up off your knees, yeah.
Please, please, please, please, ah.

So love is big
Is bigger than us.
But love is not
What you're thinking of.
It's what lovers deal
It's what lovers steal
You know I've found it
Hard to receive
'Cause you, my love
I could never believe.

PRIDE (IN THE NAME OF LOVE)

One man come in the name of love
One man come and go.
One man come he to justify
One man to overthrow.

In the name of love
What more in the name of love.
In the name of love
What more in the name of love.

One man caught on a barbed wire fence
One man he resist
One man washed up on an empty beach
One man betrayed with a kiss.

In the name of love
What more in the name of love.
In the name of love
What more in the name of love.

Early morning, April four
Shot rings out in the Memphis sky.
Free at last, they took your life
They could not take your pride.

In the name of love
What more in the name of love.
In the name of love
What more in the name of love.

In the name of love
What more in the name of love.
In the name of love
What more in the name of love.

PROMENADE

Earth, sky, scenery.
Is she coming back again?
Men of straw, snooker hall.
Words that build or destroy
Dirt dry, bone, sand and stone.
Barbed wire fence cut me down.
I'd like to be around in a spiral staircase
To the higher ground.

And I, like a firework, explode.
Roman candle, lightning, lights up the sky.
In cracked streets, trample underfoot.
Side-step, sidewalk.
I see you stare into space.
Have I got closer now, behind the face?

Oh, tell me, Cherry you dance with me
Turn me around tonight
Up through the spiral staircase to the higher ground.
Slide show, seaside town.
Coca-cola, football radio, radio, radio, radio, radio, radio.

RED HILL MINING TOWN

From father to son
The blood runs thin
Ooh, see the faces frozen (still)
Against the wind.

The seam is split
The coal-face cracked
The lines are long
There's no going back.

Through hands of steel
And heart of stone
Our labour day
Has come and gone.

They leave me holdin' on
In Red Hill Town.
See the lights go down on ...

Hangin' on
You're all that's left to hold on to.
I'm still waiting
I'm hangin' on
You're all that's left to hold on to.

The glass is cut
The bottle run dry.
Our love runs cold
In the caverns of the night.

We're wounded by fear
Injured in doubt.
I can lose myself
You I can't live without.

Yeah, you keep me holdin' on
In Red Hill Town.
See the lights go down on…

Hangin' on
You're all that's left to hold on to.
I'm still waiting
I'm hangin' on
You're all that's left to hold on to
On to.

We scorch the earth
Set fire to the sky
And we stooped so low
To reach so high.

A link is lost
The chain undone.
We wait all day
For night to come
And it comes like a hunter (child).

I'm hangin' on
You're all that's left to hold on to.
I'm still waiting
I'm hangin' on
You're all that's left to hold on to.

We see love, slowly stripped away
Our love has seen its better day.
Hangin' on
Lights go down on Red Hill
The lights go down on Red Hill.
The lights go down on Red Hill.
The lights go down on Red Hill Town.

RED LIGHT

Oh I talk to you, you walk away.
You're still on the down beat
You say you don't want my help.
But you can't escape if you're running from yourself.
I give you my love
I give you my love
Give you my love
Still you walk away.
Well

It's your own late show as you jump to the street below.
But where can you go to leave yourself behind?
Alone in the spotlight of this, your own tragedy.
I give you my love.
Love.

I give you my love.
Give you my love.
I give you my love.
I give you my love.
I give you my love.

REJOICE

It's falling, it's falling
And outside a building comes tumbling down.
And inside a child on the ground
Says he'll do it again.

And what am I to do?
What in the world am I to say?
There's nothing else to do.
He says he'll change the world some day
I rejoice.

This morning I fell out of bed
When I woke up to what he had said
Everything's crazy but I'm too lazy to lie.

And what am I to do?
Just tell me what am I supposed to say?
I can't change the world
But I can change the world in me
Rejoice.
Rejoice.

And what am I to do?
Just tell me what am I supposed to say?
I can't change the world
But I can change the world in me.

I rejoice.

RUNNING TO STAND STILL

And so she woke up
Woke up from where she was lyin' still.
Said I gotta do something
About where we're goin'.

Step on a fast train
Step out of the driving rain, maybe
Run from the darkness in the night.
Singing ah, ah la la la de day
Al la la la de day.

Sweet the sin, bitter the taste in my mouth.
I see seven towers, but I only see one way out.
You gotta cry without weeping, talk without speaking
Scream without raising your voice.
You know I took the poison, from the poison stream
Then I floated out of here, singing
Ah la la la de day
Ah la la la de day.

She walks through the streets
With her eyes painted red
Under black belly of cloud in the rain.
In through a doorway
She brings me white golden pearls
Stolen from the sea.

She is ragin'
She is ragin'
And the storm blows up in her eyes.
She will suffer the needle chill
She's running to stand still.

SALOMÉ

Baby, please, baby please don't go
I got flies to feed, they want skin and seed
And don't make me crawl.

Please
Baby don't bite your lip
Give you half what I got
If you untie the knot
It's a promise.

Salomé, Salomé
Shake it, shake it, shake it, Salomé.
Shake it, shake it, shake it, Salomé.
Shake it, shake it, shake it, Salomé.

Baby please
Baby what's that tune?
Well I heard it before
When I crawled from your door
And my blood turned blue.

Please
Baby please slow down
Baby I feel sick
Don't make me stick to a promise.

Salomé, Salomé
Salomé, Salomé
Shake it, shake it, shake it, Salomé.
Salomé, shake it, shake it, shake it, Salomé.
Salomé, shake it, shake it, shake it, Salomé.

Baby please, baby don't say no.
Won't you dance for me, under the cherry tree?
Won't you swing down low?

Please
Baby please say yes
Baby don't go away
You're spilling me
And your precious love.

Salomé, Salomé
Shake it, shake it, shake it, Salomé.
Shake it, shake it, shake it, Salomé.
Salomé, shake it, shake it, shake it, Salomé.
Salomé, shake it, shake it, shake it, Salomé.
Salomé, shake it, shake it, shake it, Salomé.

SCARLET

Rejoice
Rejoice
Rejoice

SECONDS

Takes a second to say goodbye, say goodbye
Takes a second to say goodbye, say goodbye
Oh, oh, oh, say bye-bye.
Where you going to now?
Lightning flashes across the sky
East to West, do and die.
Like a thief in the night, see the world by candlelight.
Fall, rise and...
Fall, rise and...

In an apartment on Times Square
You can assemble them anywhere.
Held to ransom, hell to pay
A revolution every day.
U.S.S.R., G.D.R., London, New York, Peking.
It's the puppets, it's the puppets pull the strings, yeah.
Fall, rise and...
Fall, rise and...

Say goodbye, say goodbye
Say goodbye, say goodbye.

It takes a second to say goodbye
Say goodbye, oh, oh, oh.
Push the button and pull the plug
Say goodbye, oh, oh, oh.

Fall, rise and...
Fall, rise and...

And they're doing the atomic bomb
Do they know where the dance comes from?
Yes they're doing the atomic bomb
They want you to sing along.

Say goodbye, say goodbye
Say goodbye, say goodbye.

SHADOWS AND TALL TREES

Back to the cold restless streets at night
Talk to myself about tomorrow night.
Walls of white protest
A gravestone in name
Who is it now?
It's always the same.

Who is it now? Who calls me inside?
Are the leaves on the trees just a living disguise?
I walk the sweet rain tragicomedy
I'll walk home again to the street melody.

But I know, oh no
But I know, oh no
But I know.

Shadows and tall trees
Shadows and tall trees
Shadows and tall trees
Shadows and tall trees.

Life through a window
Discoloured pain
Mrs Brown's washing is always the same
I walk the street rain tragicomedy
I'll walk home again to the street melody.

But I know, oh no
But I know, oh no
But I know.

Do you feel in me
Anything redeeming
Any worthwhile feeling?
Is love like a tightrope
Hanging on my ceiling?

But I know, oh no
But I know, oh no
But I know.

Shadows and tall trees
Shadows and tall trees
Shadows and tall trees
Shadows and tall trees.

Shadows, shadows, shadows.
Shadows, shadows, shadows.
Shadows and tall trees.

Shadows, shadows, shadows.
Shadows, shadows, shadows.
Shadows and tall trees.

SILVER AND GOLD

In the shithouse a shotgun
Praying hands hold me down.
If only the hunter was hunted
In this tin can town, tin can town.
No stars in the black night
Looks like the sky fall down.
No sun in the daylight
Looks like it's chained to the ground, chained to the
ground.

The warden says "The exit is sold."
If you want a way out...
Silver and gold, silver and gold.

Broken back to the ceiling
Broken nose to the floor.
I scream at the silence
It's crawling, crawls under the door.
There's a rope around my neck
And there's a trigger in your gun.
Jesus, say something!
I am someone, I am someone.

Captains and Kings in the ship's hold
They came to collect
Silver and gold, silver and gold.

I seen the coming and the going
Seen the captains and the Kings.
Seen their navy blue uniforms
Seen them bright and shiny things, bright and shiny
things.

The temperature is rising
The fever white hot
Mister I ain't got nothing
But it's more than you've got
These chains no longer bind me
Nor the shackles at my feet
Outside are the prisoners
Inside the free (set them free).

A prize fighter in a corner is told
Hit where it hurts - For Silver and Gold
You can stop the world from turning around
You just gotta pay a penny in the pound.

SLOW DANCING

My love is cruel as the night
She steals the sun and shuts out the light.
All of my colours turn to blue
Win or lose.

Slow dancing, slow dancing, slow (dancing).

Scarlet eyes and see-through heart
I saw her coming right from the start.
She picked me up, but had me down on my knees
Just a-begging her please.

(Take me) slow dancing, slow dancing, slow.

And, I don't know why a man will search for himself
In his woman's eyes.
No, I don't know why a man sees the truth
But believes the lies.

My love is restless as the wind
She moves like a shadow across my skin
She left with my conscience
And I don't want it back
It just gets in the way.

Slow dancing, etc.

SO CRUEL

We crossed the line, who pushed who over?
It doesn't matter to you, it matters to me.
We're cut adrift, but still floating.
I'm only hanging on to watch you go down, my love.

I disappeared in you
You disappeared from me.
I gave you everything you ever wanted
It wasn't what you wanted.
The men who love you, you hate the most
They pass right through you like a ghost.
They look for you, but your spirit is in the air.
Baby, you're nowhere.

Oh, love, you say in love there are no rules.
Oh, love, sweet-heart, you're so cruel.

Desperation is a tender trap
It gets you every time.
You put your lips to her lips
To stop the lie.
Her skin is pale like God's only dove
Screams like an angel for your love
Then she makes you watch her from above
And you need her like a drug.

Oh, love, you say in love there are no rules.
Oh, love, sweet-heart, you're so cruel.

She wears my love like a see-through dress
Her lips say one thing, her movements something else.
Oh, love, like a screaming flower
Love dying every hour.
Ah, you don't know if it's fear or desire,
Danger the drug that takes you higher?
Head of heaven, fingers in the mire
Her heart is racing you can't keep up.
The night is bleeding like a cut
Between the horses of love and lust we are trampled underfoot.

Oh, love, to stay with you I'd be a fool.
Oh, sweetheart, you're so cruel.

SOME DAYS ARE BETTER THAN OTHERS

Some days are dry, some days are leaky
Some days come clean, other days are sneaky.
Some days take less, but most days take more
Some slip through your fingers and on to the floor.
Some days you're quick, but most days you're speedy
Some days you use more force than is necessary.
Some days just drop in on us.
Some days are better than others.
Some days it all adds up
And what you've got is enough.
Some days are better than others.

Some days are slippy, other days are sloppy;
Some days you can't stand the sight of a puppy.
Your skin is white, but you think you're a brother.
Some days are better than others.
Some days you wake up with her complaining.
Some sunny days you wish it was raining.
Some days are sulky, some days have a grin;
And some days have bouncers and won't let you in.
Some days you hear a voice
Taking you to another place.
Some days are better than others.

Some days are honest, some days are not;
Some days you're thankful for what you've got.
Some days you wake up in the army
And some days it's the enemy.
Some days are work, most days you're lazy;
Some days you feel like a bit of a baby
Lookin' for Jesus and his mother.
Some days are better than others.
Some days you feel ahead;
You're making sense of what she said.
Some days are better than others.

Some days I hear a voice taking me to another place.
Some days are better then others.

SPANISH EYES

Wey, hey, baby hang on
Wey, hey, baby hang on.
Hang on to your heartbeat, tight as a drum
Hang on to your love, see it shines like a song
Wey, hey, hey, sugar hang on.
Our love shines like rain
In those Spanish eyes.

Wey, hey, hey, here she comes
Comes in colours now she's gonna turn the daylight on
'Cos I love the way you talk to me, and I love the way
you walk on me
And I need you more than you need me (yeah)
Our love shines like rain in those Spanish eyes.

I'll cross the world for green and gold
But, it's those Spanish eyes that get me home.
Home again.

Wey, hey, hey, sugar hang on.
Wey, hey, hey, you know that the night is as young
I'm dazzled by a light that shines in your eyes
I'm used to standing in the shadows and waiting for the night
Forever in fever, forever in heat
You re-invented me, now don't put me back on the street.

Wey, hey, hey, baby hang on
Wey, hey, hey, baby hang on
'Cause I love the way you talk to me
And I love the way you mean to me
And I need you.

STARING AT THE SUN

Summer stretching on the grass
Summer dresses pass
In the shade of a willow tree
Creeps a-crawling over me
Over me and over you
Stuck together with God's glue
It's gonna get stickier too.
It's been a long hot summer
Let's get under cover
Don't try too hard to think
Don't think at all.

I'm not the only one
Staring at the sun
Afraid of what you'd find
If you take a look inside.
Not just deaf and dumb
I'm staring at the sun

Not the only one
Who's happy to go blind.

There's an insect in your ear
If you scratch it won't disappear.
It's gonna itch and burn and sting
Do you wanna see what the scratching brings!
Waves that leave me out of reach
Breaking on your back like a beach.
Will we ever live in peace?
'Cause those that can't do often have to
And those that can't do often have to preach

To the ones staring at the sun
Afraid of what you'll find if you took a look inside.
Not just deaf and dumb, staring at the sun
I'm not the only one who'd rather go blind.

Intransigence in all around
Military's still in town
Armour plated suits and ties
Daddy just won't say goodbye
Referee won't blow the whistle.
God is good but will he listen?
I'm nearly great but there's something missing.
I left it in the duty free,
Oh, though you never really belonged to me.

You're not the only one staring at the sun
Afraid of what you'd find if you stepped back inside.
I'm not sucking my thumb, staring at the sun
Not the only one who's happy to go blind.

STAY (FARAWAY, SO CLOSE!)

Green light, Seven Eleven,
You stop in for a pack of cigarettes.
You don't smoke, don't even want to.
Hey now, check your change.
Dressed up like a car crash
Your wheels are turnin' but you're upside down.
You say when he hits you, you don't mind
Because when he hurts you, you feel alive.
Oh, is that what it is?

Red lights, grey morning
You stumble out of a hole in the ground.
A vampire or a victim
It depends on who's around.
You used to stay in to watch the adverts
You could lip synch. to the talk shows.
And if you look, you look through me
And when you talk, you talk at me

And when I touch you, you don't feel a thing.

If I could stay, then the night would give you up.
Stay, and the day would keep its trust.
Stay, and the night would be enough.

Faraway, so close
Up with the static and the radio.
With satellite television
You can go anywhere:
Miami, New Orleans
London, Belfast and Berlin.

And, if you listen, I can't call.
And, if you jump, you just might fall.
And, if you shout, I'll only hear you.

If I could stay, then the night would give you up.
Stay, and the day would keep its trust.
Stay with the demons you drowned.
Stay with the spirit I found.
Stay, and the night would be enough.

Three o'clock in the morning
It's quiet, there's no one around,
Just the bang and the clatter
As an angel runs to ground.
Just the bang and the clatter
As an angel hits the ground.

STORIES FOR BOYS

There's a place I go
When I am far away.
There's a T.V. show
And I can play.

Sometimes when a hero take me
Sometimes I don't let go
Oh, oh, oh.

There's a picture book
With colour photographs
There's a comic strip
That makes me laugh

Sometimes away he takes me
Sometimes I don't let go.

Stories for boys
Stories for boys
Stories for boys
Stories for boys

Stories for boys.

There's a place I go
And it's a part of me
There's a radio
And I will go

Sometimes a hero takes me
Sometimes I don't let go.

Stories for boys
Stories for boys
Stories for boys
Stories for boys
Stories for boys.
Stories for boys.
Stories for boys.
Stories for boys.
Stories for boys.

STRANGER IN A STRANGE LAND

Stranger, stranger in a strange land.
He looked at me like I was the one who should run.

We asked him to smile for a photograph
Waited a while to see if we could make him laugh.

The soldier asked for a cigarette
His smiling face I can't forget.
He looked at me across the street
But that's a long way here.

Oh, and I wish you were here.
Oh, and I wish you were here.

Stranger, stranger in a strange land.
He looked at me like I was the one who should run.

I watched as he watched us get back on the bus
I watched the way it was
The way it was when he was with us
And I really don't mind sleeping on the floor
But I couldn't sleep after what I saw
I wrote this letter to tell you the way I feel.

Oh I wish you were here
Oh I wish you were here
To see what I could see
To hear
And I wish you were here.

SUNDAY BLOODY SUNDAY

I can't believe the news today
I can't close my eyes and make it go away.
How long, how long must we sing this song?
How long, how long?
'Cos tonight
We can be as one, tonight.

Broken bottles under children's feet
Bodies strewn across the dead-end street.
But I won't heed the battle call
It puts my back up, puts my back up against the wall.

Sunday, bloody Sunday.
Sunday, bloody Sunday.
Sunday, bloody Sunday.
Sunday, bloody Sunday.
Oh, let's go.

And the battle's just begun
There's many lost, but tell me who has won?
The trenches dug within our hearts
And mothers, children, brothers, sisters
Torn apart.

Sunday, bloody Sunday.
Sunday, bloody Sunday.

How long, how long must we sing this song?
How long, how long?
'Cos tonight
We can be as one, tonight.
Sunday, bloody Sunday.
Sunday, bloody Sunday.

Wipe the tears from your eyes
Wipe your tears away.
I'll wipe your tears away.
I'll wipe your tears away.
I'll wipe your bloodshot eyes.
Sunday, bloody Sunday.
Sunday, bloody Sunday.

And it's true we are immune
When fact is fiction and TV reality.
And today the millions cry
We eat and drink while tomorrow they die.

The real battle just begun
To claim the victory Jesus won
On...

Sunday, bloody Sunday
Sunday, bloody Sunday.

SURRENDER

Oh, the city's alight with lovers and lies
And bright blue eyes.
Oh, the city is bright, it's brighter than day tonight.
(Surrender, surrender)
(Surrender, surrender)

Sadie said she couldn't work out what it was all about
And so she let go.
Now Sadie's on the street and the people she meets
you know.

She tried to be a good girl and a good wife
Raise a good family
Lead a good life
It's not good enough
She got herself up on the 48th floor
Gotta find out
Find out what she's living for.

Oh, the city's afire
A passionate flame that knows me by name.
Oh, the city's desire to take me for more and more.
It's in the street gettin' under my feet
It's in the air, it's everywhere I look for you.
It's in the things that I do and say
And it I wanna live I gotta die to myself someday.

SWEETEST THING

My love, she throws me like a rubber ball
(Oh, the sweetest thing.)
But she won't catch me or break my fall.
(Oh, the sweetest thing.)
Baby's got blue skies up ahead
But in this, I'm a raincloud
You know she wants a dry kind of love.
(Oh, the sweetest thing.)

I'm losin' you, I'm losin' you
Ain't love the sweetest thing?

I wanted to run, but she made me crawl
(Oh, the sweetest thing.)
Eternal fire, she turned me to straw.
(Oh, the sweetest thing.)
I know I got black eyes
But they burn so brightly for her
I guess it's a blind kind of love.
(Oh, the sweetest thing.)

I'm losin' you, I'm losin' you
Ain't love the sweetest thing?
Ain't love the sweetest thing?

Blue-eyed boy meets a brown-eyed girl.
(Oh, the sweetest thing.)

You can sew it up, but you still see the tear.
(Oh, the sweetest thing.)
Baby's got blue skies up ahead
But in this, I'm a rain-cloud,
Ours is a stormy kind of love.
(Oh, the sweetest thing.)

THE ELECTRIC CO.

Boy, stupid boy
Don't sit at the table
Until you're able to.

Toy, broken toy
Shout, shout, you're inside out
If you don't know.
Electric Co.
If you don't know
Electric Co.

Red, running red
Play for real
Talk and feel
Holding your head
You won't shout
You still beg
If you don't know
The Electric Co.

If you don't know.
Electric Co.
If you don't know
Electric Co.

THE FIRST TIME

I have a lover, a lover like no other
She got soul, soul, soul, sweet soul
And she teach me how to sing.

Shows me colours when there's none to see
Gives me hope when I can't believe
That for the first time I feel love.

I have a brother, when I'm a brother in need
I spend my whole time running
He spends his running after me.

I feel myself goin' down
I just call and he comes around.
But for the first time I feel love.

My father is a rich man, he wears a rich man's cloak.
He gave me the keys to his kingdom (coming)
Gave me a cup of gold.

He said "I have many mansions
And there are many rooms to see."
But I left by the back door
And I threw away the key
And I threw away the key.

For the first time, for the first time
For the first time, I feel love.

THE FLY

It's no secret that the stars are falling from the sky
It's no secret that our world is in darkness tonight.
They say the sun is sometimes eclipsed by the moon
Y' know I don't see you when she walks in the room.

It's no secret that a friend is someone who lets you help.
It's no secret that a liar won't believe anyone else.
They say a secret is something you tell one other person
So I'm telling you, child.

Voice 1	Voice 2
A man will beg	Love, we shine like a
A man will crawl	Burning star
On the sheer face of love	We're falling from
Like a fly on a wall	The sky... tonight
It's no secret at all	

It's no secret that a conscience can sometimes be a pest.
It's no secret ambition bites the nails of success.
Every artist is a cannibal, every poet is a thief;
All kill their inspiration and sing about their grief.

Voice 1	Voice 2
A man will rise	Love, we shine like a
A man will fall	Burning star
From the sheer face of love	We're falling from
like a fly from a wall.	The sky... tonight
It's no secret at all.	

Love, we shine like a burning star
We're falling from the sky tonight

Voice 1	Voice 2
A man will rise	Love, we shine like a
A man will fall	Burning star
From the sheer face of love	We're falling from
like a fly from a wall.	The sky... tonight
It's no secret at all.	

It's no secret that the stars are falling from the sky
The universe exploding 'cos-a one man's lie.
Look I gotta go, yeah, I'm running outta change;
There's a lot of things if I could I'd rearrange.

THE OCEAN

A picture in grey
Dorian Gray
Just me by the sea.

And I felt like a star
I felt the world could go far
If they listened to what I said.
The sea

Washes my feet
Washes my feet
Splashes the soul of my heart.

THE PLAYBOY MANSION

If coke is a mystery
Michael Jackson, history
If beauty is truth
And surgery the fountain of youth ...

What am I to do?
Have I got the gifts to get me through
The gates of that mansion?

If O.J. is more than a drink
And a Big Mac bigger than you think
And perfume is an obsession
And talk shows…confession

What have we got to lose?
Another push and we'll be through
The gates of that mansion.

I never bought a lotto ticket
I never parked in anyone's space.
The banks they're like cathedrals
I guess casinos took their place.

Love, come on down
Don't wake her she'll come around.

Chance is a kind of religion
Where you're damned for plain hard luck.
I never did see that movie
I never did read that book.
Love, come on down
Let my numbers come around.

Don't know if I can hold on
Don't know if I'm that strong.
Don't know if I can wait that long
Till the colours come flashing
And the lights go on.

Then will there be no time for sorrow
Then will there be no time for shame
Though I can't say why
I know I've got to believe.

We'll go driving in that pool
It's who you know that gets you through
The gates of the playboy mansion.

Then will there be no time for sorrow
Then will there be no time for shame
Then will there be now time for shame
Then will there be now time for pain

THE REFUGEE

Wa, war she's the refugee.
I see your face, I see you staring back at me.
Wa, war she is the refugee.
Her mama say one day she's gonna live in America.

In the morning she is waiting
Waiting for the ship to sail, sail away.

Wa, war her papa go to war.
He gonna fight but he don't know what for.
Wa, war her papa go to war.
Her mama say one day he's gonna come back from far away.

Oh help me
How can you help me?

In the evening
She is waiting
Waiting for her man to come
And take her by her hand
And take her to this promised land.

Wa, war she's a pretty face
But at the wrong time in the wrong place
Wa, war she's a pretty face
Her mama say one days she's gonna live in America.
Yeah, America.

Wa, war she is a refugee.
She coming back, she come and keep you company.
Wa, war she is a refugee.
Her mama say one day she's gonna live in America.

THE THREE SUNRISES

Spirit of the rising sun
Lift me up.
Hold me there and never let me fall.
Love me till I die, my heart won't wait
Soon thy will be done in this love song.

Love, love song
Love, love song
Hey, hey love won't find
Find its own way home.

In this love song, love
Love, love song.

Sunshine, sunshine on me
Sunshine, sunshine on me.
In this love song, love.
Love, love song.

Hey, hey, love won't find
Find its own way home.

In this love song, love
Love song, love song.
Sunshine, sunshine on me
Bring it through to my heart.
And I will give you everything
I will give you my desire
Sunshine, sunshine on me
Sunshine, sunshine on me.

THE UNFORGETTABLE FIRE

Ice, your only rivers run cold.
These city lights, they shine as silver and gold.
Dug from the night, your eyes as black as coal.

Walk on by, walk on through.
Walk till you run and don't look back
For here I am.

Carnival, the wheels fly and the colours spin through alcohol.
Red wine that punctures the skin.
Face to face in a dry and waterless place.

Walk on by, walk on through.
So sad to besiege your love ...oh hang on.

Stay this time, stay tonight in a lie.
I'm only asking, but I, I think you know.
Come on take me away, come on take me away
Come on take me home, home again.

And if the mountains should crumble
Or disappear into the sea
Not a tear, no not I.

Stay this time, stay tonight in a lie.
Ever after is a long time.
And if you save your love, save it all, save it all
Don't push me too far, don't push me too far.
Tonight, tonight.

THE WANDERER

I went out walking through streets paved with gold
Lifted some stones, saw the skin and bones
Of a city without a soul
I went out walking under an atomic sky
Where the ground won't turn and the rain it burns
Like the tears when I said goodbye.

Yeah, I went with nothing, nothing but the thought of you.
I went wandering.

I went drifting through the capitals of tin
Where men can't walk or freely talk
And sons turn their fathers in.
I stopped outside a church house
Where the citizens like to sit.
They say they want the kingdom
But they don't want God in it.

I went out riding down that old eight-lane
I passed a thousand signs looking for my own name.
I went with nothing but the thought you'd be there too,
Looking for you.

I went out there in search of experience
To taste and to touch and to feel as much
As a man can before he repents.

I went out searching, looking for one good man
A spirit who would not bend or break
Who would sit at his father's right hand.
I went out walking with a bible and a gun
The word of God lay heavy on my heart
I was sure I was the one.

Now Jesus, don't you wait up, Jesus I'll be home soon.
Yeah, I went out for the papers, told her I'd be back by noon.
Yeah, I left with nothing but the thought you'd be there too
Looking for you.

Yeah, I went with nothing, nothing but the thought of you.
I went wandering.

TOMORROW

Won't you come back tomorrow
Won't you come back tomorrow
Won't you come back tomorrow
Can I sleep tonight?

Outside, somebody's outside
Somebody's knocking at the door.
There's a black car parked at the side of the road
Don't go to the door
Don't go to the door.

I'm going out.
I'm going outside mother.
I'm going out there.

Won't you be back tomorrow,
Won't you be back tomorrow,
Will you be back tomorrow?
La, la, la, la, la, la.

Who broke the window
Who broke down the door?
Who tore the curtain
And who was it for?
Who heals the wounds
Who heals the scars?
Open the door, open the door.

Won't you come back tomorrow?
Won't you be back tomorrow?
Will you be back tomorrow?
Can I sleep tonight?

'Cause I want you
I, I want you
I really want you.
I, I want, I, I
Want you to be back tomorrow
I want you to be back tomorrow.
Will you be back tomorrow?
La la la la la la.

I want you to be back tomorrow
I want you to be back tomorrow.
Will you be back tomorrow?
Open up, open up, to the Lamb Of God
To the love of He
Who made the blind to see.

He's coming back
He's coming back
O believe Him.

TOUCH

Thank-you, don't mention it.
I'm pleased to meet you.
I don't think I'm very good at this
Let me show you, I just wanna know, I just wanna know.

Falling the world is by your side
Calling to find a place to hide
I just wanna know
I just wanna know.

She said "The twenty second floor"
I said "I can't think what it's for"
And I just wanna know
I don't wanna know.

Touching you, touching you, etc.

TRASH, TRAMPOLINE AND THE PARTY GIRL

I know a girl
A girl called Party, Party Girl.
I know she wants more than a party, Party Girl.
And she won't tell me her name.

I know a boy
A boy called Trash, Trash Can.
I know he does all that he can, wham bam.
And she won't tell me his name.

When I was three
I thought the world revolved around me
I was wrong
But you can sing, sing along
And if you dance
Then dance with me.

I know a girl
A girl called Party, Party Girl.
I know she wants more than a party, Party Girl.

I know a boy
A boy called Trampoline
You know what I mean.
I think you know what he wants
I think he knows what he wants
I think he knows what he wants.

TREASURE (WHATEVER HAPPENED TO PETE THE CHOP?)

I like to smile but I'd most like the smile to stay with you.
I like good times but I can't feel them without you.
By my side, the heart is the place we have to find.
Jump up beside me, jump up beside me.

If I should die
I couldn't tell the world how I felt about you
And I'd like more time
To describe the feeling when
I feel you in my arms
Take you in my hand
How could I let you go?
Somebody save me
Somebody save me from myself.

'Cause you sing, you sing my favourite song
'Cause you sing, my favourite song

I like good times
But the better they are the better chance they will go wrong
You sing my favourite song
You sing my favourite song

If I could swim, I'd swim in circles.
And never drown
If I did, I'd drown with you
If I had enough of my life,
It would be because
I hadn't enough of you
Then I would die
Die... die... die... die...

TRIP THROUGH YOUR WIRES

In the distance, she saw me comin' round
I was callin' out, I was callin' out.
Still shakin', still in pain
You put me back together again.
I was cold and you clothed me, honey
I was down, and you lifted me, honey.

Angel, angel or devil?
I was thirsty
And you wet my lips.
You, I'm waiting for you
You, you set my desire
I trip through your wires.

I was broken, bent out of shape
I was naked in the clothes you made.
Lips were dry, throat like rust
You gave me shelter from the heat and the dust.
No more water in the well
No more water, water.

Angel, angel or devil?
I was thirsty
And you wet my lips.
You, I'm waiting for you
You, you set my desire
I trip through your wires.

Oh I need, on I need
Oh I need, oh I need it.
Oh I need, oh I need
All I need, yeah, yeah!

Thunder, thunder on the mountain
There's a raincloud
In the desert sky.
In the distance
She saw me comin' round
I was callin' out
I was callin' out.

TRYIN' TO THROW YOUR ARMS AROUND THE WORLD

Six o'clock in the morning, you're the last to hear the warning
You been tryin' to throw your arms around the world.
You been falling off the sidewalk, your lips move but you can't talk
Tryin' to throw your arms around the world.

Gonna run to you, run to you, run to you; be still.
Gonna run to you, run to you, woman, I will.

Sunrise like a nose-bleed, your head hurts and you can't breathe
You been tryin' to throw your arms around the world.
How far are you gonna go before you lose your way back home
You been tryin' to throw your arms around the world.

Gonna run to you, run to you, run to you; be still.
Gonna run to you, run to you, woman, I will.

Yeah I dreamed that I saw Dali with a supermarket trolley
He was tryin' to throw his arms around a girl.
He took an open top beetle through the eye of a needle
He was tryin' to throw his arms around the world.

I'm gonna run to you, run to you, run to you, woman be still.
I'm gonna run to you, run to you, run to you, woman, I will.

Nothing much to say, I guess; just the same as all the rest
Been tryin' to throw your arms round the world.
And a woman needs a man like a fish needs a bicycle
When you're tryin' to throw your arms around the world.

Gonna run to you, run to you, run to you
I'm gonna run to you, run to you, run to you
I'm gonna run to you, run to you, run to you, woman be still
Woman be still, woman be still, woman I will.

TWILIGHT

I look into his eyes
They're closed but I see something.
A teacher told me why
I laugh when old men cry.

My body grows and grows
If frightens me, you know
The old man tried to walk me home
I thought he should have known.

Twilight, lost my way
Twilight, can't find my way.

In the shadow, boy meets man
In the shadow, boy meets man
In the shadow, boy meets man
In the shadow, boy meets man.

I'm running in the rain
I'm caught in a late night play.
It's all, it's everything
I'm soaking through the skin.

Twilight, darkened day
Twilight, lost my way
Twilight, night and day
Twilight, can't find my way.
Can't find your way
Can't find my way
Can't find your way.

Twilight, darkened day
Twilight, lost my way
Twilight, night and day
Twilight, can't find my way.

In the shadow, boy meets man
In the shadow, boy meets man
In the shadow, boy meets man
In the shadow, boy meets man.

TWO HEARTS BEAT AS ONE

I don't know, I don't know which side I'm on.
I don't know my right from left or my right from wrong.
They say I'm a fool, they say I'm nothing
But if I'm a fool for you oh, that's something.
Two hearts beat as one.
Two hearts beat as one.
Two hearts.

I can't stop to dance
Honey, this is my last chance
I said, can't stop to dance
Maybe this is my last chance.
Two hearts beat as one.
Two hearts beat as one.
Two hearts.

Beat on black, beat on white
Beat on anything, don't get it right.
Beat on you, beat on me, beat on love.

I don't know
How to say what's got to be said
I don't know if it's black or white
There's others see it red
I don't get the answers right
I'll leave that to you
Is this love out of fashion
Or is it the time of year?
Are these words distraction
To the words you wanna hear?
Two hearts beat as one.
Two hearts beat as one.
Two hearts.

I try to spit it out
Try to explain.
The way I wanna feel
Oh, yeah, two hearts.

Well I can't stop to dance.
Maybe this is my last chance.
And I said, I can't stop to dance.
Maybe this is my last chance.
I said don't stop to dance
Maybe this is my last chance.
I said I can't stop to dance.
Maybe this is our last chance.
I said don't stop to dance.
Maybe this is our last chance.
Oh, oh!

TWO SHOTS OF HAPPY, ONE SHOT OF SAD
(for Frank Sinatra)

Two shots of happy, one shot of sad.
You think I'm no good, will I know I've been bad.
Took you to a place, now you can't get back.
Two shots of happy, one shot of sad.

Walked together down a dead-end street
We were mixing the bitter with the sweet.
Don't try to figure out what we might have had.
Just two shots of happy, one shot of sad.

I'm just a singer, some say a sinner
Rolling the dice, not always a winner.
You say I've been lucky, well hell, I made my own
Not part of the crowd not feeling alone.

Under pressure but not bent out of shape
Surrounded, we always found an escape.

Drove me to drink but hey, that's not all bad.
Two shots of happy, one shot of sad.

Guess I've been greedy all of my life
Greedy with my children, my lovers and my wife.
Greedy for the good things as well as the bad.
Two shots of happy, one shot of sad.

Maybe it's just talk, saloon singing
The chairs are all stacked, the swingers stopped
swinging.
You say I hurt you, you put the finger on yourself
Then, after you did it, you came crying for my help.

Two shots of happy, one shot of sad.
I'm not complaining baby, I'm glad.
You call it compromise, well what's that?
Two shots of happy, one shot of sad.
Two shots of happy, one shot of sad.

ULTRA VIOLET (LIGHT MY WAY)

Sometimes I feel like I don't know
Sometimes I feel like checking out.
I wanna get it wrong
Can't always be strong
And love, it won't be long.

Oh, sugar, don't you cry.
Oh, child, wipe the tears from your eyes.
You know I need you to be strong
And the day it is dark, as the night is long.
Feel like trash, you make me feel clean.
I'm in the black, can't see or be seen.

Baby, baby, baby, light my way.
Alright now, baby, baby, baby, light my way.

You bury your treasure where it can't be found
But your love is like a secret that's been passed around.
There is a silence that comes to a house
Where no-one can sleep.
I guess it's the price of love; I know it's not cheap.

Oh, come on, baby, baby, baby, light my way.
Oh, come on, baby, baby, baby, light my way
Baby, baby, baby, light my way.

I remember when we could sleep on stones.
Now we lie together in whispers and moans.
When I was all messed up and I heard opera in my head
Your love was a light bulb hanging over my bed.

Baby, baby, baby, light my way.
Oh, come on, baby, baby, baby, light my way.

UNTIL THE END OF THE WORLD

Haven't seen you in quite a while
I was down the hold, just passing time.
Last time we met it was a low-lit room
We were as close together as a bride and groom.
We ate the food, we drank the wine
Everybody having a good time except you.
You were talking about the end of the world.

I took the money, I spiked your drink
You miss too much these days if you stop to think.
You led me on with those innocent eyes
You know I love the element of surprise.
In the garden I was playing the tart
I kissed your lips and broke your heart.
You, you were acting like it was the end of the world.

In my dream, I was drowning the sorrows
But my sorrows they'd learned to swim
Surrounding me, going down on me
Spilling over the brim
Waves of regret and waves of joy.
I reached out for the one I tried to destroy.
You, you said you'd wait till the end of the world.

VAN DIEMEN'S LAND

Hold me now, oh hold me now
Till this hour has gone around
And I'm gone, on the rising tide
For to face Van Diemen's land.

It's a bitter pill I swallow here
To be rent from one so dear.
We fought for justice and not for gain
But the magistrate sent me away.

Now kings will rule and the poor will toil
And tear their hands as they tear the soil
But a day will come in this dawning age
When an honest man sees an honest wage.

Hold me now, oh hold me now
Till this hour has gone around
And I'm gone on the rising tide
For to face Van Diemen's Land.

WAKE UP DEAD MAN

Jesus, Jesus help me
I'm alone in this world
And a fucked-up world it is too.

Tell me, tell me the story
The one about eternity
And the way it's all gonna be.

Wake up, wake up dead man
Wake up, wake up dead man.

Jesus, I'm waiting here, boss
I know you're looking out for us
But maybe your hands aren't free.

Your Father, He made the world in seven
He's in charge of heaven.
Will you put a word in for me?

Wake up, wake up dead man
Wake up, wake up dead man.

Listen to the words they'll tell you what to do
Listen over the rhythm that's confusing you
Listen to the reed in the saxophone
Listen over the hum of the radio
Listen over the sound of blades in rotation
Listen through the traffic and circulation
Listen as hope and peace try to rhyme
Listen over marching bands playing out their time.

Wake up, wake up dead man
Wake up, wake up dead man.

Jesus, were you just around the corner?
Did you think to try and warn her?
Were you working on something new?
If there's an order in all of this disorder
Is it like a tape recorder?
Can we rewind it just once more?

Wake up, wake up dead man
Wake up, wake up dead man.
Wake up, wake up dead man.

WALK TO THE WATER

She said it wasn't cold
She left her coat at home that day.
She wore canvas shoes, white canvas shoes.
Around her neck she wore a silver necklace.
"It was given to me by my father." she said.
"It was given to me."
She took the back way home
Passed the lights at Summer Hill
Turned left onto the North Strand and on
On towards the sea.

He said he was an artist
But he really painted billboards
In large capital letters.
In large capital letters.
He was telling jokes
Nobody else would listen to him.

I saw you that day, your lips of cherry red
Your legs were crossed, your arms wide open
Your hair was coloured gold
And like a field of corn
You were blown by the wind
You were blown by the wind.

Walk, walk, walk
To the water.
Walk with me awhile.
Walk, walk, walk
To the water.
Walk with me
In the light.

A room in the Royal Hotel
With sea-facing views.
A man with a suitcase
Full of things he doesn't need.
I'm looking through your window
I'm walking through your doorway.
I'm on the outside let me in.
Let me love you
Let me love you
Let me.

Walk, walk, walk
To the water.
Walk with me, yeah.
Walk, walk, walk
To the roadside
Walk with me awhile.

WHEN LOVE COMES TO TOWN

I was a sailor, I was lost at sea
I was under the waves before love rescued me.
I was a fighter, I could turn on a thread
Now I stand accused of the things I've said.

When love comes to town I'm gonna jump that train
When love comes to town I'm gonna catch that flame.
Maybe I was wrong to ever let you down
But I did what I did before love came to town.

Used to make love under a red sunset
I was making promises I was soon to forget.
She was pale as the lace of her wedding gown
But I left her standing before love came to town.

I ran into a juke-joint when I heard a guitar scream
The notes were turning blue, I was dazed and in a
dream.
As the music played I saw my life turn around
That was the day before love came to town.

When love comes to town I'm gonna jump that train
When love comes to town I'm gonna catch that flame.
Maybe I was wrong to ever let you down
But I did what I did before love came to town.

When love comes to town I'm gonna jump that train
When love comes to town I'm gonna catch that flame.
Maybe I was wrong to ever let you down
But I did what I did before love came to town.

I was there when they crucified my Lord
I held the scabbard when the soldier drew his sword.
I threw the dice when they pierced his side
But I've seen love conquer the great divide.

When love comes to town I'm gonna jump that train
When love comes to town I'm gonna catch that flame.
Maybe I was wrong to ever let you down
But I did what I did before love came to town.

WHERE DID IT ALL GO WRONG?

Did you get it, did you need it
Was it really what you wanted.
Was it good in the sun
Did you really have some fun?

Did you smash it, did you grab it
Did you jump it like a rabbit.
Did you walk, did you run
Did you slap it, did you come?

And I know that you do
Put your soul into the song.
Where did it all go wrong.
Where did it all go wrong.

Did you crack it, did you taunt it
Was it really what you wanted
Did you burn in the sun
or are you burning for someone?

Did you shoot it, did you stab it
Did you chase it like a rabbit
Did you walk, did you run
Did you come in at number one?

I know what you do
Put your soul in the song
But now it's sinking like you
Where did it all go wrong.

Did you drown it, did you clown it
Would you really have gone down on it
Did you clean it, clean it up
Did you rub it, did you soap.

Did you screen it, did you ream it
Did you ruin it, did you feed it
Is it warm in the sun
With your ear in her tounge.

WHERE THE STREETS HAVE NO NAME

I wanna run, I want to hide
I wanna tear down the walls
That hold me inside.
I wanna reach out
And touch the flame
Where the streets have no name.

I wanna feel sunlight on my face.
I see the dust-cloud
Disappear without a trace.

I wanna take shelter
From the poison rain
Where the streets have no name
Where the streets have no name
Where the streets have no name.

We're still building and burning down love
Burning down love.
And when I go there
I go there with you
(It's all I can do).

The city's a flood, and our love turns to rust.
We're beaten and blown by the wind
Trampled in dust.
I'll show you a place
High on a desert plain
Where the streets have no name
Where the streets have no name
Where the streets have no name.

We're still building and burning down love
Burning down love.
And when I go there
I go there with you
(It's all I can do).

WHO'S GONNA RIDE YOUR WILD HORSES

You're dangerous, 'cos you're honest.
You're dangerous, you don't know what you want.
Well you left my heart empty as a vacant lot
For any spirit to haunt.

You're an accident waiting to happen
You're a piece of glass left there on a beach.
Well you tell me things
I know you're not supposed to
Then you leave me just out of reach.

Who's gonna ride your wild horses?
Who's gonna drown in your blue sea?
Who's gonna ride your wild horses?
Who's gonna fall at the foot of thee?

Well you stole it 'cos I needed the cash
And you killed it 'cos I needed revenge.
Well you lied to me 'cos I asked you to.
Baby, can we still be friends?

Who's gonna ride your wild horses?
Who's gonna drown in your blue sea?
Who's gonna ride your wild horses?
Who's gonna fall at the foot of thee?

Ah, the deeper I spin
Ah, the hunter will sin for your ivory skin.
Took a drive in the dirty rain
To a place where the wind calls your name
Under the trees, the river laughing at you and me.
Hallelujah! Heaven's white rose
The doors you open I just can't close.

Don't turn around, don't turn around again.
Don't turn around your gypsy heart.
Don't turn around, don't turn around again.
Don't turn around, and don't look back.
Come on now love, don't you look back.

Who's gonna ride your wild horses?
Who's gonna drown in your blue sea?
Who's gonna taste your saltwater kisses?
Who's gonna take the place of me?
Who's gonna ride your wild horses?
Who's gonna tame the heart of thee?

WIRE

Innocent and in a sense I am
Guilty of a crime that's now in hand.
Such a nice day to throw your life away.
Such a nice day, to let it go.

Cold in his eyes, I can't believe it.
Cold in his heart and soul.
Heart and soul.

Cold man, such a cold heart
Such a cold manner, why'd you tear yourself apart.
So lay me down, my soul to keep.
So lay me down, the longest sleep.
Oh, the longest sleep.

In I come and out you go you get
Here we are again, now place your bets
Is this the time, the time to win or lose?
Is this the time, the time to choose?

Cold in his eyes, I can't believe it
So deep inside a cold fire.
Cold in his heart and soul.

Don't do it, d-d-don't do it
Don't do it, d-d-don't do it
Anytime you're on the earth... is kissing time.

You can't take me, that's right but you can keep me going.

It's so white trash if you've got the cash.
A cartoon cut out, a cut-throat, let out.
Look I'm on your side, we're both right.
Hey, I'm alright Jack, just don't piggyback.
I'm no dope, I'll give you hope.
Here's the rope.
Here's the rope...
Now swing on it.

WITH A SHOUT (JERASULEM)

Oh, where do we go
Where do we go from here?
Where to go?
To the side of a hill
Blood was spilt
We were still looking at each other.
But we're going back there?

Jerusalem
Jerusalem

Shout, shout, with a shout
Shout it out, shout
Shout it out.

I want to go, to the foot of Mount Zion
To the foot of He who made me see
To the side of a hill blood was spilt
We were filled with a love
And we're going to be there again

Jerusalem
Jerusalem

Jerusalem
Jerusalem
Jerusalem
Jerusalem
Jerusalem

Shout, shout, with a shout
Shout, with a shout.

WITH OR WITHOUT YOU

See the stone set in your eyes
See the thorn twist in your side.
I wait for you.
Sleight of hand and twist of fate
On a bed of nails she makes me wait
And I wait... without you

With or without you
With or without you.

Through the storm, we reach the shore
You gave it all but I want more
And I'm waiting for you...

With or without you
With or without you.
I can't live
With or without you.

And you give yourself away
And you give yourself away
And you give, and you give
And you give yourself away.

My hands are tied, my body bruised
She got me with nothing to win
And nothing else to lose.

And you give yourself away
And you give yourself away
And you give, and you give
And you give yourself away.

With or without you
With or without you
I can't live
With or without you.

With or without you
With or without you
I can't live
With or without you
With or without you.

ZOO STATION

I'm ready, I'm ready for laughing gas
I'm ready, I'm ready for what's next.
I'm ready to duck, ready to dive
Ready to say I'm glad to be alive
I'm ready, I'm ready for the push.

In the cool of the night, in the warmth of the breeze
I'll be crawling around on my hands and knees.
She's just down the line, Zoo Station.
Got to make it on time, Zoo Station.

I'm ready, I'm ready for the gridlock
I'm ready to take it to the street.
Ready for the shuffle, ready for the deal
Ready to let go of the steering wheel.
I'm ready, ready for the crush.

Zoo Station.

Alright, alright, alright, alright, alright
It's alright, ilt's alright, it's alright, it's alright,
Hey baby, hey baby, hey baby, hey baby,
It's alright, it's alright.

Time is a train makes the future the past
Leaves you standing in the station
Your face pressed up against the glass.

I'm just down the line from your love...Zoo Station
I'm under the sign of your love... Zoo Station
I'm gonna be there... Zoo Station
Tracing the line... Zoo Station
I'm gonna make it on time, make it on time ... Zoo Station

Just two stops down the line... Zoo Station
Just a stop down the line... Zoo Station

ZOOROPA

Zooropa, Vorsprung durch Technik.
Zooropa, be all that you can be.
Be a winner, eat to get slimmer.

Zooropa, a bluer kind of white
Zooropa, it could be yours tonight.
We're mild and green and squeaky clean.

Zooropa, better by design
Zooropa, fly the friendly skies.
Through the appliance of science
We've got that ring of confidence.

And I have no compass
And I have no map
And I have no reasons
No reasons to get back.

And I have no religion
And I don't know what's what
And I don't know the limit
The limit of what we got.

Zooropa, don't worry baby, it'll be alright.
Zooropa, you've got the right shoes
Zooropa, to get you through the night.
Zooropa, it's cold outside, but brightly lit
Zooropa, let's skip the subway,
Zooropa, let's go to the overground.
Get your head out of the mud baby
Put flowers in the mud baby,
overground.

No particular place names
No particular song
I've been hiding
What am I hiding from?

Zooropa, don't worry, baby, it's gonna be alright
Zooropa, uncertainty can be a guiding light.
Zooropa, I hear voices, ridiculous voices
Zooropa, in the slipstream.
Zooropa, let's go, let's go overground.
Zooropa, take your head out of the mud, baby.

She's gonna dream up the world she wants to live in
She's gonna dream out loud, she's gonna dream out loud,
She's gonna dream out loud, dream out loud.

additional songs

OTHER SONGS WRITTEN BY MEMBERS OF U2

A CLOCKWORK ORANGE

BONO & EDGE - written for

Royal Shakespeare Company (1990)

BILLY BOOLA

BONO, G FRIDAY, M SEEZER - written for

In The Name Of The Father (1994)

BABY PLEASE COME HOME

U2 - written for *Special Olympics Album* (1987)

CAPTIVE

EDGE Solo - *soundtrack for movie* (1986)

CONVERSATION ON A BAR STOOL

U2 Cover version in the film *Short Cuts* (1993)

GOLDENEYE

BONO & EDGE - covered by Tina Turner

for film soundtrack (1995)

HAVING A WONDERFUL TIME

(WISHING YOU WERE HER)

BONO and T-BONE BURNETTE (1984)

HOLD ONTO YOUR DREAMS

EDGE and JAH WOBBLE (1983)

IN THE NAME OF THE FATHER

BONO, G FRIDAY, M SEEZER - written for

In The Name Of The Father (1994)

JAH LOVE

BONO and CYRIL NEVILLE (1990)

J SWALLO

U2 (1981)

LUCILLE

BONO

MISERERE

BONO and ZUCCHERO (1992)

MY WILD IRISH ROSE

BONO - appeared in *Bringing It All Back Home* programme (1991)

NEW DAY

BONO and WYCLEF JEAN - written for NetAid (1999)

NORTH & SOUTH OF THE RIVER

BONO, EDGE and CHRISTY MOORE (1995)

ORIGINAL SOUNDTRACKS 1

PASSENGERS (1995)

PURPLE HEART

BONO & T-BONE BURNETT (1988)

PUT 'EM UNDER PRESSURE

LARRY, DENIS WOODS and JOHN DONNELLY

with THE HORLSIPS (1990)

SHE'S A MYSTERY TO ME

BONO & EDGE - written for Roy Orbison (1989)

SWEET FIRE OF LOVE

U2 & ROBBIE ROBERTSON (1989)

YOU MADE ME THE THIEF

OF YOUR HEART

BONO, G FRIDAY, M SEEZER - written for

In The Name Of The Father (1994)

"40"

Words & Music by U2

Tune guitar down a semitone

♩ = 72

N.C.

Two, three, four.

1. I waited patiently for the Lord. He inclined and heard my cry.___ He brought me up___ out of the pit, out of the miry clay. I will sing, sing a new___ song.___ I will sing, sing a new___ song.___ How long___ to sing___ this___ song?___ How long___ to sing___ this___ ___ song?___ How long, how long, how long, how

long _____ to sing ___ this _____ song? _____

2. You

set my feet u - pon a rock _____ and made my foot - steps firm.

Ma - ny will see, _____ ma - ny will see and hear. _____ I will

sing, _____ sing a new ___ song. _____ I will sing, _____ sing a new

1.
___ song. _____

2.
I will ___ song. ___ How

long _____ to sing ___ this _____ song? ___ How

Repeat ad lib. to fade

long _____ to sing ___ this _____ song? ___ How

11 O'CLOCK TICK TOCK

Words & Music by U2

Tune guitar down a semitone

♩= 144

1. It's cold out - side, it gets so hot in here
(Verse 2 see block lyric)

the boys and girls col - lide to the

mus - ic in my ear. I hear the chil - dren cry - ing

and I know its time to go, I hear the chil -

- dren cry - ing take me home.

Oh

Verse 2:
A painted face
And I know we haven't long
We thought that we had the answers
It was the questions we had wrong.

I hear the children crying *etc.*

4TH OF JULY

Music by U2

A CELEBRATION

Words & Music by U2

(And) _____ And _____ you _____ can _____

go, _____ go, _____ go, _____ go! _____ Shake!

Shake! _____ Shake! _____ Shake!

1.

Guitar

2.

And we don't have the time,

_____ and ev - 'ry - thing _____ goes round _____ and round. _____ And

we don't have the time _____ to watch the world _____ go tum -

- bl - ing _____ down. _____

Guitar

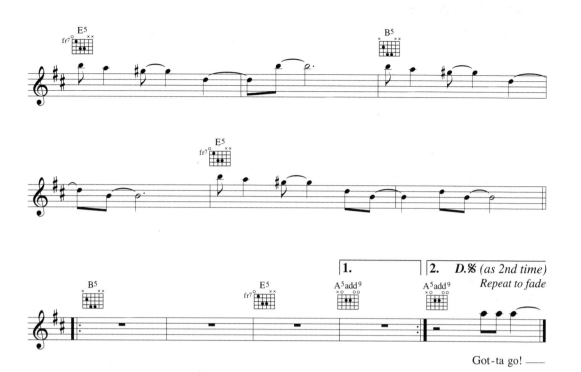

Got-ta go! —

Verse 2:
I believe in the Third World War
I believe in the atomic bomb.
I believe in the powers-that-be
But they won't overpower me.

And you can go there too, etc.

Verse 3:
I believe in the bells of Christchurch
Ringing for this land.
I believe in the cells of Mountjoy
There's an honest man.

And you can go there too, etc.

Verse 4:
I believe in the walls of Jericho
I believe they're coming down.
I believe in this city's children
I believe the trumpet's sound.

And you can go there too, etc.

A DAY WITHOUT ME
Words & Music by U2

you're a - - - wake. If I was—

— sleep - ing—— what's— at stake?——

A day with - out—— me.

Guitar

1.

What-ev - er the feel - ings, I keep feel - ing,

what are the feel - ings, you left be - hind?

2.

Guitar and Drums only

Start-ed a land - slide in my e - go,

looked from the out - side _____ to the world _____ I left be - hind.

_____ In the world _____ I left be - hind, _____ wipe their

eyes _____ and then let _____ go, in the world _____ I left be - hind,

_____ shed a tear _____ and let love _____

_____ go. _____

Drums

Ba, ba, ba, ba, ba, ba,

Repeat ad lib. to fade

ba, ba, ba, ba, ba.

A ROOM AT THE HEARTBREAK HOTEL

Words & Music by U2

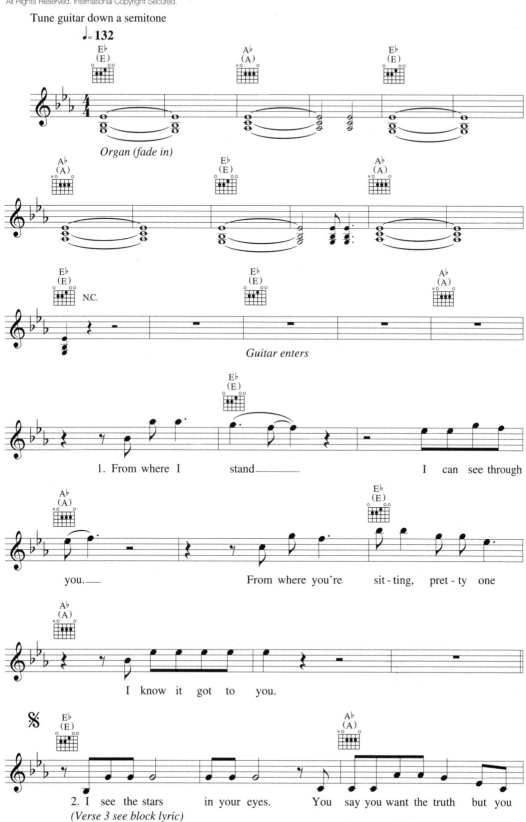

Vere 3:
You say it's love, it's not the money
You let them suck your life out like honey
Turning tricks you're on the street
Selling your kisses so bittersweet.

A SORT OF HOMECOMING

Words & Music by U2

2° only

O com - a way, o com - a way o com, o com - a way, I say— I.

O com - a way, o com - a way, o com, o com - a way, I say— I.

Oh,— oh,— oh,— on bor - der - land— we—

— run.—

I'll be there,— I'll— be there— to - night,

— a high-road, a high-road out— from here.—

1.

2. The ci - ty walls

121

2.

Cmaj7

there   so high.— I'll be there— to - night,— to -

- night.

O com-a way, I   say,— I say um ha.   O com-a way, I   say.— The wind— will— crack

—— in win-ter   time,— this bomb-blast light - ning   waltz.— No spo-ken words,

—— just a   scream. Yeah. Ooh,

— ah, oh, to -

- night—— we'll build a— bridge— a - cross the sea and land.—

See the sky,— the burn - ing   rain,—— she— will die— and live a - gain— to -

Verse 2:

The city walls are all come down
The dust a smoke screen all around
See faces ploughed like fields that once
Gave no resistance.

And we live by the side of the road
On the side of a hill as the valleys explode
Dislocated, suffocated
The land grows weary of its own.

O com-a way *etc.*

Oh, oh on borderland we run
And still we run, we run and don't look back
I'll be there, I'll be there
Tonight, tonight
I'll be there tonight, I believe
I'll be there so high
I'll be there tonight, tonight.

ACROBAT

Words & Music by U2

throw it up or choke on it, and you can dream, so dream out loud, you

know that____ your time is com-ing____ 'round,____ so

1.
don't let____ the bas-tards grind you down.____

2.
____ down._____ Oh._____ save me!

What are we go-ing to do now it's all been said?_ No new i-deas in the house, and ev-'ry book's been read.

Guitar

And

I must be— an ac-ro-bat— to talk like this _ and act_ like that.— And

you can dream,_ so dream out loud,_ and you can find_ your own way out.— And

you can build,_ and I can will,_ and you can call,_ I can't wait un-til— you_

— can stash_ and you can seize_ in dreams_ be-gin re-spon-si-bi-li-ties, and

I can love,_ and I can love._ And I know_____ that the tide is turn-ing—

rit.

— 'round,_____ so don't let— the bas-tards— grind you down._____

Verse 2:
No, nothing makes sense, nothing seems to fit.
I know you'd hit out if you only knew who to hit.
And I'd join the movement if there was one I could believe in
Yeah, I'd break bread and wine if there was a church I could receive in.
'Cause I need it now, to take the cup
To fill it up, to drink it slow.
I can't let you go.
And I must be an acrobat
To talk like this and act like that.
And you can dream, so dream out loud
And don't let the bastards grind you down.

ALL I WANT IS YOU

Words by Bono
Music by U2

Tune guitar down a semitone

1. You say you want diamonds on a ring of gold. You say you want your story to remain untold.

(Verses 3 & 5 see block lyric)

All the promises we make, from the cradle to the grave, when all I want is you.

2. You say you'll give me a highway with no-one on

(Verse 4 see block lyric)

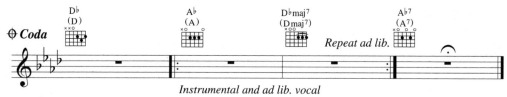

Instrumental and ad lib. vocal

Verse 3:
You say you'll give me eyes in the moon of blindness
A river in a time of dryness
A harbour in the tempest.
All the promises we make, from the cradle to the grave
When all I need is you.

Verse 4:
You say you want your love to work out right
To last with me through the night.

Verse 5:
You say you want diamonds on a ring of gold
Your story to remain untold
Your love not to grow cold.
All the promises we break, from the cradle to the grave
When all I want is you.

AN CAT DUBH

Words & Music by U2

Tune guitar down a semitone

♩ = 112

1. Say good - night,— she waits for—
(Verse 2 see block lyric)

me to turn out the light.—

Real - ly still,— she waits to

break my will. Woah, oh,—

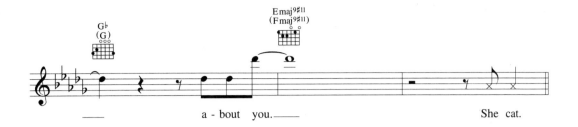

_____ a - bout you.____ She cat._

Guitar

Bass

Guitar ad lib.

Segue

Verse2:
And in the daylight
A blackbird makes a violent sight
And when she is done
She sleeps beside the one.

Woah-oh-oh
Yes, and I know the truth about you
She cat.

ANGEL OF HARLEM

Words by Bono
Music by U2

won't let me go._____ So long,__ An - gel of__

1.

Har - lem.__ *(Brass)*

2. An - gel of__ Har - lem,__ yeah.__

Ooh,_____ ooh._____ She says

heart,_____ heart__ and soul,_____ yeah, yeah.__

3. Blue light__ on the a - ve - nue,__ God__ knows__ they got__ to you.__
(Verse 4 see block lyric)

1.

Emp - ty glass, the la - dy sings,__ eyes swol - len like a bee - sting.__

133

fall-ing to the ci-ty in broad day-light. An-gel in de-vil's shoes, sal-va-tion in the blues, you ne-ver looked like an an-gel, yeah, yeah, An-gel of Har-lem.

Repeat to fade

An-gel, An-gel of Har-lem.

Verse 2:
Birdland on Fifty-Three
The street sounds like a symphony
We got John Coltrane and a love supreme
Miles and she's got to be an angel.
Lady Day got diamond eyes
She sees the truth behind the lies
Angel.
Soul love, *etc.*

Verse 3:
Blinded, you lost your way
In the side streets and the alleyways
Like a star exploding in the night
Filling up the city with broad daylight.

ANOTHER DAY
Words & Music by U2

way. Oh, oh,___ oh.___

2. Day-light, Mo-ther stands___ in the hall.___
(Verse 3 see block lyrics)

Last night, head a-gainst___ the___ wall.

Oh, oh,___ oh.___ When

night turns to day___ and the child-ren come out___ to play.___

___ A-no-ther day.___

Stop, shout. They come my___ way.___ Oh,___

___ oh.___ Oh,___

Verse 3:
Boy, salute in a street uniform
Toy, soldier ripped and torn
Oh, oh, oh.

ANOTHER TIME, ANOTHER PLACE

Words & Music by U2

1. Bright morn-ing lights wipe the sleep from an-oth-er day's eye.
(Verse 2 see block lyric)

Turn a-way from the wall and there's no-

-thing at all. Be-ing na-ked and a-fraid

in the o-pen space of my bed.

I'll be with you now,____ I'll be with you

now, I'll be with you now.____ We____

lie on a cloud, we lie._____

An-oth-er time,___ an-oth-er place.___ We____

____ lie. An-oth-er time,___ an-oth-er place,

____ we____ lie. An-oth-er time,___ an-oth-er place,

____ we____ lie. Your time, your

Play 6 times

Instrumental

place.

Verse 2:
Just as I am
I awoke with a tear on my tongue
I awoke with a feeling of never before
In my sleep, I discovered the one
But she left with the morning sun.

*Original recording has improvised lyrics.

BABYFACE

Words by Bono
Music by U2

(Chorus 2 see block lyric)

Ba - by - face,— Ba - by - face,— slow down child, let me un - tie your lace.— Ba - by - face,— Ba - by - face,— co - ver girl— with na - tu - ral grace.— How could beau - ty be— so kind— to an or - di - na - ry guy?— — Yeah!—

2. Com - in' home late— at— night— to turn— you on— — love, check - in' out ev - 'ry— frame,— — I've got slow mo - - - tion on my side.—

Turn-in' a - round____ and a - round,__ with the sound__

____ and co-lour un-der my con - trol.__ Round____ and a - round,__

D.%. al Coda

____ go - in' down,__ dressed up like a love - ly day.__

⊕ *Coda*

Do do do do do do__

____ do do do do do do do do.

Do do do do do do do do do do do

do do do do. Ba - by - face,__
(Choruses 4 - 6 see block lyric)

1, 2, 3.

Ba - by - face,__ slow down child, let me un - tie your lace.__

143

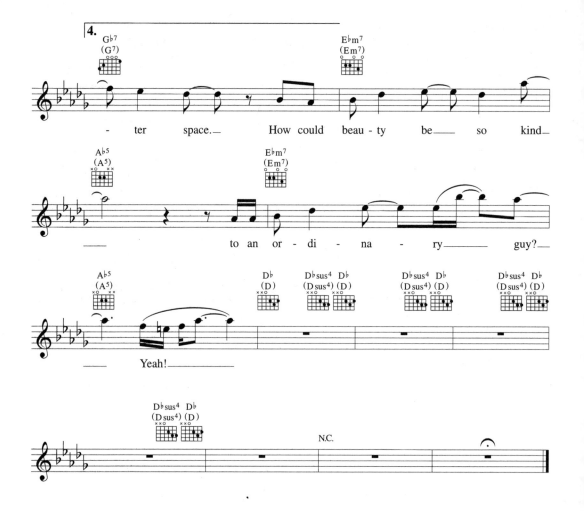

4.

-ter space.— How could beau-ty be— so kind— — to an or-di-na-ry— guy?— — Yeah!—

Chorus 2:
Babyface, Babyface
Tinfoil hair all tied up in lace
Babyface, Babyface
Bitter-sweet girl, won't you give me a taste
How could beauty be so kind
To an ordinary guy?

Chorus 4:
Babyface, Babyface
Open that door, let me unpack my case.

Chorus 5:
Babyface, Babyface
You're everywhere, child, you're all over the place.

Chorus 6:
Babyface, Babyface
You're comin' to me from outer space.

BAD

Words & Music by U2

1. If you— twist and— turn a - way.—

If you— tear your - self in two a - gain.

If I could,— yes I would,– if I could, I— would let it go.–

—— Sur - ren - der,— dis - lo -

- cate.

2. If I— could throw this life - less life - line— to the wind.— Leave this

heart of clay,— see you walk,— walk— a-way— in-to the

— night,———— and through— the—— rain — in-to the

— half— light— and through— the—— flame.—

If I— could, through my-self,— set your— spir-it free,— I'd lead your

heart a - way,— see you break,— break— a-way— in-to the

— light——— and to the day.———

1. **2.**

To let it go

Repeat 2° only

and— so to find a way.——— To let it go—

and— so find a way.—

—— I'm wide a-wake.—— I'm wide a-wake,

To Coda ⊕

—————— wide a-wake.———— I'm not—

—— sleep - ing.— Oh,— no,— no,— no.

3. If you— should ask,— then may-be they'd— tell you what I——would say,— true

col-ours fly— in blue and black,— blue silk-en sky,— and burn-ing flag.—

BASS TRAP

Music by U2

BOOMERANG I

Music by U2

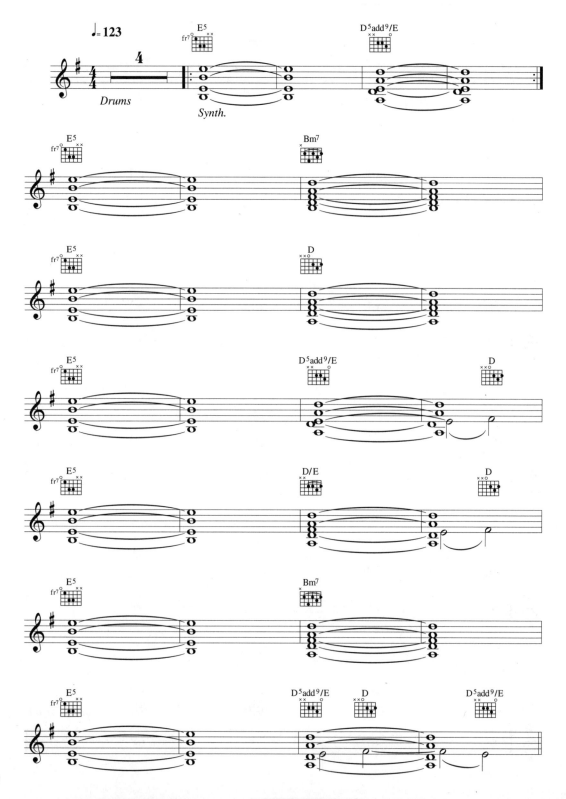

BOOMERANG II

Words & Music by U2

Soul wind blow, soul wind blow. 1. Un-der her skin I feel her laugh-ing, un-der her

(Verses 2 & 3 see block lyrics)

nails a piece of me, un-der her weight I feel weight-less, un-der her

eyes I dis-ap-pear. Soul wind blow, soul wind blow.

Soul wind blow, soul wind blow.

Verse 2:
Under her wings I feel I'm flying
Under her breath I hear my name
Under her spell I'm going under
Under her eyes… I disappear.

Soul wind blow, *etc.*

Verse 3:
Under her roof I feel shelter
Under her hands I feel as clay
Under her weight I feel weightless
Under her clock time goes away.

Soul wind blow, *etc.*

BOY/GIRL

Words & Music by U2

Tune guitar down a semitone

♩ = 176

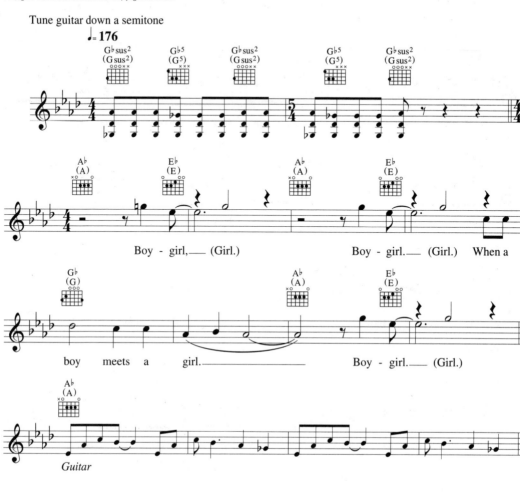

Boy - girl,___ (Girl.)   Boy - girl.___ (Girl.)   When a

boy   meets   a   girl._____   Boy - girl.___ (Girl.)

Guitar

1. Find - ing   out,   I'm   find - ing   out   the   things   that   I've   been___

___   talk - ing a-bout.   I'm   find - ing   out   the   things   that   I've   been___

___   miss - ing   out.   Find - ing   all   the   things,   that   blow   my

mind. I some-times fall be - hind.____

2. You and I,____ we live on the big ship and____
(Verse 3 see block lyric)

____ time sails by. You make up and I be - lieve mi -

- la - dy's lie. The skin-heads call it straw-ber-ries and cream.

Some-times I scream._____ Boy - girl,__

____ (Girl.) Boy - girl.__ (Girl.) When a boy meets a

girl._____ Boy - girl.__ (Girl.)

Guitar

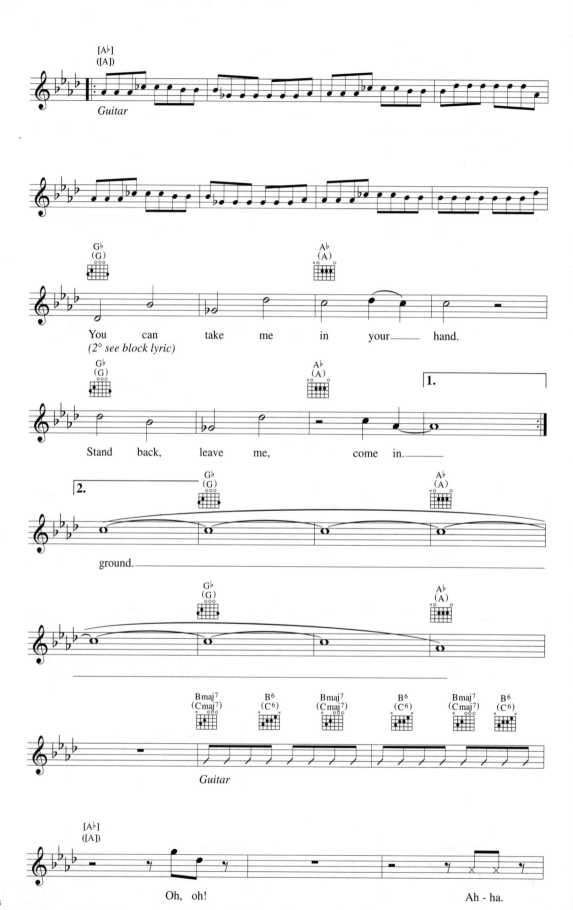

You can take me in your ___ hand.
(2° see block lyric)

Stand back, leave me, come in. ___

ground. ___

Oh, oh!   Ah - ha.

Boy - girl._____ (Girl.)   boy - girl.___

_____ (Girl.)   When a   boy   meets   a   girl._____

_____   Boy - girl___ boy   meets,   when a   boy   meets,   when a

boy   meets   girl._____

Verse 3:
We go out
A picture or a disco or a roundabout
I walk you home, I hold you there
You're giving out
I open doors so I can shut your face
Know your place.

2°:
Up and down and all around
Swinging sideways to the ground.

BULLET THE BLUE SKY

Words & Music by U2

bul-let the blue.___ Oh,_____ oh._____

2.

(Acc. tacet) Ah,____ ah.____ Drum fill

3. Suit and tie comes up to me,_ his face red like a rose on a thorn bush,_ like all the co-lours_
(Half spoken)

____ of a roy-al flush, and he's peel-in' off those dol-lar bills,_ (slap-pin' 'em down:)

one hun-dred, two hun-dred. And I can see those fight-er planes,_

and I can see those fight-er planes,_ a-cross the tin huts as chil-dren sleep,_

through the al-leys of a quiet_ ci-ty street._ Up___ the stair-case to the first floor,

we turn the key_ and slow-ly un-lock the door, as a man breathes in-to his sax-o-phone,

Verse 2:

In the locust wind comes a rattle and hum.
Jacob wrestled the angel, and the angel was overcome.
You plant a demon seed, you raise a flower of fire.
We see them burnin' crosses, see the flames, higher and higher.

Woh, woh, bullet the blue sky *etc.*

DADDY'S GONNA PAY FOR YOUR CRASHED CAR

Words by Bono
Music by U2

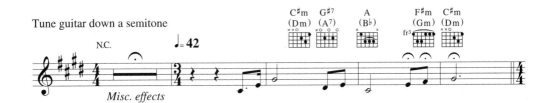

Tune guitar down a semitone

a tempo (♩=120)

pre-cious stone,— you're out on your own.— You know ev-

-'ry-one in the world,— but you feel a - lone.— Dad-dy

won't let you weep,— Dad-dy won't let you ache,—

Dad-dy gives you— as much as you can take.— A-

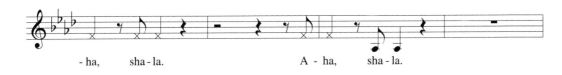

- ha, sha - la. A - ha, sha - la.

Dad-dy's gon-na pay for your crashed car.

2. A

[A♭]
([A])

lit-tle up - tight, you're a ba-by's fist,
(Verse 3 see block lyric)

but-ter-fly kiss-es up an' down your wrist. When you

see Dad-dy com-in', you're lick-in' your lip,

To Coda ⊕

nails bit-ten down to the quick. A - ha, sha-la.

A - ha, sha-la. Dad-dy's gon-na pay for your

crashed car. Dad-dy's gon-na pay for your

D.%. al Coda

crashed car. *Loop effect* 3. You've got a

⊕ *Coda*

Dad-dy's a com - fort,— Dad-dy's

your best— friend,— Dad-dy'll hold your hand— right up—

— to the end. A - ha, sha-la.

A - ha, sha-la. Dad-dy's gon-na pay for your—

— crashed car.—

Dad-dy's gon-na pay for your— crashed— car. —

Repeat to fade

Sun-day, Mon-day, Tues-day, Wedn's-day, Thurs-day, Fri-day, Sa-tur-day's al - right.

Verse 3:
You've got a head full of traffic, you're a siren's song.
You cry for Mama, and Daddy's right along.
He gives you the keys to a flamin' car.
Daddy's with you wherever you are.

Daddy's a comfort, *etc.*

DEEP IN THE HEART

Words & Music by U2

Oh, an - gel, ev-'ry-thing's gon-na be al - right._____ Oh,

an - gel ev - 'ry-thing's gon - na work out to - night._____

1. Thir-teen years old, sweet as a rose,___ ev-'ry pet-al of her___ wa-fer___ thin.
(Verse 2 see block lyric)

Love will make you___ blind, creep up from be-hind, get you jump-ing out of your skin.___

An - gel, it's___ sink or swim.___ Deep in the heart,

___ deep___ in the heart of this___ place. Deep in the heart,

165

Verse 2:
The scent of cedar
I can still see her
You can't return to the place you never left.

Angel, we'll make it work out tonight
Angel, I wanna be home tonight.

The door is closed behind me now
The window's sealed, to shut out the light
Green as the leaves and the cure for the nettle sting
Do your work and you'll work out right.

DESIRE

Words by Bono
Music by U2

DIRTY DAY

Words by Bono & The Edge
Music by U2

Tune guitar down a semitone

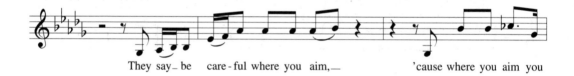

You can't____ e - ven re - mem - ber what I'm

try - ing to__ for-get.

It was a dir - ty day,__

dir - ty day.__

Look-ing for ex - pla - na - tions I__ don't ev - en

un - der - stand.__ If you need__ some - one to blame,

throw a rock__ in the air, you'll hit some - one guil - ty.

From fa - ther to____ son,__

in one___ life_____ has_____ be - gun___

___ a___ work_____ that's_ ne - ver done,_

___ Love, _____ it won't last_

fa - ther to son.

kiss-in' time.___ Love,_____ it won't last_

1. | **2.** **D.%. al Coda**

kiss - in' time.___

⊕ *Coda*

"The

Repeat to fade

days,_ days,_ days___ run a-way like_ hor-ses ov - er the hill."_ "The

Verse 2:
Get it right, there's no blood thicker than ink.
Hear what I say, nothing's as simple as you think.
Wake up, some things you can't get around
I'm in you, more so when they put me in the ground.

DISCOTHÈQUE

Words by Bono & The Edge
Music by U2

1.

- ey - dov - ey stuff ___

You get con-fused, ___ but you know ___ it. ___ Yeah, you hurt ___

___ for it, work ___ for it, love, ___ you don't al-ways show ___ it - *love.* Let ___

___ go, let's ___ go ___ dis - co - thèque, ___ ha. ___ (Go,) go, ___

___ let ___ go, ___ dis - co - thèque. ___

Look-ing for the one, ___ but you know ___ you're some -

- where else ___ in - stead; ___ you want to be the song, ___ the song ___

___ that you hear ___ in your ___ head, ___ love ___

hi,— hi,— hi,— hi,— hi.— Boom-cha, boom-

-cha, dis - co-thèque. Boom-cha, boom - cha, dis - co-thèque

Boom-cha, boom - cha, dis - co-thèque. Boom-cha, boom -

N.C.

Repeat to fade

-cha, dis - co-thèque. *Guitar (8ve bassa)*

Verse 3:
It's not a trick, you can't learn it
It's the way that you don't pay that's okay
'Cause you can't earn it - *love.*

You know you're chewing bubble gum
You know what that is
But you still want some
You just can't enough of that lovey-dovey stuff.

DO YOU FEEL LOVED

Words by Bono & The Edge
Music by U2

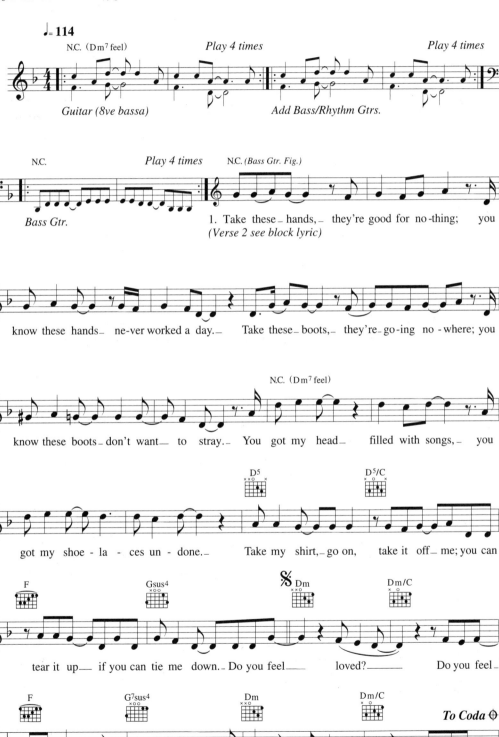

♦ *Coda*

like the sun, but it feels like rain, and there's heat

in the sun to see us through the rain. Do you feel

loved? Do you feel loved? Do you feel

loved? Do you feel loved?

N.C. (*Bass Gtr. Fig.*)

Ooh.

Guitar (8ve bassa)   *Repeat to fade*

Verse 2:
Take the colours of my imagination
Take the scent hanging in the air
Take this tangle of a conversation
Turn it into your own prayer.
With my fingers as you want them
With my nails under your hide
With my teeth at your back
And my tongue to tell you the sweetest lies.

Do you feel loved? *etc.*

DROWNING MAN

Words & Music by U2

I have pro-mised, for to be——— with you to-night——— and for———

——— the time— that will come.———

1.

Violin

2.

Hold on, and hold on tight - ly.

Hold on,——— and don't let go——— of my

love._____

The storms will pass,_____

The storms will pass_____

storms will pass_____

it won't be   it won't be   long_____

it won't be long_____ now.

_____ now.   This   love will last,_____   this love will last_____

_____ for - ev - er._____

3. And

take my   hand,_   you   know I'll be_ there.   If you   can_

_____ I'll cross the sky_____ for your_____ love.   Give you what I_____

_____ hold_ dear._____   Hold   on,_____

hold on tight - ly. Hold on,_____

_____ and hold on tight - ly.

Rise up, rise up with

wings like ea - gles. You run,

you run. You run and_____ not grow

wea - ry. (Take my hand, take my

Hold on. and hold on tight - ly. Hold on,_____
hand)

_____ hold on tight - ly to this love,_____

Verse 2:
Take my hand
You know I'll be there
If you can
I'll cross the sky for your love
And I understand
These winds and tides
This change of times
Won't drag you away.

ELVIS PRESLEY AND AMERICA
Words & Music by U2

so cold— when I'm with you.   And you feel— like

no-one told— you to.—   And your— time— is on— side.   And your

time   with me,   oh don't   talk   to   me.   Oh don't

talk   to me.   Don't talk   to me.—   You know

—   like   no - one told   you how.   But you know—   though the

king that howls has howled. But you feel———   like— sen - ti - men - tal   but you don't care_

To Coda ⊕

— if   I   just— share it   in— your   heart.—————

Heart.————————————————   Hope - less - ly,—   so

hope-less-ly— I'm break-ing through for you— and me. And you know,

some-thing in your heart, it beats— like some-thing new. —

*wordless vocals

2°:

And you know
Though no one told you to
And you found out
Where you were going, where to
You're through with me
But I know that you will be back
For more.

And you know
And though no one told you so
And you know, blue sky
Like a harder shade of blue
And you walk
When you want
To let go.

Me, I'm the outside, don't let me fade away
Drop me down but don't break me
In your sleep
In your sleep, inside
It's in your heart and mind.

Whole sea is dark
It's in your heart and mind
Sweetly, those will come
Loving is on your side walking through
Something in your heart
It beats like something new.

ENDLESS DEEP
Words & Music by U2

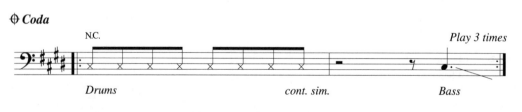

EVEN BETTER THAN THE REAL THING

Words & Music by U2

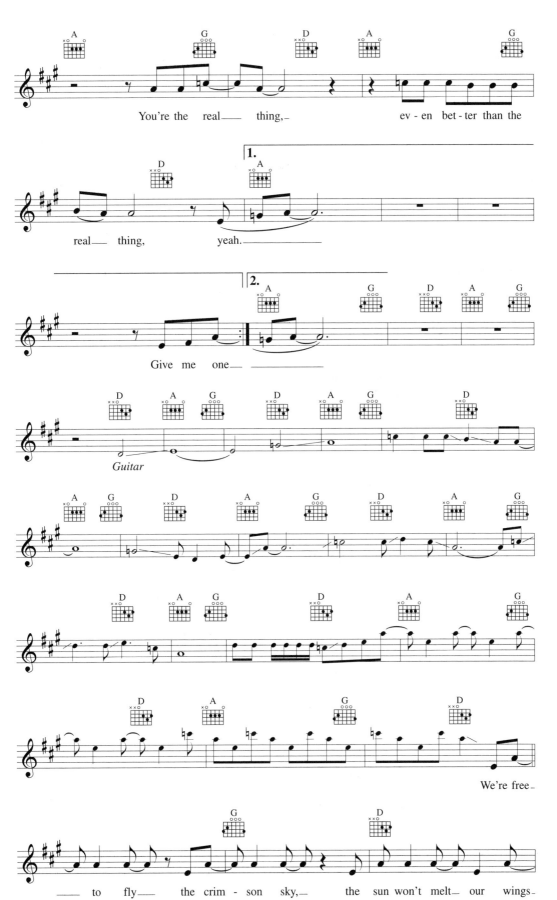

You're the real____ thing,__   ev - en bet - ter than the

real____ thing,   yeah._____

Give me one____ _____

Guitar

We're free_

____ to fly____ the crim - son sky,___   the sun won't melt_ our wings_

Verse 2:
Give me one last chance, and I'm gonna make you sing
Give me half a chance to ride on the waves that you bring
You're honey child to a swarm of bees
Gonna blow right through ya like a breeze
Give me one last dance, we'll slide down the surface of things

You're the real thing *etc.*

EXIT

Words & Music by U2

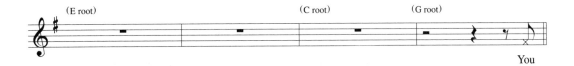

You

know he got the cure,— but then he went a-stray,— he

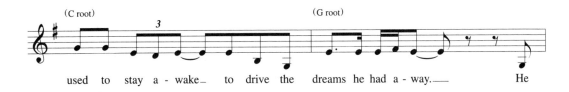

used to stay a-wake— to drive the dreams he had a-way.— He

want-ed to— be-lieve— in the hands of love.—

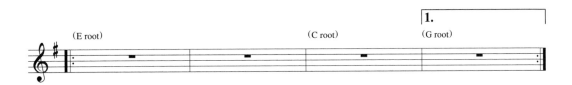

His head it felt hea-vy as he came a-cross the land.— A

195

(C root)   (G root)

dog— start-ed cry-in' like a brok-en heart-ed man   at the

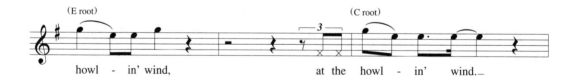

(E root)   (C root)

howl - in' wind,   at the howl - in' wind.—

(G root)   (E root)

He went deep-er in - to black,   deep-er in - to white.— He could

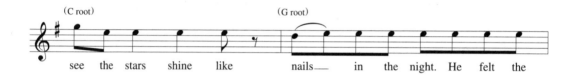

(C root)   (G root)

see the stars shine like   nails—— in the night. He felt the

(E root)   (C root)

heal-ing, heal-ing, heal-ing, heal-ing hands of love, like the stars shin-y

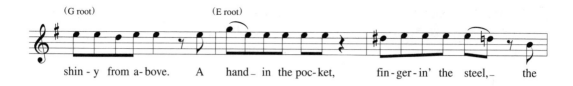

(G root)   (E root)

shin - y from a- bove.   A hand— in the poc-ket, fin-ger-in' the steel,— the

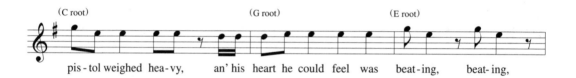

(C root)   (G root)   (E root)

pis - tol weighed hea-vy, an' his heart he could feel was beat-ing,   beat-ing,

(C root)   (G root)

beat-ing,   beat-ing, oh my love, oh my love, oh my love, oh my love.—

So   hands that build

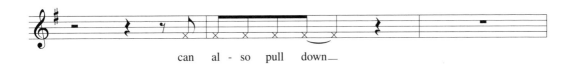

can   al - so   pull   down⸺

the hands of   love.⸺

Instrumental

Play 7 times   **16**

FIRE

Words & Music by U2

1. Call - ing, call - ing ___ the sun ___ is burn - ing black. ___

(Verses 2 & 3 see block lyrics)

Call-ing, call - ing, ___ it's beat - ing on ___ my back. ___ With a

fi - re, ___ with a

fi - re. ___

But there's a fi - re in - side,

and I'm fall - ing ov - er, ____ there's a

fi - re in me. When I call out, ____

____ you built a fi - re, fi - re. I'm go - ing ____

D.%. al Coda

____ home.

⊕ Coda

Guitar solo

But there's a fi - re in - side ____

____ and I'm fall - ing ov - er, ____ there's a

fi - re in me. ____ When I call out, ____ there's a

199

Verse 2:
Calling, calling, the moon is running red
Calling, calling, it's pulling me instead
With a fire, fire.

Verse 3:
Calling, calling, the stars are falling down
Calling, calling, they knock me to the ground
With a fire, fire.

GLORIA
Words & Music by U2

Tune guitar down a semitone

-ly in you I'm com - plete.

Glo - ri - a, in te do - mi - ne.

Glo - ri - a, ex - ul - ta - te.

Glo - ri - a, glo - ri - a.

Oh Lord, loos - en my lips.

I'd give it to you.

Instrumental

202

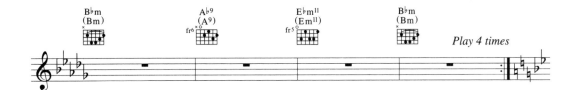

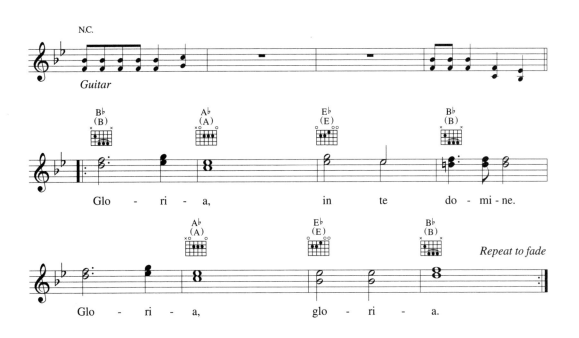

Glo - ri - a, in te do - mi - ne.

Glo - ri - a, glo - ri - a.

Verse 2:
I try to sing this song
I, I try to get in but I can't find the door
The door is open, you're standing there, you let me in.

Gloria
In te domine
Gloria
Exultate
Oh, Lord, if I had anything, anything at all
I'd give it to you.

GOD PART II

Words by Bono
Music by U2

Tune guitar down a semitone

♩ = 112

N.C.

Bass Guitar

1. Don't be-lieve— the de-vil,— I don't be-lieve his book;— but the
(Verses 2 & 4 see block lyric)

truth is not— the same— with-out— the lies—— he made— up.—

Don't be-lieve— in ex - cess, suc-cess is to give.—

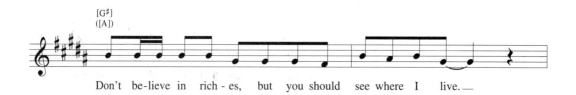

Don't be-lieve in rich - es, but you should see where I live.—

I,—————— I————— be-lieve— in love.—

3. Don't be-lieve in co-caine, got a speed-ball in my head;— I could
(Verse 5 see block lyric)

cut and crack— you op-en, did you hear what I said? Don't be-

-lieve them when they tell me there ain't no cure;— the rich stay heal-thy, the

sick stay poor.— I,—— I—— be-lieve— in love.—

Oh.——

Verse 2:
Don't believe in forced entry, don't believe in rape
But every time she passes by wild thoughts escape.
Don't believe in Death Row, skid row or the gangs.
Don't believe in the Uzi, it just went off in my hands.
I, I believe in love.

Verse 4:
Don't believe in Goldman, his type like a curse
Instant karma's gonna get him if I don't get him first.
Don't believe that Rock 'n' Roll can really change the world
As it spins in revolution, yeah, it spirals and turns.
I, I believe in love.

Verse 5:
Don't believe in the sixties, the golden age of pop
You glorify the past when the future dries up.
Heard a singer on the radio late last night
Says he's gonna kick the darkness till it bleeds daylight.
I, I believe in love.

GONE

Words by Bono & The Edge
Music by U2

Tune guitar down a semitone

Keyboards

1. You

get to feel so guil - ty, got so much for so — lit - tle,—
(Verse 2 see block lyric)

then you find that feel-ing just— won't go— a - way.— You're hold-

- ing on— to ev - 'ry lit - tle thing— so tight - ly,

till there's no-thing left— for you a - ny-way.—

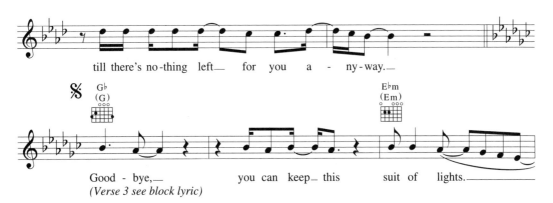

Good - bye,— you can keep— this suit of lights.—
(Verse 3 see block lyric)

I'll be up with the sun.

I'm not com-ing down, I'm not com-ing down,

ooh, I'm not com-ing down.

2. You 'Cause I'm al-

- rea-dy gone, felt that way all a-

- long. Clo-ser to you ev-'ry day,

I did-n't want it that much a-ny-way.

You're tak-ing steps that make you feel diz-zy,

then you learn to like the way it feels._____ You hurt your-self, you hurt your lo-ver,

D.%. al Coda

then you dis-co-ver_____ what you thought was free-dom is just_____ greed.

Coda

I'm not com-ing down, oh yeah, I'm not com-ing down.

Ah,

sun, sun,_____ sun._____ Come,

sun._____ Come_____ sun,_____ sun._____

N.C.

Verse 2:
You wanted to get somewhere so badly
You had to lose yourself along the way.
You changed your name, well that's okay, it's necessary
And what you leave behind you don't miss anyway.

Verse 3:
Goodbye, and it's an emotional.
Goodnight, I'll be up with the sun.
Are you still holding on?
I'm not coming down…

HALLELUJAH HERE SHE COMES

Words & Music by U2

1. I see you dressed to kill. I know I can't wait un-til Hal-le-

(Verse 2 see block lyric)
(Verse 3 as Verse 1)

-lu - jah, (hal -le - lu - jah,) here she comes.

I see you dressed in black. I guess I'm not com-ing back. Hal-le-

-lu - jah, (hal-le - lu - jah,) here she comes.

Born and raised on the wrong side of town.

You get so high that you can't come down.

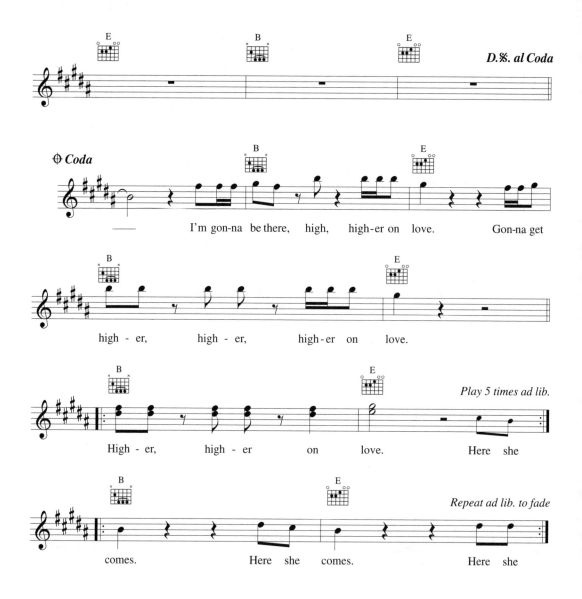

1.
2.
Yeah!
I'm go - in'
B
E
high - er, high - er, high-er on love.
B
1.
E
High - er, high - er, high-er on love.
2.
E
B
love. I'm gon-na be there when that
E
B
light gon-na shine. I'm gon-na be there when her heart
E
B
kin-dles next to mine. I'm gon-na be…
E
B
Here she comes.
E
B
Yeah here she comes.

Verse 2:
I see the road is rough
You know I'm not giving up
Hallelujah, here she comes
I know where the lady goes
I know she got rings on her toes
Hallelujah, here she comes.

HAWKMOON 269

Words by Bono
Music by U2

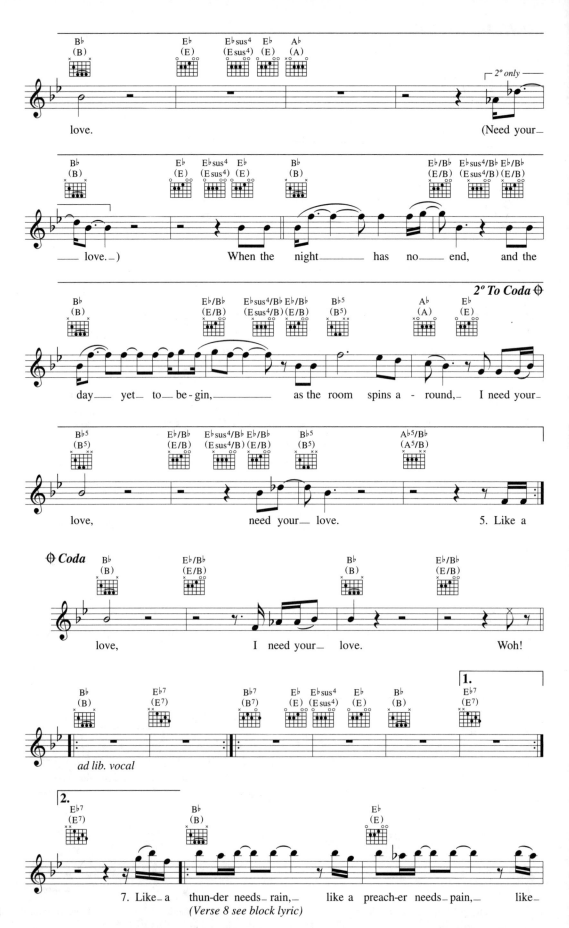

love.   (Need your

___ love.___)   When the   night_____   has   no___   end,   and the

day___ yet__ to__ be - gin,_____ as the room   spins a - round,_ I need your_

love,   need your_ love.   5. Like a

love,   I   need your_   love.   Woh!

ad lib. vocal

7. Like_ a   thun-der needs_ rain,_   like a preach-er needs_ pain,_   like_
(Verse 8 see block lyric)

Verse 4:
Like coming home and you
    don't know where you've been
Like black coffee, like nicotine
I need your love, I need your love.

When the night has no end, *etc.*

Verse 5:
Like a Phoenix rising needs a holy tree
Like the sweet revenge of a bitter enemy
I need your love.

Verse 6:
Like heat needs the sun, like honey on her tongue
Like the muzzle of a gun, like oxygen
I need your love, I need your love.

When the night has no end, *etc.*

Verse 8:
Like a needle needs a vein, like someone to blame
Like a thought unchained, like a runaway train
Need your love, I need your love.

HEARTLAND

Words by Bono
Music by U2

HOLD ME, THRILL ME, KISS ME, KILL ME

Words by Bono
Music by U2

don't _ know what you're do-in', babe, ___ it must be art. You're a

head-ache___ in a suit-case, you're a_____ star.___

(Guitar)

Oh no, don't be shy,_____ you don't

have to go_ blind._____ Hold_ me, thrill_ me,

To Coda ⊕

kiss_ me, kill_ me. Synth.

1.

3. You

2.

(Guitar)

(Synth.)

Verse 3:
You don't know how you got here
You just know you want out
Believing in yourself almost as much as you doubt.
You're a big smash, you wear it like a rash
Star.
Oh no, don't be shy
You need a crowd to cry.
Hold me, thrill me, kiss me, kill me.

Verse 4:
They want you to be Jesus
They'll got down on one knee
But they'll want their money back
If you're alive at thirty-three.
And you're turning tricks
With your crucifix.
You're a star, oh child
Of course you're not shy
You don't have to deny love.
Hold me, thrill me, kiss me, kill me.

HOLY JOE

Words by Bono & The Edge
Music by U2

work-ing my way   to get   to   you.—   Come

on, come on,—   come on, come on,—   be good to me.—   Come

on, come on,—   come on, come on,—   be good to me.—

Here it comes,   here it comes, Ho - ly Joe.—

_____   2. Please

____   don't   make me   say   please,—————

to   cham - pagne—   and ice - cream,—————

it's not what I want— it's what I need,   de - vo -

223

-tion, a lit-tle ap-pre-ci-a -tion,

a lit-tle hea-vy ro-ta -tion__ oh aye looks good on

me. I'm hav-ing the best__ of a-ny-bo-dy's life

clo-ser than ev - er to ev-'ry-bo-dy's wife yeah. Come

on, come on,__ come on, come on,__ be good to me.__

Come on, come on,__ come on, come on__ be

good to me.__ Here it comes, here it comes, Ho - ly Joe.__

Guitar

I FALL DOWN

Words & Music by U2

Tune guitar down a semitone

1. Ju-lie says— John I'm get-ting no-where.
(Verses 2 & 3 see block lyrics)

I wrote this let-ter, hope to get— to some

— place soon.— I want to get up—

when I wake— up,— but when I

get up,— I fall— down.—

227

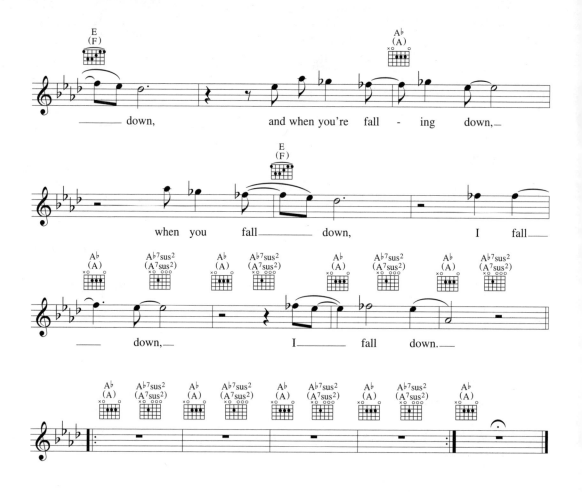

down, and when you're fall - ing down,—

when you fall_____ down, I fall___

___ down,— I_____ fall down.___

Verse 2:
Julie wake up, Julie tell the story
You wrote the letter, said you were gonna
Get there someday
Gonna walk in the sun
And the wind and the rain
Never look back again
Now you fall down
You're falling down
You fall down
You fall down.

Verse 3:
Julie say something, Julie say you're sorry
You're gonna get better, you better not
Leave me here anyway
I want to get up, when you wake up
But when I get up
I fall down
I'm falling down
I fall down
I broke myself.

I STILL HAVEN'T FOUND WHAT I'M LOOKING FOR

Words & Music by U2

_____ Mm, but I still_____ have-n't found_____ what I'm look-

- ing for._____ But I still_____ have-n't found_____ what I'm look-

- ing for._____

Verse 2:
I have kissed honey lips, felt the healing in her finger tips
It burned like fire, (I was) burning inside her.
I have spoke with the tongue of angels
I have held the hand of a devil
It was warm in the night, I was cold as a stone.

But I still haven't found *etc.*

Verse 3:
I believe in the Kingdom Come, then all the colours will bleed into one
Bleed into one. But yes, I'm still running
You broke the bonds and you loosed the chains
Carried the cross of my shame
Oh my shame, you know I believe it.

But I still haven't found *etc.*

I THREW A BRICK THROUGH A WINDOW

Words & Music by U2

2.

Tom-toms

Instrumental

Bass and Drums enter

No - one,— no-one is blind - er— than he—

— who will not— see.— No - one,—

D.%. al Coda

no-one is blind - er— than me.—

⊕ Coda

N.C.

Tom-toms

cont. sim.

Verse 2:
I was walking, I was walking into walls
And back again
I just keep walking
I walk up to a window to see myself
And my reflection, when I thought about it
My direction, going nowhere, going nowhere.

Verse 3:
I was talking, I was talking in my sleep
I can't stop talk, talk, talking
I'm talking to you, it's up to you
Be my brother, there is no other way out of here
Be my brother
Got to get out, got to get out
Got to get out of here.

I WILL FOLLOW

Words & Music by U2

stops to think— he starts to cry,— oh—— why? If you

walk a-way, walk a-way, I walk a-way, walk a-way,— I— will fol - low. If you

walk a - way, walk a-way I walk a-way, walk a-way,—— I— will fol-

- low, I— will fol - low.

Your

—— eyes—— make a— cir - cle.—

I see— you when I go in—— there.——

234

Your___ eyes   y - y - your___ eyes.

Your___ eyes,   y - y - y - y - your___

___ eyes.___

D.%. al Coda

If   you

⊕ *Coda*

Play 4 times

I ___ will   fol - low.

Verse 3:
I was on the inside
When they pulled the four walls down
I was looking through the window
I was lost, I am found.

I'M NOT YOUR BABY

Words by Bono
Music by U2

1. It's a beau-ti-ful day___ to-day, ev'-ry-thing___ is goin' my way;
(Verse 2 see block lyric)

ev-en the words___ are do-in' what I say,___ oh babe,___ got to get a-way.

To be im-pos-si-ble is-n't that dif-fi-cult. In the

ci-ty you're___ in-vi-si-ble,___ when you come from a small___ town.

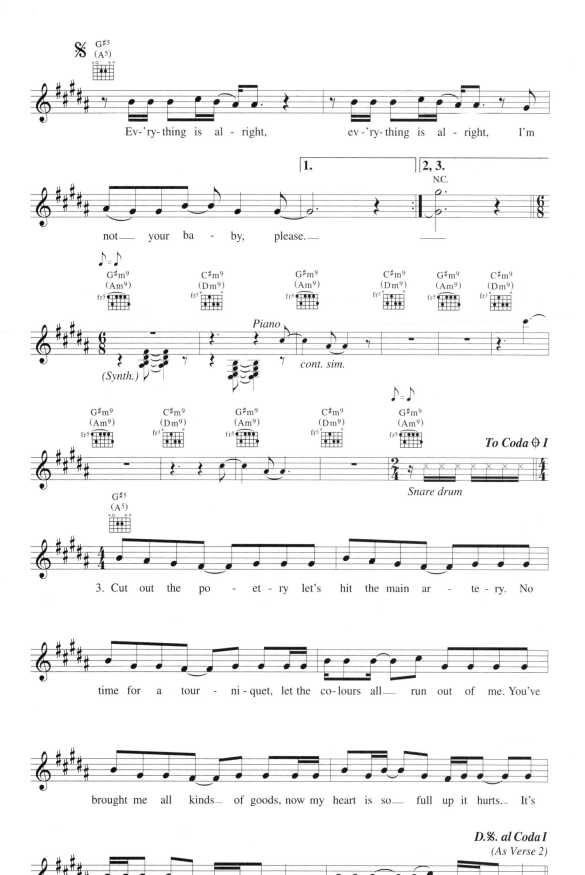

Ev-'ry-thing is al - right, ev-'ry-thing is al - right, I'm

1.

not___ your ba - by, please.___

2, 3.

N.C.

Piano

(Synth.)

cont. sim.

To Coda I

Snare drum

3. Cut out the po - et - ry let's hit the main ar - te - ry. No

time for a tour - ni - quet, let the co - lours all___ run out of me. You've

brought me all kinds___ of goods, now my heart is so___ full up it hurts.___ It's

D.%. al Coda I
(As Verse 2)

hea-vy as___ a shop-ping bag,___ full of things___ I___ should give back.

⊕ *Coda I*

Guitar

4. Don't

𝄋𝄋

want you to co - ver me, smo-ther me— or mo-ther me. I

(Verse 5 see block lyric)

like to feel this in - com- plete, I'm not your ba - by.

Ev- 'ry-thing is al - right, ev- 'ry-thing is al - right. I'm

To Coda ⊕⊕ *II*

not your ba - by. *Guitar*

Drum rhythm, overlay Synth/Piano　　　　　　*Spoken:* Not dizzie,

just busy.　　　Didn't drink nothing fizzy,　　no pills to feel easy;　　don't

know what got into me.　　Daylight a kinda robbery, the night is your geography.

238

you're not white, you're pink an' rosy; you could be right but you're way above me.

I'm   in   recovery,   a   star   of   pornography.   I'm   a

tourist, there's a lot to see. You don't   like   the   photographs   of   me;

so   you've   got   a   lot   to   say.   You don't   sleep   around   but   sometimes   you   stray.   You

Drum fill

don't believe, but oftentimes you pray for something…what is it, babe?

D. 𝄌 𝄌 al Coda II

Bass Guitar

Don't

Coda II

Play 7 times ad lib. N.C.

Guitar   I'm— not   your   ba - by.—   *Guitar*

Verse 2:
Tourist in a traffic jam, Babycham and handicam.
I'm not your mother, you're not my man.
I'm not your baby.
Don't treat me like I'm a trick
I won't treat you like you're a prick.
Don't need no doctor, I'm not ill.
I'm not your baby.
Everything is alright, *etc.*

Verse 5:
Don't treat me like I'm a trick
I won't treat you like you're a prick.
Don't need no doctor, I'm not sick.
I'm not your baby.
Everything is alright, *etc.*

IF GOD WILL SEND HIS ANGELS

Words by Bono & The Edge
Music by U2

cops___ col-lect-ing for the cons.___ So where is___ the hope___ and

where is___ the faith and the___ love?___ What's that you say to me? Does___

___ love___ light up your___Christ-mas tree? The next___ min-ute you're

blow-ing___ a fuse,___ and the car-toon net-work turns in-to the news. If___

God will send___ his an - gels,___ and if God___ will send___ a___ sign,___

___ well if God___ will send___ his___ an - gels,

D.%. al Coda

where do we go,_____ where do we go?_____

242

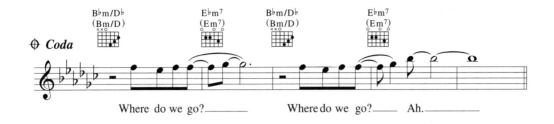

Where do we go?———— Where do we go?——— Ah.————————

Keyboards

Repeat to fade

Guitar

Verse 2:
Nobody made you do it
No one put words in your mouth.
Nobody here taking orders
When love took a train heading south.

Verse 4:
See his mother dealing in a doorway
See Father Christmas with a begging bowl.
And Jesus' sister's eyes are a blister
The High Street never looked so low.

Verse 5:
Jesus never let me down
You know Jesus used to show me the score.
Then they put Jesus in show business
Now it's hard to get in the door.
It's the stuff, it's the stuff of country songs
But I guess it was something to go on.
Hey, if God will send his angels
I sure could use them here right now
Well, if God will send his angels…

Vocal ad lib.

IF YOU WEAR THAT VELVET DRESS

Words by Bono & The Edge
Music by U2

you? It's her day-light___ that gets___ me through.___ 3. We've been here be-

wear___ that___ vel - vet dress,___ if you

wear___ that___ vel - vet dress___

To Coda ⊕

To - night,___ the moon's___

drawn its cur - tains.___ It's a pri - vate show,___ no one else___ gon-na

know___ I'm want - - - ing.

Guitar solo

Sun - light,___ sun-light fills___ my room.___
(Chorus 3 see block lyric)

It's sharp and it's clear, but no-thing at all like the moon. It's But if you

To - night, the moon is a mir-ror - ball, — light flic- kers— from a - cross the hall. —

Who'll catch the star— when it falls?

Repeat to fade

If you wear that vel - vet dress.

Verse 3:
We've been here before
Last time you scratched at my door
The moon was naked and cold
I was like a two-year-old
Who just wanted more.
If you wear that velvet dress.

Chorus 3:
It's okay
The struggle for things not to say
I never listened to you anyway
And I got my own hands to pray.

IN GOD'S COUNTRY

Words & Music by U2

Yeah, _____ yeah. _____

2.

Sleep_ comes like a drug_ in ____ God's coun - try.

Sad_ eyes, crook-ed cross - es, in ____ God's coun - try, ____

_ yeah. _

Guitar solo

Play 4 times

Nak-ed_ flame, she stands_ with a nak-ed_ flame;_ I stand_ with the

sons_ of_ Cain, burned_ by the fire_ of_ love, burned_ by the fire_ of_ love._

Whoa, _____ whoa. _____

Verse 2:
Set me alight, we'll punch a hole right through the night.
Every day the dreamers die to see what's on the other side.
She is liberty, and she comes to rescue me.
Hope, faith, her vanity; the greatest gift is gold.

Sleep comes like a drug *etc.*

INDIAN SUMMER SKY

Words & Music by U2

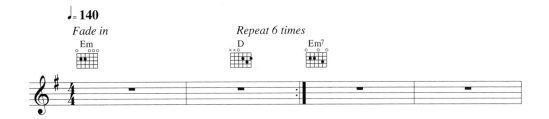

1. In the o-cean cuts— ring deep,— the sky.—

—— Like there, I don't know why. In the for-est there's— a clear - ing, I,—

—— I run there— to-wards the light. Sky,———

it's a blue— sky.———

2. In the earth the hole

—— deep, deep,— de - cide.— If I— could I would. Up for air to

swim a - gainst the tide. Hey, hey, hey.

Up to - wards the sky.

It's a blue sky.

To lose a - long the way the spark that set the

flame, to flick-er and to fade on this the long - est

day.

So wind go through to my heart. So wind blow through my soul.

(Repeat 3 times on %)

So wind go through to my heart.

(So wind-blow in my soul.)

250

INTO THE HEART

Words & Music by U2

IS THAT ALL?

Words & Music by U2

Tune guitar down a semitone

1. Oh_____ to sing this song_ makes me an-gry, I'm not_ an-gry with you._ Is that all?_____ Is that all?__ Is that all?

2. Oh_____ to sing this song_ makes me hap-py, I'm not_ hap-py with you.

Oh_____ to sing this song— makes me dance.   Is that

2. B♭m (Bm)

Instrumental

(2º) Is that

all?____   Is it   all?_____   Is that

all?_____   Is that   all   you   want— from me?_____

Play 6 times

Vocals ad lib.

LADY WITH THE SPINNING HEAD

Words by Bono
Music by U2

1. Here she comes, la - dy luck a - gain,— fig - ure of eight,—

(Verse 2 see block lyric)

six and nine— a - gain. I,——— I,——— I my

la - dy with the spin - ning head.——— 2. What - —

La la la la la la la la la la la la la - dy with the spin-ning head.

3. She's been gone— but I knew she'd— be back.

She's got the rent,— she put me in the black. I,———— I—

———— need you la - dy with the spin-ning head.——

Mean old man — took a - way my car, those cre-dit guys, — they've

got the pow'r,— I'm—— on top when she's a-round,

she's the tick-et out of town.

Guitar

Repeat ad lib.

257

La la la la la la   la la la la la la - dy with the spin-ning head.

Play 3 times ad lib.

Guitar

Verse 2:
Whatever the deal
She won't let me down
Wherever I go
She's always hanging round.

LAST NIGHT ON EARTH

Words by Bono & The Edge
Music by U2

it takes to-day. You got-ta give it a-way,

you got-ta give it a-way, you got-ta give it a-way, give it a-way,

you got-ta give it a-way, you got-ta give it a-way. (1, 2.) Well she
(3.) She al-

don't care what it's worth; she's
-read-y knows it hurts;

liv-ing like it's the last night on earth,

the last night on earth.

1.
N.C.(D♭sus² feel)

2. She's not waiting on a sa-viour to come,

she's at the bus-stop with the

News Of The World and The Sun. Sun, here it comes.

She's not wait - ing for a - ny - one.

2.

You got - ta give it a - way,

Slip - ping a - way, slip slide,

too ma - ny slip - ping

a - way. The world turns and we get

diz - zy, slip - ping a - way.

LEMON

Words by Bono
Music by U2

I_____ feel__ like I'm hold-ing on__ to noth-
- ing. 2. She wore le-mon__ to co-lour in the cold__ grey__
night. She had hea-ven,__ and she held__ on so tight.
3. A man__ makes a pic-ture, a mov-ing pic-ture;
(Verses 4 & 5 see block lyric)
through the light pro-jec-ted, he__ can see__ him-self__ up close.__
A man cap-tures co-lour, a man likes to stare.__

To Coda ⊕ ⊕ *II*

He turns his mo-ney in-to light__to look__ for her.__
And I____ feel like I'm drift-ing, drift-ing, drift-ing from the__ shore.__

Verse 4:

A man builds a city, with banks and cathedrals
A man melts the sand so he can see the world outside
A man makes a car, and builds a road to run (them) on
A man dreams of leaving, but he always stays behind
And these are the days when our work has come asunder
And these are the days when we look for something other

You're gonna meet her there
She's your destination
You gotta get to her
She's imagination

Verse 5:

A man makes a picture, a moving picture
Through light projected, he can see himself up close
A man captures colour, a man likes to stare
He turns his money into light to look for her.

Gotta meet her there
She's your destination
There's no sleeping there
She's imagination

LIKE A SONG...

Words & Music by U2

2. And in lea - ther, lace— and— chains— we
(Verses 3 & 4 see block lyrics)

stake our claim.— Re - vo - lu - tion once— a - gain,

no I won't,

I won't wear— it on my sleeve,— I can

see through this— ex - pres - sion and you know— I don't be - lieve.—

To Coda ⊕

Too old to be told,— ex -

1.

- act - ly who are you?— To - night, to -

- mor - row's too— late.—

268

right to be wrong,— in this re-bel song.———— Let the

bells ring out.———— Let the

bells ring— out.———— Is there

no-thing left?— Is there, is there no-thing, is there

no-thing left?— (Is honesty what you want?)

Play 3 times
D.%. al Coda

⊕ Coda

time— to— go. It's your— time.——— An - gry

words won't stop the fight,—— two—— wrongs won't make it right.

A new heart— is what I need.— Oh,— God

make it bleed._____ Is there no-thing left?—

Drums

Verse 2:
And we love to wear a badge, a uniform
And we love to fly a flag
But I won't let others live in hell
As we divide against each other
And we fight amongst ourselves
Too set in our ways to try to rearrange
Too right to be wrong, in this rebel song
Let the bells ring out
Let the bells ring out
Is there nothing left?
Is there, is there nothing?
Is there nothing left?
Is honesty what you want?

Verse 4:
A generation without name, ripped and torn
Nothing to lose, nothing to gain
Nothing at all
And is you can't help yourself
Well take a look around you
When others need your time
You say it's time to go… it's your time.

LOVE COMES TUMBLING

Words & Music by U2

down a - gain.

D.C. al Coda

⊕ *Coda*

___ you___ are.___

1.

2.

Verse 2:
The seed is split, the bed defiled
For you a virgin bride
Find yourself in someone else
Don't find yourself in me
I can't lift you up again
Love comes tumbling down again.

Verse 3:
Love don't need to find a way
You'll find your own way
I forget that you can't stay
But I know that
All roads lead to where you are
All roads lead to where you are.

LOVE IS BLINDNESS

Words & Music by U2

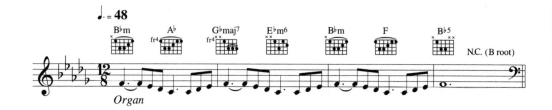

Double tempo

1. Love is

blind-ness,_ I don't want to see;_ won't you wrap the night a-round me?_
(Verses 2-6 see block lyric)

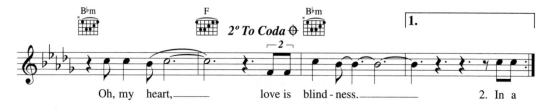

Oh, my heart,_____ love is blind-ness._____ 2. In a

3. Love is   4, 6. Love is blind ____   A lit-tle

death__ with-out mourn-ing;_ no call__ and no warn-ing__ ba-by, a

Verse 2:
In a parked car, in a crowded street
You see your love made complete.
Thread is ripping, the knot is slipping
Love is blindness.

Verse 3:
Love is clockworks and cold steel
Fingers too numb to feel.
Squeeze the handle, blow out the candle
Love is blindness.

Verse 4:
Love is blindness, I don't want to see
Won't you wrap the night around me?
Oh, my love,
Blindness.

Verse 5:
Love is drowning in a deep well
All the secrets, and no one to tell.
Take the money, honey…
Blindness.

Verse 6:
Love is blindness, I don't want to see
Won't you wrap the night around me?
Oh, my love,
Blindness.

LOVE RESCUE ME

Words by Bono & Bob Dylan
Music by U2

1. Love,___ res - cue___ me,___ come forth and___ speak to
(Verses 3, 4, 5 & 6 see block lyric)

me, raise me up___ and don't___ let me fall.___

No man is my___ e - ne - my,___ my own

hands im - pri - son me.___ Love,___

res - - - cue me. 2. Ma-ny And the

sun in the sky makes a sha-dow of you and I,

stretch-ing out as the sun sinks in the sea.

I'm here with - out a name, in the pa-

- lace of my shame. I said love,

res - cue me. 3. In the cold

Yeah, though I walk in the val - ley of the

sha - dow, yet I will fear no

277

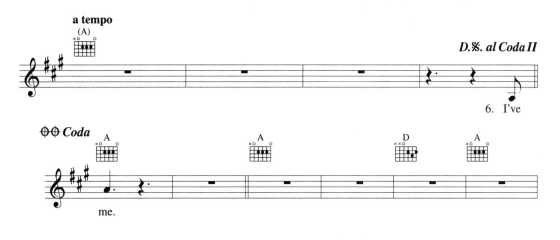

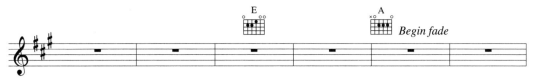

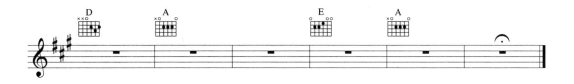

Verse 2:
Many strangers have I met
On the road to my regret
Many lost who seek to find themselves in me.
They ask me to reveal
The very thoughts they would conceal.
Love, rescue me.

Verse 3:
In the cold mirror of a glass
I see my reflection pass
I see the dark shades of what I used to be.
I see the purple of her eyes
The scarlet of my lies.
Love, rescue me.

Verse 4:
Sha la la la *etc.*
I said love, love, rescue me.

Verse 5:
(ad lib. lyrics)

Verse 6:
I've conquered my past
The future is here at last
I stand at the entrance to a new world I can see.
The ruins to the right of me
Will soon have lost sight of me.
Love, rescue me.

LUMINOUS TIMES (HOLD ON TO LOVE)

Words & Music by U2 & Brian Eno

1. Hey,— sis-ter love.— Hey,— sis-ter soul.—
(Verses 2 & 3 see block lyrics)

Hey,— on - ly love.— can turn me 'round

— to - night.— Hey,— sis-ter love.

Save my— soul.

Save my— soul.— Hold on to love.—

To Coda
Am
Hold on to love.
Love won't let you go.
C
Love won't let you go.
Hold on to love.
Am
C
1.
G
See the sun - shine in her song.
2. Hey, sis - ter love.
Hey, sweet sur -
2.
G
soul.
Whoa!
F
G
D.%. al Coda
3. She is the gun - fire.
She is the car crash.

$\oplus$ *Coda*

Hold on to love. Oh,

see the sun-light in her song. See the sun-light in her

song, yeah!

Verse 2:
Hey sister love, hey, sweet surrender
She comes like carnival
She is the big wheel
She turned my head around
She turned my head around
She is the speedway
She is the slipstream
She is coming 'round.

Hold on to love, hold on to love
Love won't let you go
Hold on to love, hold on to love
See the sunlight in her song
See the sunlight in her song.

Verse 3:
She is the gun fire
She is the car crash
She is the avalanche
She is the thunder
She is the waves
And she pulls me under.

I love you 'cause I need to
Not because I need you
I love you 'cause I understand
That God has given me your hand
It holds me in a tiny fist
And still I need your kiss.

MIAMI

Words by Bono & The Edge
Music by U2

Tune guitar down a semitone

Drum solo

1. Wea-ther 'round here chop-pin' and chang-in',
(Verse 3 see block lyric)

sur-ge-ry in the air;   print shirts and sou-thern ac-cents,   ci-gars— and big— hair.—

We got the wheels, pe-trol's cheap,   we on-ly went there for a   week.—

Got the sun, got the sand, got the batt'ries   in the han-di-cam.—

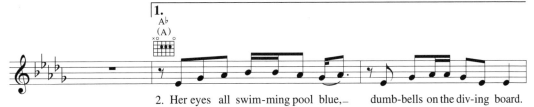

2. Her eyes all swim-ming pool blue,—   dumb-bells on the div-ing board.

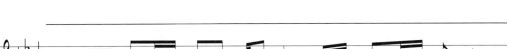

Ba-by's al-ways at-trac-ted to——   the things— she's a-fraid of.

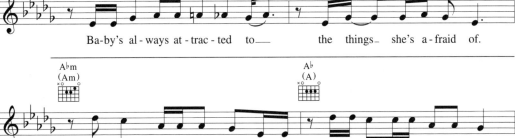

Big girl   with a sweet tooth watch-es   skin-ny girl in the pho-to shoot.

Fresh-men, squea-ky clean, she tastes of chlo-rine. Ba ba ba ba ba ba ba ba.

Ba ba ba ba ba ba ba. My mam-my.

2.

Ba ba ba ba ba ba ba ba.   Ba ba ba ba ba ba ba ba.

Ba ba ba ba ba ba ba ba.

Ba ba ba ba ba ba ba ba.   4. I bought

two new suits,   Mi - a - mi;   pink and blue,

(Verse 5 see block lyric)

Mi - a - mi.   I took a pic-ture of you,   my

mam-my,   get-ting hot in a pho-to booth,   Mi-a-mi.   5. I said, "You

2.

Ba - by." We could make some-thing beau-ti - ful, some-thing that would-n't be a prob-lem. We could make some-thing beau-ti-ful, some-thing that would-n't be a prob - lem, least not in Mi-a-mi. You know, some pla-ces are like your aun - tie, but there's no place like Mi-a-mi, my mam-my, Mi - a-mi, my mam-my. Ba ba ba ba ba ba ba ba.

Repeat to fade

Ba ba ba ba ba ba ba ba.

Verse 3:

Love the movies, babe; love to walk through movie sets
Get to shoot someone in the foot, get to smoke some cigarettes.
No big deal, we know the score, just back from the video store.
Got the car and the car chase. What's he got inside that case?
I want a close-up of that face. Here comes the car chase.

Verse 5:

I said, You looked like a madonna.
You said, Maybe.
You said, I wanna have your baby, baby.

MISS SARAJEVO

Words & Music by Passengers
(Brian Eno, Bono, The Edge, Adam Clayton & Larry Mullen Jnr.)

here she comes,___ to take her__ crown._

3. Is there a time___ to run for cov - er a time

(Verse 4 see block lyrics)

__ for kiss and tell.___ a time__ for dif-f'rent col -

1.

- ours, dif-f'rent names_ you find hard to spell. 4. Is there a time_

2.

Here she comes._ Ooh,__ ooh,__

beau - ty plays the clown,___ here she comes,_

sur - re - al in her crown._ Di - ci che il fiu -

- me ____ tro - va la vi - a al ma - re ____

Che co me il fiu - me _____ giun - ge - ra -

- i a me. _____ Ol - tre i con - fi - - - ni e le ter - re as - se

- ta - te. _____ Di - ci che co - me fiu - me, _____

co - me fiu - me _____ l'a - mor - - e

giun - ge - rà, _____ l'a - mor - - - -

- - - - - - e. E non so più _____

_____ preg - are E nell' - l'a- mor - e _____

non su più spe - ra - re. E quell' a-

Verse 2:
Is there a time for kohl and lipstick
Is there a time for cutting hair
Is there a time for high street shopping
To find the right dress to wear.

Verse 4:
Is there a time for first communion
A time for East 17
Is there time to turn to Mecca
Is there time to be a beauty queen.

MLK

Words & Music by U2

MOFO

Words by Bono & The Edge
Music by U2

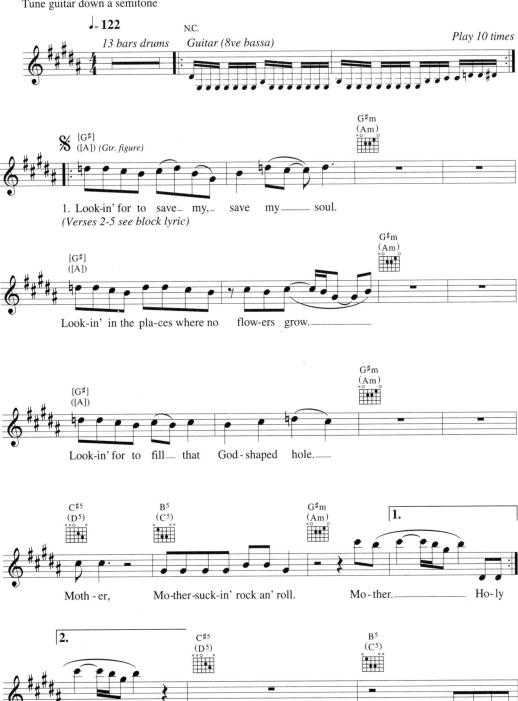

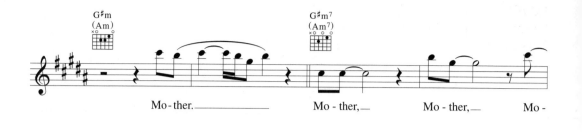

Mo - ther._____ Mo - ther,— Mo - ther,— Mo -

- ther,_____ Mo - ther,— Mo - ther,— Mo -

To Coda ⊕

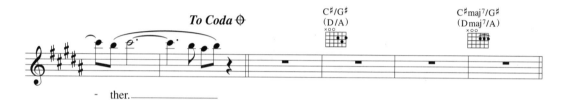

- ther._____

3. Mo - ther,_____ am I still your_ son?_____ You know I've
(Verse 4 see block lyric)

wait - ed— for so long— to hear— you— say so._____

Guitar (8ve bassa)

D.%. al Coda
(as verse 2)

292

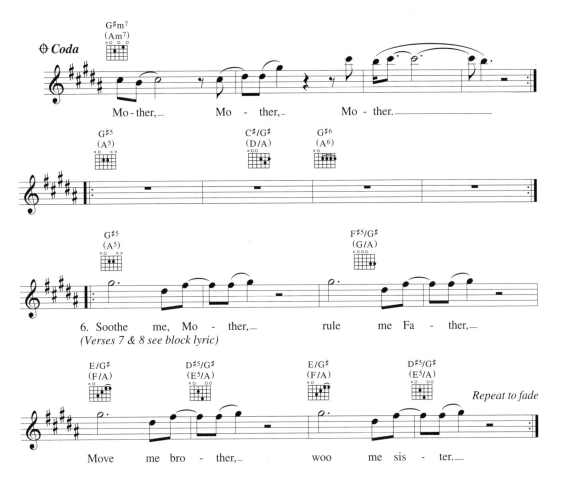

Mo - ther,—   Mo - ther,—   Mo - ther.——

6. Soothe me, Mo - ther,—   rule me Fa - ther,—
(Verses 7 & 8 see block lyric)

Repeat to fade

Move me bro - ther,—   woo me sis - ter.—

Verse 2:
Holy dunc, space junk comin' in for the splash
White dopes on punk staring into the flash.
Lookin' for the baby Jesus under the trash
Mother, mother-suckin' rock an' roll.
Mother.

Verse 4:
Mother, you left and made me someone.
Now I'm still a child, but no one tells me no.

Verse 5:
Lookin' for a sound that's gonna drown out the world.
Lookin' for the father of my two little girls.
Got the swing, got the sway, got my straw in lemonade.
Still lookin' for the face I had before the world was made.
Mother, mother-suckin' rock an' roll
Mother.

Verse 7:
Soothe me Mother, rule me Father
Show me Mother, show me Mother.

Verse 8:
Show me Mother, show me Mother,
Show me Mother, show me Mother.

MOTHERS OF THE DISAPPEARED

Words & Music by U2

1. Mid - night, our sons and daugh - ters
(Verse 2 see block lyric)

were cut— down and tak - en from — us. Hear their heart - beat,

we hear their heart - beat.

Ooh,———— ooh.———

Ooh,———— ooh.———

Night hangs like a pri-so-ner, stretched — ov - er black and blue.— Hear their

heart - beats, we hear their heart - beats.

In— the trees our sons stand na - ked, through— the walls our

daugh-ters cry.—— See their—— tears——————— in the

rain - fall.———— Ooh,———————— ooh.—

Play 6 times   *Repeat to fade*

Instrumental

Verse 2:
In the wind we hear their laughter
In the rain we see their tears.
Hear their heartbeat, we hear their heartbeat.

MYSTERIOUS WAYS

Words & Music by U2

Tune guitar down a semitone

Guitar (8ve bassa)

1. John-ny, take a walk with your sis-ter, the moon;_ let her pale light in, to
(Verse 2 see block lyric)

fill up your room._ You've been liv-ing un-der-ground, eat - ing from a can;_ you've been

run-ning a-way_ from what you don't un-der - stand._ she's slip-py,

you're slid-ing down. She'll be_ there when you hit the ground._

It's al-right,— it's al-right,— it's al-right. She moves— in mys-

-te-ri-ous ways.— It's al-right,— it's al-right,— it's al-right.

To Coda ⊕ **1.**

She moves— in mys-te-ri-ous ways,— oh.—

2.

-te-ri-ous ways.— Yeah, oh,— ah.—

Lift my days, light up my nights,— oh.—

Verse 2:

Johnny, take a dive with your sister in the rain
Let her talk about the things you can't explain.
To touch is to heal, to hurt is to steal.
If you want to kiss the sky, better learn how to kneel
On your knees, boy!
She's the wave, she turns the tide
She sees the man inside the child.

NEW YEAR'S DAY

Words & Music by U2

1. All is qui - et on— New— Year's Day.—
(Verses 2 & 3 see block lyrics)

A world in white___ gets un-der-way.___

I want to be___ with you,___ be with you night and day.

No-thing chan-ges on New Year's Day.

To Coda ⊕

1st time only

On___ New___ Year's Day.___

2nd time only

True, it's___ true.___ And we can break___ through.___ Through

torn in___ two___ we can be___ one.___

I will be with you a-gain.___

I will be with you a-gain.___

Verse 2:
Under a blood-red sky
A crowd has gathered in black and white
Arms entwined, the chosen few
The newspapers says, says
Say it's true, it's true…
And we can break through
Though torn in two
We can be one.

I… I will begin again
I… I will begin again.

Verse 3:
And so we are told this is the golden age
And gold is the reason for the wars we wage
Though I want to be with you
Be with you night and day
Nothing changes
On New Year's Day
On New Year's Day

NUMB

Words by The Edge
Music by U2

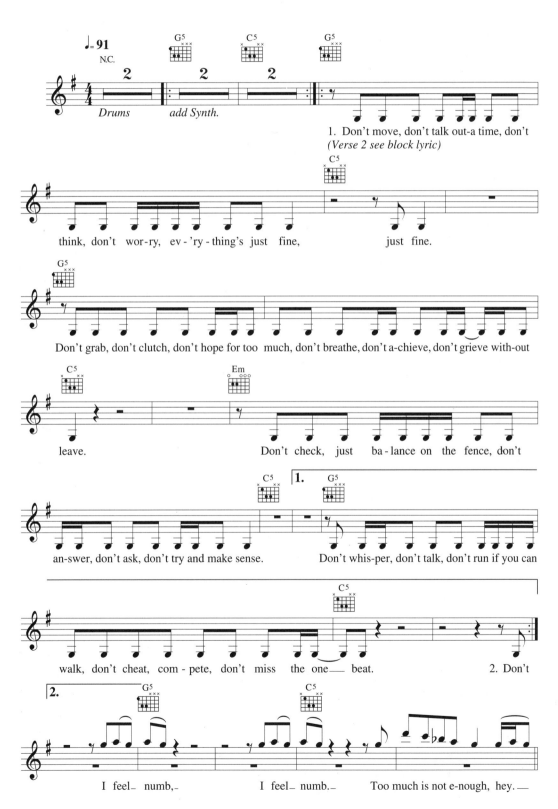

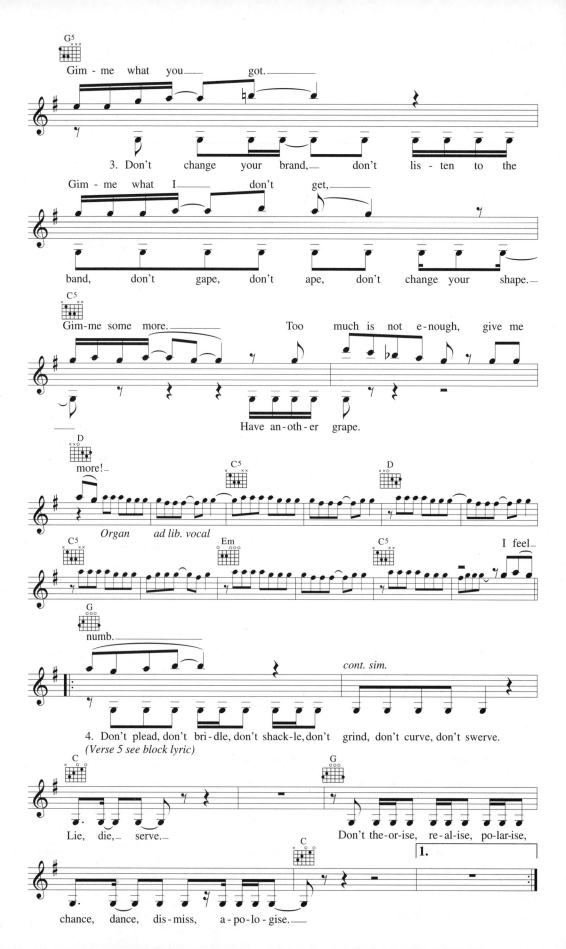

Gim - me what you___ got.___

3. Don't change your brand,___ don't lis - ten to the

Gim - me what I___ don't get,___

band, don't gape, don't ape, don't change your shape.___

Gim - me some more.___ Too much is not e - nough, give me

Have an - oth - er grape.

more!___

Organ ad lib. vocal

I feel___

numb.___

cont. sim.

4. Don't plead, don't bri - dle, don't shack - le, don't grind, don't curve, don't swerve.
(Verse 5 see block lyric)

Lie, die,___ serve.___

Don't the - or - ise, re - al - ise, po - lar - ise,

1.

chance, dance, dis - miss, a - po - lo - gise.___

2. Em

Don't pro-ject,— don't con-nect, pro-tect. Don't ex-pect, sug-gest.—

C

Don't pro-ject,— don't con-nect, pro-tect. Don't ex-pect, sug-gest.—

G

7. Don't strug-gle, don't jerk, don't col-lar, don't work, don't wish, don't fish, don't teach, don't
(Verses 8 & 9 see block lyric)

C **1.** **2.** **3.**

reach. 9. Don't Don't pro-ject,— don't con-nect, pro-tect.

G C/G G C/G G

Don't ex-pect, sug-gest.— Don't pro-ject,— don't con-nect, pro-tect.

C/G G I feel— numb.—

Don't ex-pect, sug-gest.—

Verse 2:
Don't travel by train, don't eat, don't spill
Don't piss in the drain, don't make a will.
Don't fill out any forms, don't compensate
Don't cover, don't crawl, don't come around late
Don't hover at the gate.
Don't take it on board, don't fall on your sword
Just play another chord if you feel you're getting bored.

Verse 5:
Don't spy, don't lie, don't try, imply
Detain, explain, start again.
Don't triumph, don't coax, don't cling, don't hoax
Don't freak, peak, don't leak, don't speak.

Verse 8:
Don't borrow, don't break, don't fence, don't steal
Don't pass, don't press, don't try, don't feel.

Verse 9:
Don't touch, don't dive, don't suffer, don't rhyme
Don't fantasise, don't rise, don't lie.

OCTOBER

Words & Music by U2

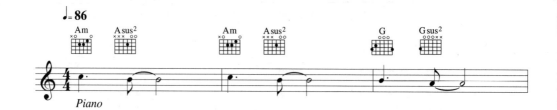

ONE

Words & Music by U2

2.

C   Am   D   F   G

- ry each oth - er...   one!____

3.

C   Am

do it a-gain. You say   love   is a tem-ple,   love___ a high-er law;_   love_

C   Am   C

___ is a tem - ple,   love___ the high-er law._   You ask me_ to en-ter,   but

G

then you   make_ me crawl;_   and I can't_ be hold - ing on___

Fmaj7   C

___ to what_ you_ got,_   when all_ you got_ is hurt.___   One love,_

Am   Fmaj7   C   *D.%. al Coda*

one blood,_   one life,_ you got to   do what you should._

⊕ *Coda*

C   Am   Fmaj7   C

- ry each oth - er.   One,_____   one.___

Guitar

Am   Fmaj7   C

309

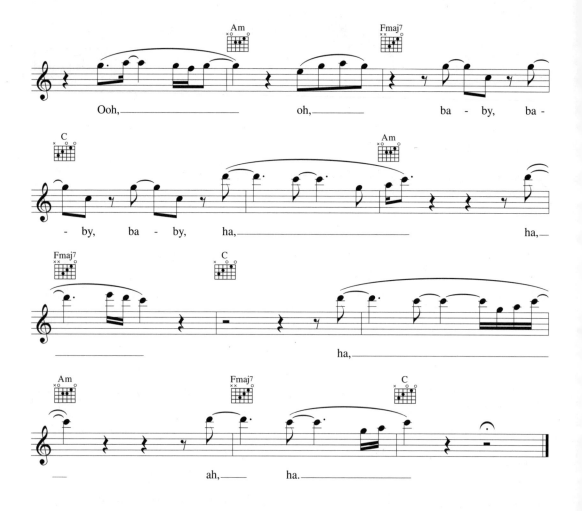

Ooh,_____ oh,_____ ba - by, ba -

- by, ba - by, ha,_____ ha,___

_____ ha,___

___ ah,___ ha._____

Verse 2:

Did I disappoint you or leave a bad taste in your mouth?
You act like you never had love and you want me to go without.
Well, it's too late tonight to drag the past out into the light.
We're one, but we're not the same.
We get to carry each other, carry each other... one.

Verse 3:

Have you come here for forgiveness, have you come to raise the dead
Have you come here to play Jesus to the lepers in your head
Did I ask too much, more than a lot
You gave me nothing, now it's all I got.
We're one, but we're not the same.
Well, we hurt each other, then we do it again.

D.𝄋.:

One life with each other: sisters, brothers.
One life, but we're not the same.
We get to carry each other, carry each other.
One, one.

ONE TREE HILL
Words & Music by U2

Verse 2:
And in the world, a heart of darkness
A fire-zone where poets speak their heart then bleed for it
Jara sang, his song a weapon in the hands of love.
You know his blood still cries from the ground.
It runs like a river runs to the sea.
It runs like a river to the sea.

Verse 3:
I don't believe in painted roses or bleeding hearts
While bullets rape the night of the merciful.
I'll see you again when the stars fall from the sky
And the moon has turned red over One Tree Hill.
We run like a river runs to the sea.
We run like a river to the sea.

OUT OF CONTROL

Words & Music by U2

Tune guitar down a semitone

♩ = 150

1. Mon - day— morn - ing, eight-een years _____ dawn - ing, I said

(Verse 3 see block lyric)

how long.— Say how long.— It was

one dull— morn - ing I woke the world— with— bawl - ing. I was

so sad.— They were so glad.—

I had— the feel - ing it was out of con - trol, I was of the

o - - - pin - ion it was out of con - trol.

To Coda ⊕

(Oh_____)

2. Boys and— girls——— go to school and— girls——— they make

chil - dren,— not like this one.— And

I had — the feel- ing it was out of con - trol, I was of the

o - - - pin - ion it was out of con - trol._____

(Oh_____)

Guitar ad lib.

Verse 3:
I fought fate
There's blood at the garden gate
The man said childhood
It's in his childhood
One day I'll die
The choice will not be mine
Will it be too late?
You can't fight fate.

PLEASE

Words by Bono & The Edge
Music by U2

Tune guitar down a semitone

♩ = 102

Keyboards/Bass Gtr.   Keyboards only   Add Drums/Bass

1° Keyboards/Bass Gtr. only

1. So you nev-er— knew love— un-til you crossed— the line of— grace,—
(Verse 2 see block lyric)

and you nev-er felt want-ed till you'd some-one slap your— face.—

So you nev-er— felt— a-live— un-til you'd al-most wast-ed a-way. You

had to win, you could-n't just pass:— the smart-est ass— at the top of— the class,— your

fly-ing co-lours, your fa-mi-ly tree, and all your les-sons in his-to-ry.— Please,—

_____ please,— please— get up off— your knees. Please,—

317

is big, — is big-ger — than us. — But love — is — not what — you're think - ing of. — It's what lov-ers deal, — it's what lov-ers steal, — you know I've found it hard — to re - ceive, — 'cause you, — my — love, I could nev - er — be - lieve. —

rall.

Verse 2:
And you never knew how low you'd stoop to make that call
And you never knew what was on the ground till they made you crawl.
So you never knew that the heaven you keep you stole.
Your Catholic blues, your convent shoes,
Your stick-on tattoos now they're making the news
Your holy war, your northern star
Your sermon on the mount from the boot of your car.

Please *etc.*

Verse 4:
October, talk getting nowhere.
November, December; remember
We just started again.

Please *etc.*

PRIDE (IN THE NAME OF LOVE)

Words & Music by U2

1. One man come in the name of love, one man come and go.
(Verse 2 see block lyric)

One man come he to jus-ti-fy, one man to ov-er-throw. In the name

of love, what more in the name of love. In the name

of love, what more in the name of love.

3. Ear-ly morn-ing, Ap - ril four,— shot rings out— in the Mem-phis sky.—

Free at last,— they— took your life, they— could not take your— pride.— In the name—

———— of love,— what more— in the name of— love.— In the name—

———— of love,— what more— in the name of love.— In the name — Oh

1.

2.

Repeat to fade

oh— oh, oh oh— oh, oh oh— oh, oh oh— oh. Oh

Verse 2:
One man caught on a barbed wire fence
One man he resist
One man washed up on an empty beach
One man betrayed with a kiss.

In the name of love *etc.*

PROMENADE

Words & Music by U2

In

cracked streets,— tram - ple——— un - der - foot.——

Side - step,— side - walk. I see you— stare——— in - to——

—— space.— Have I got— clo - ser now, be - hind—— the face?—

Oh, tell me, Cher-ry you dance with me,—— turn me a -

- round to - night,—— up through the spi - ral—— stair - case to the

high - er—— ground.—— Slide - show,—— sea - side— town.

Co-ca co - la, foot - ball ra - di - o, ra - di - o, ra-di-o, ra-di-o, ra - di - o, ra - di - o.

Repeat to fade

RACE AGAINST TIME

Words & Music by U2

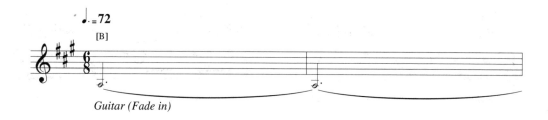

Guitar (Fade in)

Bass

Play 8 times

Guitar (Bass cont. sim.)

Fade in

Oh   la.   Oh   la,

Oh la. Oh la. Oh la. Oh la.

Oh la, say oh la. Oh la.

Oh race a - gainst___ time.___

To Coda ⊕

Bass

D.%. al Coda
Play 10 times ad lib.

⊕ *Coda*

Repeat ad lib. to fade

RED HILL MINING TOWN

Words & Music by U2

1. From fa-ther to — son, the blood — runs — thin. —

Ooh, — see the fa - ces fro - zen (still) a -

- gainst — the wind. —

2. The seam is — split, — the coal - face — cracked,
(Verse 3 see block lyric)

the lines are — long, there's no go - ing back.

Through hands of — steel and heart of — stone, —
(Verse 4 see block lyric)

our la - bour day____ has come and____

gone._____ They leave__ me hold - in' on____ in

Red____ Hill Town.__ See lights____ go__ down on...

Hang - in' on,_____ you're all that's left to

hold__ on__ to. I'm still wait - ing.__

__ I'm hang - in' on,_____ you're all__ that's left to

To Coda ⊕ | 1. | 2.

hold__ on__ to. on __

(Half spoken)

to. We scorch __ the earth, set fire__ to the sky,__

and we stooped so low, to reach so high.

⊕ Coda

Love, slow - ly stripped a - way;

love has seen its bet-ter day.

Hang-in' on, lights go down on Red Hill.

The lights go down on Red Hill.

The lights go down on Red Hill Town.

The lights go down on Red Hill Town.

Verse 3:
The glass is cut, the bottle run dry.
Our love runs cold in the caverns of the night.
We're wounded by fear, injured in doubt.
I can lose myself, you I can't live without.
Yeah, you keep me holdin' on in Red Hill Town.
See the lights go down on…

Hangin' on *etc.*

Verse 4:
A link is lost, the chain undone.
We wait all day for night to come
And it comes like a hunter child.
I'm hangin' on *etc.*

RED LIGHT

Words & Music by U2

Tune guitar down a semitone

♩ = 128

(Da da da da da da   da da da da da da.) (Da da da   da da da da   da da da da da da.) (Da

da da   da da da   da   da da   da da da.) (Da   da da   da da da   da   da da   da da da.) (Da

da da.)   Ooh. —   1. Oh   I

talk — to you,   you — walk a - way.   You're still on the

down beat,   you say — you don't want my   help. —   But you can't es -

- cape —   if you're run-ning from your - self. —   I give you my

love, —   I give you my — love. —   Give — you my

love,_____ still you_____ walk a - way._____ Well.

It's your

own late show_____ as you jump to the_____ street be -

- low. But where can_____ you go_____ to

leave your - self be - hind? A - lone_____ in the spot - light

of this,_____ your own_____ tra - ge - dy._____ I give you my

love._____ Love._____

(Love, love, love, love, love, love, love, love, love._____)

REJOICE

Words & Music by U2

1. It's fall-ing, it's fall-ing and out-side a build-ing comes tum-bl-ing down.
(Verse 2 see block lyrics)

And in-side a child on the ground says he'll do it a-gain. And what am I to do? What in the world am I to say? There's noth-ing else to do.

He says he'll change the world some day, I re-

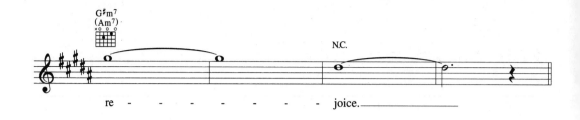

re - - - - - joice.

Tom-toms and bass only

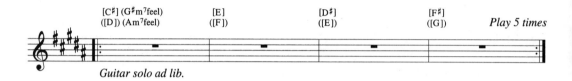

Guitar solo ad lib.

Drums only

Vocals ad lib.

Verse 2:
This morning I fell out of bed
When I woke up to what he had said
Everything's crazy but I'm too lazy to lie.

And what am I to do?
Just tell me what am I supposed to say?
I can't change the world
But I can change the world in me
Rejoice.

RUNNING TO STAND STILL

Words & Music by U2

hooh, ooh, hooh, ooh,

hooh. She walks through the streets

with her eyes paint-ed red, un-der black bel - ly of cloud in the rain.

In through a door - way, she brings me white gold-en pearls

sto - len from the sea. She is rag - in', she is rag - in', and the storm

blows up in her eyes. She will suf-fer the nee - dle chill,

she's run-ning to stand still.

Repeat to fade

Verse 2:
Sweet the sin, bitter the taste in my mouth.
I see seven towers, but I only see one way out.
You gotta cry without weeping, talk without speaking
Scream without raising your voice.
You know I took the poison, from the poison stream
Then I floated out of here, singing

Ah la la la *etc.*

SALOMÉ

Words by Bono
Music by U2

- mé.   Sa - lo - mé,   shake

it, shake it, shake it, Sa - lo - mé.___   3. Ba - by please

⊕ *Coda*   Sa - lo - mé,___   shake___

___ it, shake it, shake it, Sa - lo - mé.___

Ooh,   ooh.   *Drums*

Guitar

Bass   5. Ba - by please,

(Verse 6 see block lyric)

ba - by don't__ say no.

Won't you dance__ for me, 'neath the cher - ry tree? Won't you swing

1.

2.

__ down low?__ 6. Please Sa - lo -

- mé,__ Sa - lo - mé,__ shake__

__ it, shake it, shake it Sa - lo - mé.__ Shake__

__ it, shake it, shake it, Sa - lo - mé.__ Sa - lo -

- mé,__ shake__ it, shake it, shake it, Sa - lo -

1.

2.

N.C.

- me.__ Sa - lo -

339

N.C. [A]
Guitar solo ad lib.

Play 6 times

Bass

Backing vocals ad lib.

Repeat ad lib. to fade

Verse 2:
Please
Baby don't bite your lip
Give you half what I got
If you untie the knot
It's a promise.

Verse 3:
Baby please
Baby what's that tune?
Well I heard it before
When I crawled from your door
And my blood turned blue.

Verse 4:
Please
Baby please slow down
Baby I feel sick
Don't make me stick to a promise.

Verse 6:
Please
Baby please say yes
Baby don't go away
You're spilling me
And your precious love.

SCARLET

Words & Music by U2

SECONDS

Words & Music by U2

Tune guitar down a semitone

♩ = 96

Drums   cont. sim.

Bass   cont. sim.

1. Takes a se-cond to say good-bye,— say good-bye,

oh, oh, oh. Takes a se-cond to say good-bye,— say good-bye,

oh, oh, oh. Say bye - bye.—

Where you go - ing to— now?— Light-ning

flash-es a-cross the sky,— East to West, do and die.— Like a
(Verse 3 see block lyric)

Fall, _____ rise, ____ and... ____ Say good-

Say good-bye, say good-bye,— say good-bye.—
-bye, say good - bye, say good - bye.—

Radio Broadcast

D.%. al Coda

Drums   *Bass*

3. It takes a

⊕ *Coda*

Say— good-bye,   say— good-bye,   say— good-bye,   say— good-bye.

Verse 3:
It takes a second to say goodbye
Say goodbye, oh, oh, oh
Push the button and pull the plug
Say goodbye, oh, oh, oh.

Fall, rise and...
Fall, rise and...

Verse 4:
And they're doing the atomic bomb
Do they know where the dance comes from?
Yes they're doing the atomic bomb
They want you to sing along.

Say goodbye, say goodbye
Say goodbye, say goodbye.

SHADOWS AND TALL TREES

Words & Music by U2

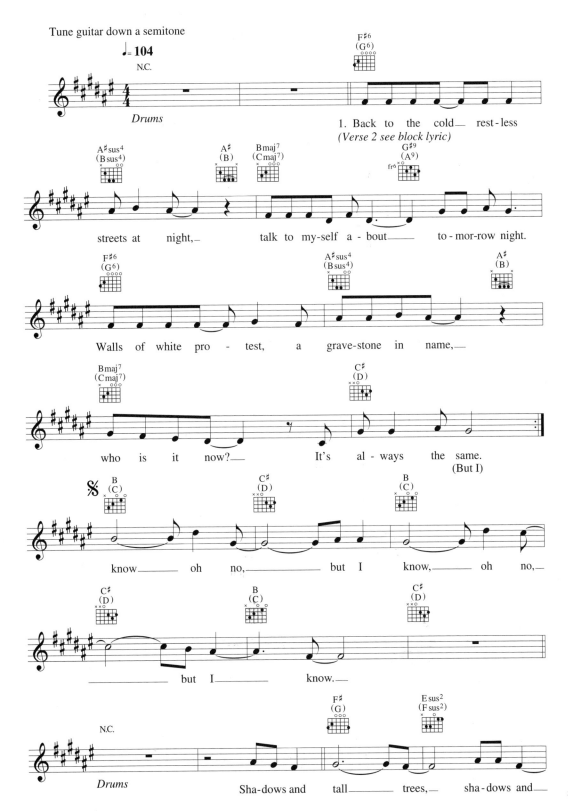

tall _____ trees, _____ sha - dows and tall _____ trees, -

sha - dows and _____ tall _____ trees. _____

To Coda ⊕

3. Life through a win-dow, dis - col -oured pain. _____ Mrs _____ Brown's wash-ing is al -

- ways the same, _____ I walk the street rain _____ tra - gi - com - e - dy, _____ I'll

walk home a - gain _____ to the street _____ me - lo - dy. _____ But I

know, _____ oh no, _____ but I know, _____ oh no, -

_____ but I _____ know. _____

Drums

Guitar

Do you

Verse 2:
Who is it now? Who calls me inside?
Are the leaves on the trees just a living disguise?
I walk the sweet rain tragicomedy
I'll walk home again to the street melody.

SILVER AND GOLD

Words by Bono
Music by U2

1. In the shit-house, a shot-gun, pray-ing hands— hold me down.

If on-ly the hunt-er was hunt-ed in this—

tin can town,— tin can town.—

No stars— in the black night,

looks like the sky fall down.— No sun— in the day-

-light, looks like it's chained to the ground,— chained to the ground.

The war-den says "the ex-it is sold." — If you want a way out... — sil-ver and gold, sil-ver and gold. Whoa!

Bass *cont. sim.*

2. Bro-ken back to the ceil-ing, bro-ken nose — to the floor.
(Verse 3 see block lyric)

— I scream — at the si-lence, it's crawl-ing, crawls un-der the door. — There's a rope a-round my neck — and there's a trig-ger in your gun. —

Je-sus, say some-thing! I am— some - one,— — I am some - one.— Cap-tains and Kings in the ships hold.— They came to col - lect— sil-ver and gold, sil - ver and gold.

Bass *cont. sim.*

I seen the com - ing and the go - ing, seen the cap - tains and the Kings.— Seen their na - vy blue u - ni - forms, seen them

To Coda

Verse 3:
The temperature is rising
The fever white hot
Mister I ain't got nothing
But it's more than you've got
These chains no longer bind me
Nor the shackles at my feet
Outside are the prisoners
Inside the free (set them free).

A prize fighter in a corner is told
Hit where it hurts — For Silver and Gold
You can stop the world from turning around
You just gotta pay a penny in the pound.

SIXTY SECONDS IN KINGDOM COME

Music by U2

SLOW DANCING

Words by Bono & The Edge
Music by U2

eyes and see-through heart,— I saw her com-ing right from the start.—
(Verse 3 see block lyric)

— She picked me up, but had me down on my knees,— just a-beg-ging her—

— please.— (Take me) Slow—— danc-ing,——

slow—— danc-ing,—— slow.——

(danc-ing.) And I don't—

— know why—— a man— will search— for him-self— in his wo-man's eyes.——

— No, I don't— know why—— a man

sees— the truth,— (but) be-lieves the lies.—— 3. My— love is

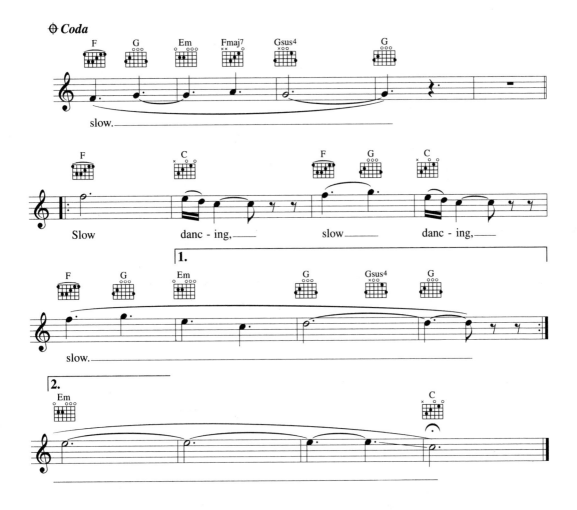

⊕ *Coda*

Slow danc - ing,___ slow___ danc - ing,___

slow.___

1.

slow.___

2.

Verse 3:
My love is restless as the wind
She moves like a shadow across my skin
She left with my conscience
And I don't want it back
It just gets in the way.

Slow dancing, *etc.*

SO CRUEL

Words & Music by U2

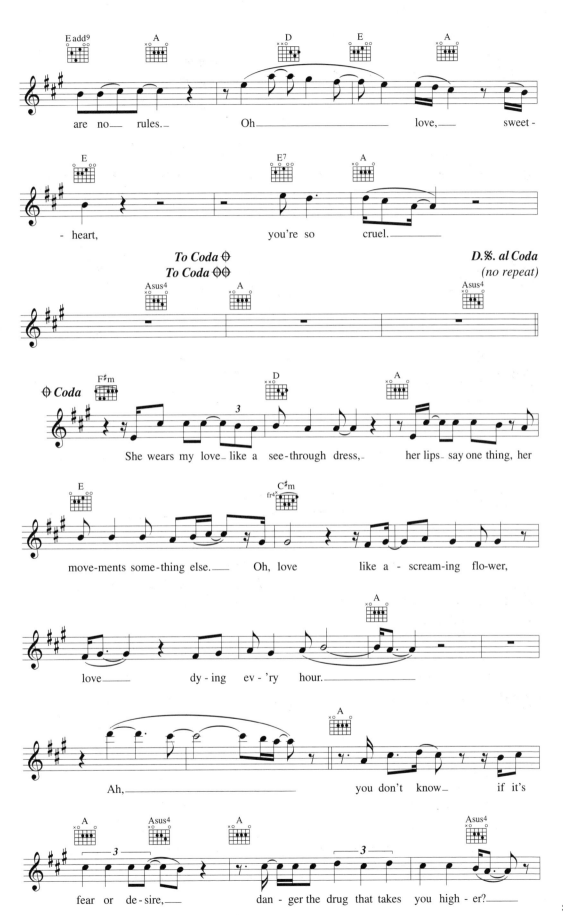

are no— rules.— Oh———————————— love,—— sweet-

-heart, you're so cruel.———

To Coda ⊕
To Coda ⊕⊕

D.%. al Coda
(no repeat)

⊕ **Coda**

She wears my love— like a see-through dress,— her lips— say one thing, her

move-ments some-thing else.— Oh, love like a-scream-ing flo-wer,

love——— dy-ing ev-'ry hour.———————

Ah,———————————— you don't know— if it's

fear or de-sire,——— dan-ger the drug that takes you high-er?———

Verse 2:
I disappeared in you
You disappeared from me.
I gave you everything you ever wanted
It wasn't what you wanted.
The men who love you, you hate the most
They pass right through you like a ghost.
They look for you, but your spirit is in the air.
Baby, you're nowhere.

Verse 3:
Desperation is a tender trap
It gets you every time.
You put your lips to her lips
To stop the lie.
Her skin is pale like God's only dove
Screams like an angel for your love
Then she makes you watch her from above
And you need her like a drug.

SOME DAYS ARE BETTER THAN OTHERS

Words by Bono
Music by U2

Tune guitar down a semitone

1. Some_days are dry, some_days are lea-ky; some_days come clean, oth-
(Verses 2 & 3 see block lyric)

- er days are snea - ky. Some_days take less, but most_days take more; some

slip_through your fin-gers and on_ to the floor._ Some_days you're quick, but

most_ days you're spee - dy; some_ days you use more_ force_

_ than is ne - ces-sa-ry. Some_ days_ just drop

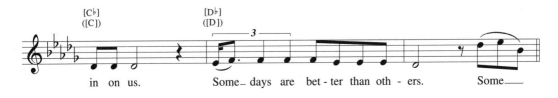

in on us. Some_days are bet - ter than oth - ers. Some_

Verse 2:

Some days are slippy, other days are sloppy;
Some days you can't stand the sight of a puppy.
Your skin is white, but you think you're a brother.
Some days are better than others.
Some days you wake up with her complaining.
Some sunny days you wish it was raining.
Some days are sulky, some days have a grin;
And some days have bouncers and won't let you in.
Some days you hear a voice
Taking you to another place.
Some days are better than others.

Verse 3:

Some days are honest, some days are not;
Some days you're thankful for what you've got.
Some days you wake up in the army
And some days it's the enemy.
Some days are work, most days you're lazy;
Some days you feel like a bit of a baby
Lookin' for Jesus and his mother.
Some days are better than others.
Some days you feel ahead;
You're making sense of what she said.
Some days are better than others.

SPANISH EYES

Words & Music by U2

1. Wey, hey, hey,   mm.___   Ba - by hang on,___
(Verses 2 & 3 see block lyrics)

___   mm.___   Wey, hey, hey,   mm.___

⊕ *Coda*

Wey, hey, hey, ooh. Ba-by hang on, hang on. Wey, hey, hey, oh. Ba-by hang on, hang on. Cos I love the way you talk to me, and I love the way you mean to me. And I need you.

Verse 2:
Wey, hey, hey, here she comes
Comes in colours now she's gonna turn the daylight on
'Cos I love the way you talk to me, and I love the way you walk on me
And I need you more than you need me (yeah)
Our love shines like rain in those Spanish eyes.

Verse 3:
Wey, hey, hey, sugar hang on.
Wey, hey, hey, you know that the night is as young
I'm dazzled by a light that shines in your eyes
I'm used to standing in the shadows and waiting for the night
Forever in fever, forever in heat
You re-invented me, now don't put me back on the street.

STARING AT THE SUN

Words by Bono & The Edge
Music by U2

(Verse 2 see block lyric)

(Chorus 3 see block lyric)

left it in___ the____ du - ty - free,__ oh,_____ though you

ne - ver real - ly be - longed to me.__ You're not the on - ly one__

D.%. al Coda

Coda

blind._____ Ooh.__

Ah, ah, ah, oh,_____ ah, ah, ah, ah._____

Repeat to fade

___ Ah, ah, ah, oh,_____ ah, ah, ah, ah.__

Verse 2:

There's an insect in your ear
If you scratch it won't disappear.
It's gonna itch and burn and sting
Do you wanna see what the scratching brings!
Waves that leave me out of reach
Breaking on your back like a beach.
Will we ever live in peace?
'Cause those that can't do often have to
And those that can't do often have to preach
To the ones staring at the sun
Afraid of what you'll find if you took a look inside.
Not just deaf and dumb, staring at the sun
I'm not the only one who'd rather go blind.

Chorus 3:

You're not the only one staring at the sun
Afraid of what you'd find if you stepped back inside.
I'm not sucking my thumb, staring at the sun
Not the only one who's happy to go blind.

STAY (FARAWAY, SO CLOSE!)

Words by Bono
Music by U2

Stay, and the night would be e - nough. Oh,

oh. Oh.

Three o' clock in the morn - ing; it's qui -

- et, there's no one a - round, just the bang and the clat-

- ter as an an - gel runs to ground. Just the bang

and the clat-ter as an an - gel hits the ground.

Crash cymbal

Verse 2:
Red lights, grey morning
You stumble out of a hole in the ground.
A vampire or a victim
It depend's on who's around.
You used to stay in to watch the adverts
You could lip synch. to the talk shows.

Verse 3:
Faraway, so close
Up with the static and the radio.
With satellite television
You can go anywhere:
Miami, New Orleans
London, Belfast and Berlin.
And, if you listen, I can't call.
And, if you jump, you just might fall.
And, if you shout, I'll only hear you.

If I could stay *etc.*

STORIES FOR BOYS
Words & Music by U2

Tune guitar down a semitone

1. There's a place I go — when I — am far a - way. —
(Verses 2 & 3 see block lyrics)

There's a T. V. show — and I — can — play.

Some-times when a he-ro takes — me. Some-times I don't let — go. —

Oh, oh, — oh. —

Verse 2:
There's a picture book
With colour photographs
There's a comic strip
That makes me laugh
Sometimes away he takes me
Sometimes I don't let go.

Verse 3:
There's a place I go
And it's a part of me
There's a radio
And I will go
Sometimes a hero takes me
Sometimes I don't let go.

STRANGER IN A STRANGE LAND

Words & Music by U2

was the one who should run. We

asked him to smile for a pho - to - graph, — wait - ed a while to
(Verse 2 see block lyric)

see if we — could make — him laugh.

Whoa. — The sold - ier asked for a cig - ar - ette — his —

— smil - ing face I can't for - get. He looked at me ac -

- ross the street — but that's a long — way here. —

Oh — and I wish you were — here.

Oh — and I wish you were — here,

to   see   what I___   could see___   to

hear   and I   wish you were here.

Whoa.___

Repeat to fade

Verse 2:
I watched as he watched us get back on the bus
I watched the way it was
The way it was when he was with us
And I really don't mind sleeping on the floor
But I couldn't sleep after what I saw
I wrote this letter to tell you the way I feel.

Oh I wish you were here *etc.*

SUNDAY BLOODY SUNDAY

Words & Music by U2

we can be as one— to - night.

2. Bro - ken bot - tles un - der child - ren's— feet,—
(Verses 3 & 4 see block lyrics)

bod - ies strewn a - cross— the dead - end street.—

But I— won't heed— the bat - tle call,

it puts my back up, puts my back up a - gainst the wall.—

Sun - day,— blood - y Sun - day.—

Sun - day,— blood - y Sun - day.—

To Coda

1.

Sun - day,— blood - y Sun - day.—

Sun - day,— blood - y Sun - day.—

377

Sun - day blood - y Sun - day.
Sun - day,— blood - y Sun -

- day.— Ah.

D.℈. al Coda

⊕ Coda

Sun - day,— blood - y Sun - day.—

Sun - day,— blood - y Sun - day.—

Verse 3:

And the battle's just begun
There's many lost, but tell me who has won?
The trenches dug within our hearts
And mothers, children, brothers, sisters
Torn apart.

Sunday, bloody Sunday
Sunday, bloody Sunday.

Verse 4:

And it's true we are immune
When fact is fiction and TV reality
And today the millions cry
We eat and drink while tomorrow they die.

Sunday, bloody Sunday.

The real battle just begun
To claim the victory Jesus won
On…

Sunday, bloody Sunday
Sunday, bloody Sunday.

SURRENDER

Words & Music by U2

(Sur-

-ren - der.____) (Sur - ren - - - der.____)

To Coda ⊕

Bass

2. Sa-

- die said she could-n't work____ out what it was all a-bout____

____ and so she let go.____ Now____ Sa-die's on the____ street

D.%. al Coda

____ and the peo-ple she meets____ you know.____ She

⊕ *Coda*

Oh,_____ oh._____ Oh,_____

381

oh.＿＿＿＿＿＿＿ To -

- night.＿＿＿＿＿＿＿＿＿＿＿＿＿ 4. Oh,＿ the ci-ty's a - fire,-

＿ a pas-sion-ate flame＿ that knows me by name.＿ Oh,

＿ the ci-ty's de - sire＿ to take me for more＿ and more.-

It's in the street＿ get-tin' un-der my feet, it's

in the air,＿ it's ev-'ry-where I＿＿＿ look for you.＿

＿ It's in the things＿ that I do and say,＿ and

if I wan-na live I got-ta die to my - self some-day.＿

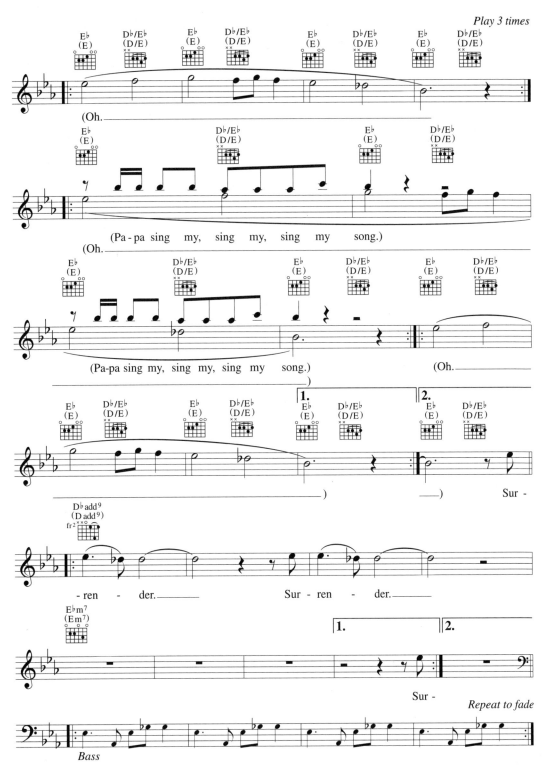

Verse 3:
She tried to be a good girl and a good wife
Raise a good family
Lead a good life
It's not good enough
She got herself up on the 48th floor
Gotta find out
Find out what she's living for.

SWEETEST THING

Words & Music by U2

1. My love, she throws me like a rub-ber ball; (Oh, the sweet-est thing.)
(Verse 3 see block lyric)

But she won't catch me or break my fall. (Oh, the sweet-est thing.)

Ba-by's got blue skies up a-head, but in this, I'm a rain cloud,

To Coda

you know she wants a dry kind of love. (Oh, the sweet-est thing.)

I'm los-in' you, I'm los-in' you.

Ain't love the sweet-est thing? 2. I want-ed to run but she made me

Verse 3:
Blue-eyed boy meets a brown-eyed girl.
(Oh, the sweetest thing.)
You can sew it up, but you still see the tear.
(Oh, the sweetest thing.)
Baby's got blue skies up ahead
But in this, I'm a rain-cloud,
Ours is a stormy kind of love.
(Oh, the sweetest thing.)

THE ELECTRIC CO.

Words & Music by U2

shout, shout___ you're in - side out___ if you

don't know,___ E - lec - tric___ Co.,___ if you

don't___ know,___ E - lec - tric___ Co.___

Guitar

Instrumental

Guitar

388

Guitar

Voice ad lib.

If___ you don't

know,_____ E - lec - tric_ Co,_____ if__ you don't

know,_____ E - lec - tric_ Co._____ If__ you don't

1, 2.

3.

Drums   Guitar

Play 19 times

Vocal/Instrumental ad lib.

Verse 2:
Red, running red
Play for real
Talk and feel
Holding your head
You won't shout
You still beg
If you don't know
The electric co.

THE FIRST TIME

Words by Bono
Music by U2

-in' down, I just call and he comes a-round. But for the

first time I feel love.

Hey, hey-

-ey ey- -ey. Hooh,

ooh. 5. My

fa-ther is a rich man, he wears a rich man's cloak.
(Verse 6 see block lyric)

He gave me the keys to his king-dom (com-ing,) gave me a cup

1.
of gold. He said "I

2.
and I threw

392

Verse 2:
Shows me colours when there's none to see
Gives me hope when I can't believe
That for the first time I feel love.

Verse 6:
He said "I have many mansions
And there are many rooms to see".
But I left by the back door
And I threw away the key
And I threw away the key *etc.*

THE FLY

Words & Music by U2

child.   1. It's no se-cret that the stars_ are fall-ing from the sky._ It's no

se-cret that our world is in dark-ness to-night. They say the sun is some-times_ e-

-clipsed by the moon._ Y' know I don't see you when she walks in the room. 2. It's no

se-cret that a friend is some-one who lets you help. It's no se-cret that a liar_ won't be-lieve
(Verse 3 see block lyric)

Love, _____ we shine like a burn - ing star,_ we're fall-

- ing from_ the sky_____ to - night._____

⊕ *Coda*

Oh yeah It's no se-cret that the stars_ are fall-ing from the sky,_ the u -

- ni-verse ex - plod - ing 'cos_ a one man's lie._ Look_ I got-ta go,_ yeah, I'm

run - ning out-ta change; there's a lot of things_ if_ I could I'd re - ar - range._

Verse 3:
It's no secret that a conscience can sometimes be a pest.
It's no secret ambition bites the nails of success.
Every artist is a cannibal, every poet is a thief;
All kill their inspiration and sing about their grief.
A man will rise, a man will fall
From the sheer face of love like a fly from a wall.
It's no secret at all.

THE OCEAN

Words & Music by U2

THE PLAYBOY MANSION

Words by Bono & The Edge
Music by U2

no— time for shame.— And though I can't— say why,

D.%. al Coda

I know I've got— to be - lieve._____ We'll—

⊕ *Coda*

the play - boy man - sion._____ Then will there be—
(Then there will be no time for sorrow)

no— time— for pain, _ then will there be— no— time for sor-

- row, then will there be— no— time— for shame.—

Guitar (8ve bassa)   N.C.   *(Bass & Drums tacet)*

Verse 2:
If O.J. is more than a drink
And a Big Mac bigger than you think
And perfume is an obsession
And talk shows… confession
What have we got to lose?
Another push and we'll be through
The gates of that mansion.

Verse 4:
Chance is a kind of religion
Where you're damned for plain hard luck.
I never did see that movie
I never did read that book.
Love, come on down
Let my numbers come around.

Chorus 3:
We'll go driving in that pool
It's who you know that gets you through
The gates of the playboy mansion.

THE REFUGEE

Words & Music by U2

(Wa, war. _____) She is a re-fu-gee. She com-ing back, she come

_____ and keep you com-pa-ny. (Wa, war. _____) She is a re-fu-gee.

Her ma - ma say one day — she's gon-na live in A - me - ri - ca.

Repeat to fade

(Vocals ad lib.)

On 𝄋:
In the evening
She is waiting
Waiting for her man to come
And take her by her hand
And take her to this promised land.

(Wa, war) She's a pretty face
But at the wrong time in the wrong place
(Wa, war) She's a pretty face
Her mama say one day she's gonna live in America.

THE THREE SUNRISES

Words & Music by U2

Spi - rit of___ the ris - ing sun

lift me up.___ Hold me there___ and nev-

-er let___ me fall.___

Love me till___ I die, my heart can't wait.___

Soon Thy will___ be___ done in this

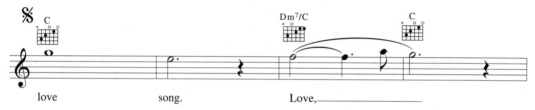

love song. Love,___

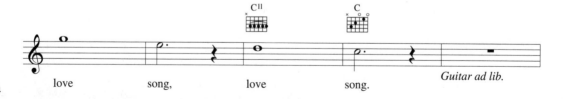

love song, love song.

Guitar ad lib.

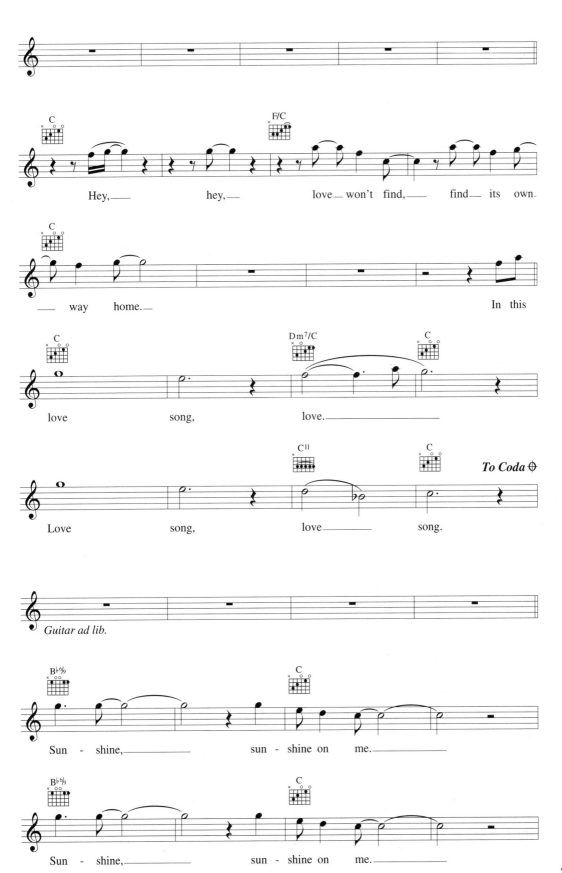

Guitar ad lib.

D.%. al Coda

In this

⊕ *Coda*

Sun - shine__ on____ me,__ bring it through_ to my__ heart.__ And

I will give__you ev - 'ry-thing, I will give you my__ de - sire.__

Guitar ad lib.

Sun - shine,_____ sun - shine on me._____

Sun - shine,_____ sun - shine on me._____

Repeat to fade

Guitar

THE UNFORGETTABLE FIRE

Words & Music by U2

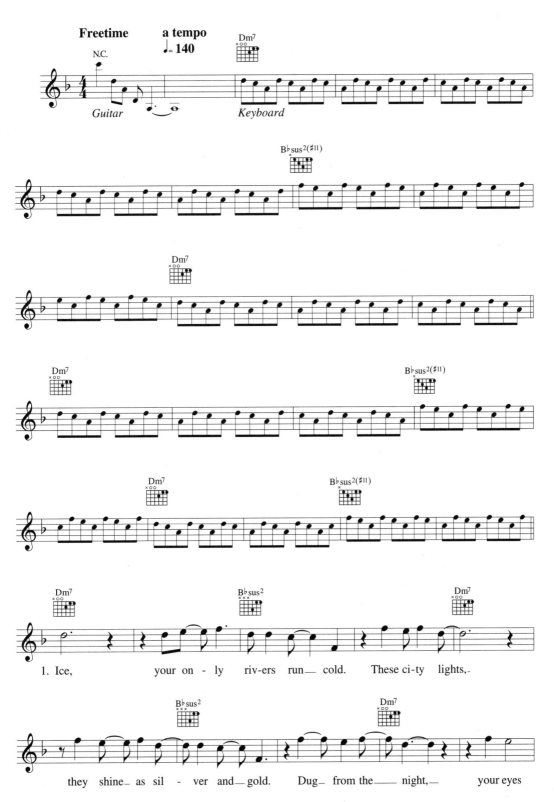

1. Ice, your on - ly riv-ers run— cold. These ci-ty lights,—

they shine— as sil - ver and— gold. Dug— from the—— night,— your eyes

as black as coal.

Walk on by,— walk on through.— Walk till— you run

— and— don't look— back for— here— I— am.

2. Car - ni - val, the wheels fly and the col-ours spin

— through al - co-hol,— red wine that punc-tures— the— skin.

Face to face— in a dry and wa-ter-less— place.

Walk on by,— walk on through,- so

sad to — be - siege— your love... oh hang——— on.———

THE WANDERER

Words by Bono
Music by U2

Tune guitar down a semitone

♩ = 120

(Vocal sounds 2 octaves lower)

1. I went out walk-ing through streets paved with gold,___ lift-ed some stones,_ saw the

(Verses 2 & 3 see block lyric)

skin and_ bones___ of a ci-ty with-out_ a soul.___

I went out walk-ing un-der an a-tom-ic___ sky,_ ___ where the ground won't turn and the rain it burns_ like the

tears when I said good-bye.___ Yeah, I went_ with no-thing, no-thing but the thought of___ you.___ I went wan-

-der-ing.——

2, 3.
I went out rid-ing down that old—— eight——

lane,—— I—— passed by—— a thou-sand signs—

look-ing for my—— own—— name.—— I went with——

no-thing but the thought—you'd be—— there—— too, look-ing for

To Coda ⊕

you.

4

(Spoken) I went out there in

search of ex - pe - ri-ence, to taste and to touch

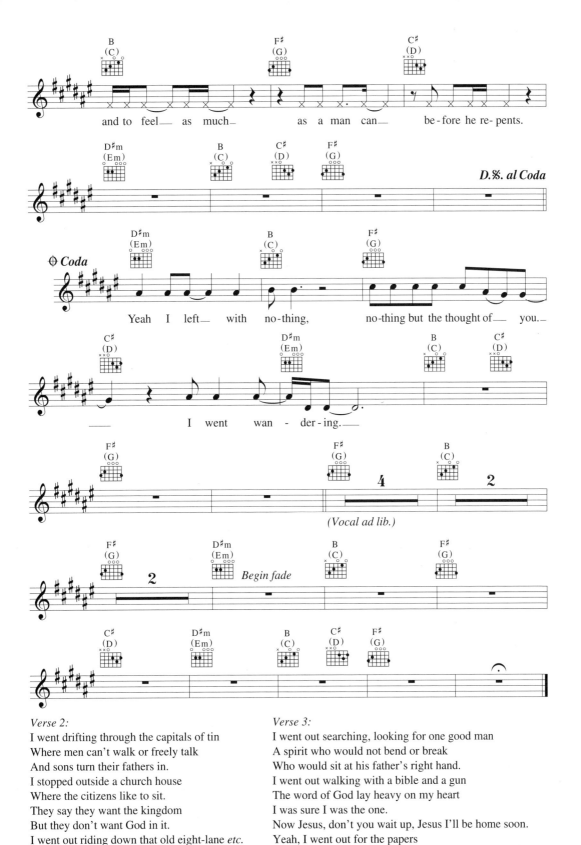

and to feel— as much— as a man can— be - fore he re - pents.

D.%. al Coda

Coda

Yeah I left— with no-thing, no-thing but the thought of— you.—

—— I went wan - der - ing.——

(Vocal ad lib.)

Begin fade

Verse 2:
I went drifting through the capitals of tin
Where men can't walk or freely talk
And sons turn their fathers in.
I stopped outside a church house
Where the citizens like to sit.
They say they want the kingdom
But they don't want God in it.
I went out riding down that old eight-lane *etc.*

Verse 3:
I went out searching, looking for one good man
A spirit who would not bend or break
Who would sit at his father's right hand.
I went out walking with a bible and a gun
The word of God lay heavy on my heart
I was sure I was the one.
Now Jesus, don't you wait up, Jesus I'll be home soon.
Yeah, I went out for the papers
Told her I'd be back by noon.
Yeah, I left with nothing but the thought you'd be there too
Looking for you.

THINGS TO MAKE AND DO

Music by U2

Tune guitar down a semitone

♩ = 144

Guitar

2.

[D♭]
([D])

TOMORROW

Words & Music by U2

1. Won't you come back to - mor - - - row,
(Verse 2 see block lyric)

won't you come back to - mor - row,_____ won't you come back to - mor -

- - row, can I sleep to - night?

Out-side, some-bo-dy's out-side, some-bo-dy's knock-ing at the door. There's a black car parked at the side of the road, don't go to the door, don't go to the door. I'm go-ing out.

(2nd time instrumental)

I'm go-ing out - side moth-er, I'm go-ing out there, ooh, ooh.

Won't you come back to-mor-row, won't you be back to-mor-row. Will you be back to-mor-row, can

417

who made — the blind — to see. —

He's com-ing back,— he's com-ing back. O Be -

- lieve —— Him. —

Je - sus com - ing.

Instrumental, vocal ad lib.

Repeat ad lib. to fade

Verse 2:
Won't you be back tomorrow,
Won't you be back tomorrow,
Will you be back tomorrow?
La, la, la, la, la, la.

Who broke the window
Who broke down the door?
Who tore the curtain
And who was it for?
Who heals the wounds
Who heals the scars?
Open the door, open the door.

TOUCH

Words & Music by U2

Guitar

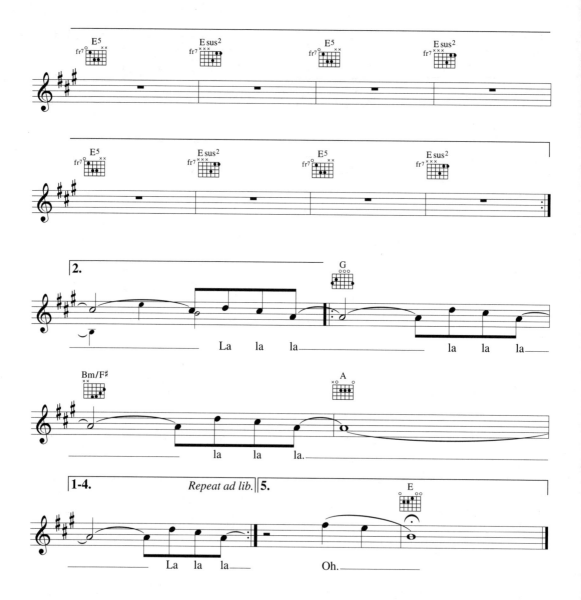

Verse 2:
Falling… the world is by your side
Calling… to find a place to hide
I just wanna know
I just wanna know.

Verse 3:
She said "The twenty second floor"
I said "I can't think what it's for"
And I just wanna know
I just wanna know.

TRASH, TRAMPOLINE AND THE PARTY GIRL
Words & Music by U2

2. I know a boy,— a boy— called Trash,— Trash Can.— I know he does— all that he can.—

Wham bam. And she won't tell— me his

[B] name. *Piano*

[E]

1, 2. *Repeat ad lib.* 3.
[B]

D.%. al Coda

Coda

— a - - - long. And if you dance

then— dance with— me.—

Verse 3:
I have a heart
A heart that's beating inside
When I was three
I thought the world revolved around me
I was wrong
But you can sing, sing along
And if you dance
Then dance with me.

TREASURE (WHATEVER HAPPENED TO PETE THE CHOP?)

Words & Music by U2

You sing,_____ Sing my,___ fav-'rite___ song._____

_____ You sing___ my fav-'rite song___

Mm,_____ mm._____

Play 4 times ad lib.

Smile_____ though_ your heart_ breaks in two.

Touch_____ me when can I be with you?

D.%. al Coda

427

⊕ *Coda*

4. If I could swim,____ I'd swim in cir-cles and ne-ver drown (If I did,) I'd drown with you. If____ I had____ e-nough____ of____ my____ life,____ it would be, be-cause I had-n't en-ough___ of you___(Then) I would die.

Play 3 times ad lib.

Die,_____ die,_____ die,_____ die.____

Verse 2:
If I should die
I couldn't tell the world how I felt about you
And I'd like more time
To describe the feeling when
I feel you in my arms
Take you in my hand
How could I let you go?
Somebody save me
Somebody save me from myself.

Verse 3:
I like good times
But the better they are
The better the chance they will go wrong
You sing my favourite song
You sing my favourite song.

TRIP THROUGH YOUR WIRES

Words & Music by U2

thirs - ty_____ and you wet_ my_ lips._____

You,_____ I'm wait - ing for_____ you._____

You,_____ you set my de - sire,_____ I trip through your

wi - res._____ Whoa, yeah!

Play 4 times

Play 4 times

Harmonica   Guitar

I_ was bro-ken, bent_ out of shape,_ I_ was na-ked in the clothes you made._

Lips were dry,___ throat like_ rust,_ you gave me shel - ter from the heat and the dust._

TRYIN' TO THROW YOUR ARMS AROUND THE WORLD

Words & Music by U2

1. Six o'-clock in the morn-ing, you're the last to hear the warn-ing, you been
(Verses 2 & 3 see block lyric)

tryin' to throw your arms a-round the world. You been

fall-ing off the side-walk, your lips move but you can't talk,

To Coda

tryin' to throw your arms a-round the world. Gon-na

run to you, run to you, run to you; be still.

Gon-na run to you, run to you, run to you; wo-man, I

will. ___ Ah.___ ___ will. Yeah, I

dreamed that I___ saw Da-li with a su-per-mar-ket trol-ley; he was

tryin' to throw his arms a-round a girl.___ He took an op-en top bee-tle through the

eye of a nee-dle; he was tryin' to throw his arms___ a-round the world.___ I'm gon-na

run to you,___ run___ to you,___ run___ to you;___ wo-man___ be still.___

I'm gon-na run to you,___ run___ to you,___ run___ to you;___ oh,___ wo-man, I___

___ will. Oh. And you've just got-ta, you've just got-ta make the

best of it. Oh,_____ ooh,_____ ooh,___

D.%. al Coda

yeah,— yeah, yeah,—yeah, yeah,— yeah, yeah, yeah.

⊕ Coda

run to you,— run— to you,— run— to you,— I'm gon-na run to you,— run—to you,— run—

— to you,—— I'm gon-na run to you,— run— to you,— run— to you,— wo-man be

still, wo-man— be still,— be still,

wo-man—be still,— wo-man I—— will.————

Verse 2:
Sunrise like a nose-bleed, your head hurts and you can't breathe
You been tryin' to throw your arms around the world.
How far are you gonna go before you lose your way back home.
You been tryin' to throw your arms around the world.

Gonna run to you *etc.*

Verse 3:
Nothing much to say, I guess; just the same as all the rest
Been tryin' to throw your arms round the world.
And a woman needs a man like a fish needs a bicycle
When you're tryin' to throw your arms around the world.

I'm gonna run to you *etc.*

TWILIGHT

Words & Music by U2

Guitar

Twi - light.

Twi - light_____ lost__ my way Twi - light_____ can't find__ my way.__

Guitar and Bass

In the sha - dow,__ boy__ meets man,__ in the

sha - dow,__ boy__ meets man,__ in the sha - dow,__ boy__ meets man,__ in the

sha - dow,__ boy__ meets__ man.__

Guitar and Bass

Guitar solo ad lib.

Guitar solo ad lib.

Twi-light,   dark - ened day. Twi - light,   lost— my way.

Twi - light,   night— and day. Twi - light,

can't find— my way. *Guitar and Bass*   In the

sha - dow——   boy— meets man,— in the sha - dow,——   boy-

—— meets man,— in the sha - dow,——   boy— meets man,— in the

sha - dow,——   boy—— meets- man. *Guitar and Bass*

Play 5 times

Verse 2:
My body grows and grows
If frightens me, you know
The old man tried to walk me home
I thought he should have known.

438

TWO HEARTS BEAT AS ONE

Words & Music by U2

to the words— you— wan - na hear?—

Two hearts_____ beat as_____ one.—

Two hearts_____ beat as_____ one._____ Two—

1. hearts.

2. hearts. Beat on black, beat on white,

beat on an - y-thing, don't get it right. Beat on you, beat on me, beat

on love.—

D.%. al Coda

440

⊕ *Coda*

I try to spit it out, try to ex - plain the way I wan - na feel. Oh, yeah. Two hearts.

Well I can't stop to dance. May-be this is my last chance.

1. **2.**

And I said I I said don't stop to dance.

Verse 2:
I can't stop to dance
Honey, this is my last chance
I said, can't stop to dance
Maybe this is my last chance.

Verse 3:
I don't know
How to say what's got to be said
I don't know if it's black or white
There's others see it red
I don't get the answers right
I'll leave that to you
Is this love out of fashion
Or is it the time of year?
Are these words distraction
To the words you wanna hear?

TWO SHOTS OF HAPPY, ONE SHOT OF SAD

For Frank Sinatra

Words by Bono. Music by Bono & The Edge

Don't try to fi-gure out___ what we might have had.___

Just two shots of hap-py,___ one___ shot of sad.

1. I'm___ just a sing-er,___ some___ say a sin-ner,___
(Tag 2 see block lyric)

roll-ing the dice,___ not al-ways a win-ner.

To Coda

You_ say I've been luck-y,___ well hell, I___ made my own,___

not part of the crowd___ not feel-ing a - lone.___

2.
(Instrumental)

D.%. al Coda I

444

⊕ *Coda I*

then, af-ter you did it, you came cry-ing— for my— help.—

D.%%. al Coda ⊕⊕ II

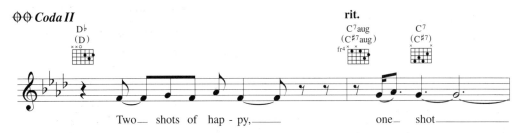

⊕⊕ *Coda II*

rit.

Two— shots of hap-py,—— one— shot————

of— sad.————

Verse 3:
Under pressure but not bent out of shape
Surrounded, we always found an escape.
Drove me to drink but hey, that's not all bad.
Two shots of happy, one shot of sad.

Guess I've been greedy all of my life
Greedy with my children, my lovers and my wife.
Greedy for the good things as well as the bad.
Two shots of happy, one shot of sad.

Tag 2:
Maybe it's just talk, saloon singing
The chairs are all stacked, the swingers stopped swinging.
You say I hurt you, you put the finger on yourself
Then, after you did it, you came crying for my help.

Verse 3:
Two shots of happy, one shot of sad.
I'm not complaining baby, I'm glad.
You call it compromise, well what's that?
Two shots of happy, one shot of sad.
Two shots of happy, one shot of sad.

ULTRA VIOLET (LIGHT MY WAY)
Words & Music by U2

Ba - by, ba - by, ba - by, light my way. Al-right now,

ba - by, ba - by, ba - by, light my way.

2. You bu-ry your trea - sure where it can't be found,

but your love is like a se-cret that's been passed a - round.

There is a si - lence that comes to a house where no one can sleep.

I guess it's the price of love; I know it's not cheap.

Oh, come on ba - by, ba - by, ba - by, light my way.

Oh, come on ba - by, ba - by, ba - by, light my way.

447

Oh, ah, _____ ah, _____ ah, _____

ah. _____

Ba - by, ba - by, ba - by, light my _____ way. _____

3. I _____ re -

- mem - ber _____ when we could sleep on _____ stones. _____

Now we lie _____ to-geth-er in whis-pers and _____ moans. _____

When I was all messed _____ up and I _____ heard op-era in _____ my head, _____

your _____ love _____ was a light bulb _____ hang-ing ov-er my bed. _____

448

UNTIL THE END OF THE WORLD
Words & Music by U2

Verse 2:
I took the money, I spiked your drink
You miss too much these days if you stop to think.
You led me on with those innocent eyes
You know I love the element of surprise.
In the garden I was playing the tart
I kissed your lips and broke your heart.
You, you were acting like it was the end of the world.

Verse 3:
In my dream, I was drowning the sorrows
But my sorrows they'd learned to swim
Surrounding me, going down on me
Spilling over the brim
Waves of regret and waves of joy.
I reached out for the one I tried to destroy.
You, you said you'd wait till the end of the world.

VAN DIEMEN'S LAND

Words by The Edge
Music by U2

Verse 2:
It's a bitter pill I swallow here
To be rent from one so dear.
We fought for justice and not for gain
But the magistrate sent me away.

Verse 3:
Now kings will rule and the poor will toil
And tear their hands as they tear the soil
But a day will come in this dawning age
When an honest man sees an honest wage.

Verse 4:
Hold me now, oh hold me now
Till this hour has gone around
And I'm gone on the rising tide
For to face Van Diemen's Land.

WAKE UP DEAD MAN

Words by Bono & The Edge
Music by U2

-fus-ing you.— Listen to the reed in the sax - o - phone,—

lis-ten ov-er the hum of the ra - di - o.— Listen ov - er sounds of

blades in ro - ta-tion, lis-ten through the traf-fic and cir-cu-la-tion. Lis-ten as hope and

peace try to rhyme, lis-ten ov-er march-ing bands play-ing out— their— time.

Wake up, wake up,— dead man.

Wake up,——— wake up,— dead man.

To Coda ⊕

3. Je - sus,— were you just a-round the cor - ner?— Did you think to try and

warn her?— Were you work-ing on some-thing— new?— If there's an

454

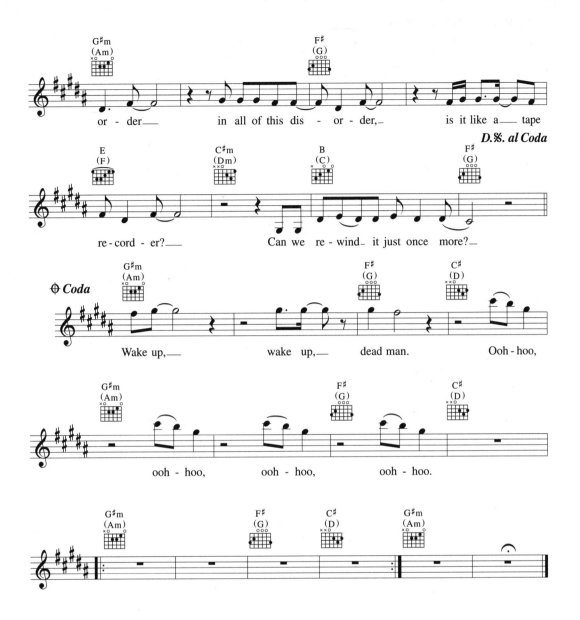

or - der____ in all of this dis - or - der,_ is it like a____ tape

D.%. al Coda

re - cord - er?____ Can we re - wind_ it just once more?_

⊕ *Coda*

Wake up,____ wake up,____ dead man. Ooh - hoo,

ooh - hoo, ooh - hoo, ooh - hoo.

Verse 2:
Jesus, I'm waiting here, boss
I know you're looking out for us
But maybe your hands aren't free.
Your Father, He made the world in seven
He's in charge of heaven.
Will you put a word in for me?

WALK TO THE WATER

Words & Music by U2

Drums   cont. sim. Bass   cont. sim.

1. (Spoken) She said it wasn't cold,

she left her coat at home that day.   She wore canvas shoes,   white canvas shoes.

Around her neck she wore a silver necklace.   "It was given to me by my father." she said.

"It was given to me."   She took the back way home   passed the lights at Summer Hill.

Turned left onto the North Strand and on,   on towards the sea. 2. He said he was an artist
(Verse 3 see block lyric)

but he really painted billboards in large capital letters.   In large capital letters.

He was telling jokes, nobody else would listen to him.

Walk, walk, walk to the wa-ter. Walk with— me a-

- while.— Walk, walk, walk to the wa-ter.

Walk with me in the light. 4. A room in the Royal Ho-tel

with sea fac-ing views.— A man with a suit-case

full of things he does-n't need.— I'm look-ing through your win-dow,

I'm walk-ing through your door-way. I'm on the out-side, let—

Verse 3:
I saw you that day, your lips of cherry red
Your legs were crossed, your arms wide open
Your hair was coloured gold
And like a field of corn
You were blown by the wind
You were blown by the wind.

WHEN LOVE COMES TO TOWN

Words by Bono
Music by U2

Guitar Solo

— came to town.— When love— —comes to town— I'm gon-na jump that train. When love— comes to town— I'm gon-na catch that flame._ May-be I was wrong— to ev-er let you down,— but I did what I did— be-fore love———— came to town.

Guitar Solo

When love——   Guitar Solo

D.%. al Coda *Play 5 times*

Coda

— — came to town.   Guitar Solo

Repeat to fade

Verse 2:
Used to make love under a red sunset
I was making promises I was soon to forget.
She was pale as the lace of her wedding gown
But I left her standing before love came to town.
I ran into a juke-joint when I heard a guitar scream
The notes were turning blue, I was dazed and in a dream.
As the music played I saw my life turn around
That was the day before love came to town.

Verse 3:
I was there when they crucified my Lord
I held the scabbard when the soldier drew his sword.
I threw the dice when they pierced his side
But I've seen love conquer the great divide.
When love comes to town, *etc.*

WHERE DID IT ALL GO WRONG?

Words by Bono
Music by U2

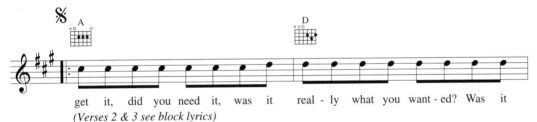

1. Did you get it, did you need it, was it real-ly what you want-ed? Was it

(Verses 2 & 3 see block lyrics)

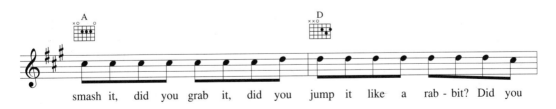

good in the sun, did you real-ly have some fun? Did you

smash it, did you grab it, did you jump it like a rab-bit? Did you

walk, did you run? Did you slap it, did you come? And

D.%. al Coda

Coda

3. Did you

Play 4 times
ad lib.

Repeat to fade

Verse 2:

Did you crack it, did you taunt it
Was it really what you wanted?
Did you burn in the sun
Or are you burning for someone?
Did you shoot it, did you stab it
Did you chase it like a rabbit?
Did you walk, did you run
Did you come in at number one?

I know that you do
Put your soul in the song
But now it's sinking like you
Where did it all go wrong?

Verse 3:

Did you drown it, did you clown it
Would you really have gone down on it?
Did you clean it, clean it up
Did you rub it, did you soap?
Did you screen it, did you ream it
Did you ruin it, did you feed it
Is it warm in the sun
With your ear in her tongue?

WHERE THE STREETS HAVE NO NAME
Words & Music by U2

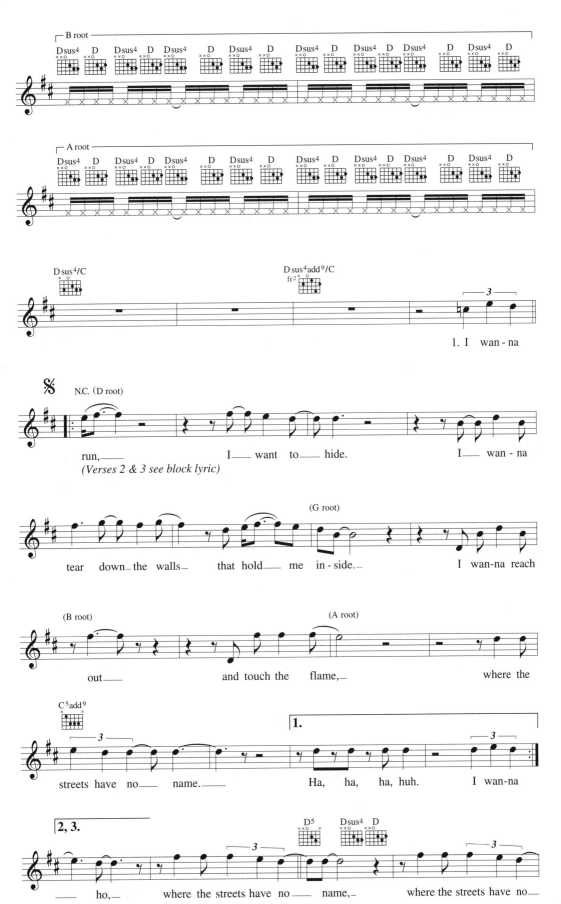

(Verses 2 & 3 see block lyric)

wind. Oh,___ I___ go there,___ I go there with___ you;

(it's all I can___ do.) *Guitar*

Verse 2:
I wanna feel sunlight on my face.
I see the dust-cloud disappear without a trace.
I wanna take shelter from the poison rain
Where the streets have no name.

Verse 3:
The city's a flood, and our love turns to rust.
We're beaten and blown by the wind, trampled in dust.
I'll show you a place high on a desert plain
Where the streets have no name.

WHO'S GONNA RIDE YOUR WILD HORSES

Words & Music by U2

Guitar

1. You're dan-

- ger - ous,— 'cos you're hon - est. You're dan-

(Verses 2 & 3 see block lyric)

- ger - ous,— you don't know what you want.— Well you left

— my heart— emp - ty as a va - cant lot, for

an - y— spi - rit to haunt.

1.

2, 3.

Hey,— hey,— sha - la la,— hey,— hey. 2. You're an ac - — sha la - la.

Verse 2:
You're an accident waiting to happen
You're a piece of glass left there on a beach.
Well you tell me things I know you're not supposed to
Then you leave me just out of reach.

Verse 3:
Well you stole it 'cos I needed the cash
And you killed it 'cos I needed revenge.
Well you lied to me 'cos I asked you to.
Baby, can we still be friends?

WIRE

Words & Music by U2

1. In - no - cent — and in —— a sense — I —— am ——

(Verse 2 see block lyric)

guil-ty of a crime that's now in hand.

Such a nice day to throw your life a - way.

Such a nice day, to let it go.

2° only

Em⁷

Ah

Ah

C#m⁷ D sus² C#m⁷ D sus²

Cold in his eyes, I can't be - lieve it.

C#m⁷ D sus² *To Coda* ⊕ Em⁷

Cold in his heart and soul. Heart and—

soul.

Cold____ man,__ such a cold____ heart,__ such a

cold____ man,__ I watch you__ tear your - self__ a - part._____

So lay me down, my soul__ to keep.____

So____ lay__ me down,__ the long - est____ sleep.

Oh,_____ the__ long - est sleep.

D.%. al Coda

⊕ *Coda*

cold____ fire._____ Cold__ in his heart__ and

soul.

Don't do ___ it, d-d-don't do it ___

Don't do ___ it d-d-don't do it   A - ny - time ___   you're

on   the   earth...   kiss him.   *Vocal ad lib.*

You can't take me, that's right but you can keep me going.

It's so white trash if you've got the cash. A car-toon cut out, a cut-throat let out.

Look I'm on your side, we're both right.___ Hey, I'm al - right Jack, just don't pig - gy - back.

I'm no dope, I'll give you hope. Here's ___ the rope. Here's the rope... Now swing on it.

Verse 2:
In I come and out you go you get
Here we are again, now place your bets
Is this the time, the time to win or lose?
Is this the time, the time to choose?
Ah, ah.
Cold in his eyes, I can't believe it
So deep inside a cold fire.

WITH A SHOUT (JERUSALEM)

Words & Music by U2

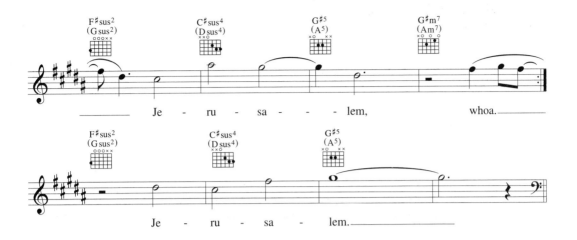

Je - ru - sa - - - lem, whoa.___

Je - ru - sa - lem.___

Bass Guitar

Shout,___ shout,___ with a shout, whoa,___

___ shout,___ with a shout.___

Play 5 times

Bass Guitar

Verse 2:
I want to go, to the foot of Mount Zion
To the foot of He who made me see
To the side of a hill blood was spilt
We were filled with a love
And we're going to be there again, Jerusalem.

WITH OR WITHOUT YOU

Words & Music by U2

1. See the stone set in your eyes, see the thorn twist in your side. I wait for you.

2. Sleight of hand and twist of fate, on a bed of nails she makes me wait.
(Verse 3 see block lyric)

And I wait.... with-out you, with or with-out you, with or with-out you.

Verse 3:
Through the storm, we reach the shore
You gave it all but I want more
And I'm waiting for you…

With or without you *etc.*

ZOO STATION

Words & Music by U2

to - be a - live. I'm rea - dy,— I'm rea - dy for the

1. push. In the cool of the night,———— in the

warmth of the breeze,———— I'll be crawl - ing a - round————

on my hands— and knees.————————

She's just down the line, Zoo Sta - tion. Got to

make it on time, oh, Zoo Sta - tion. 2. I'm

2. crush. Zoo Sta - tion,————

Zoo Sta - tion.————————

make it on time,— make it on time,— make it on time,—

make it on time.— I'm gon-na be there for your love.

It's al - right, don't wor - ry,

I'm gon-na be there. Just two stops down the line, don't

wor-ry. Just a stop down the line.

Guitar

Verse 2:
I'm ready, I'm ready for the gridlock
I'm ready to take it to the street.
Ready for the shuffle, ready for the deal
Ready to let go of the steering wheel.
I'm ready, ready for the crush.

ZOOROPA

Words by Bono
Music by U2

Tune guitar down a semitone

D.%%. al Coda ⊕⊕

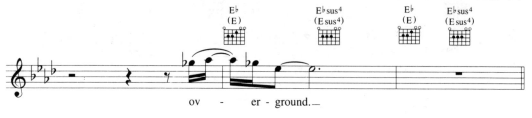

ov - er - ground. —

She's gon - na dream — up the world — she wants to live in, she's gon - na

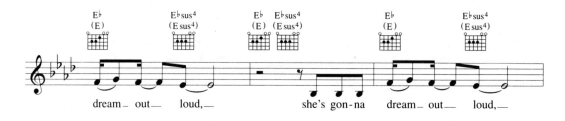

dream — out — loud, — she's gon - na dream — out — loud, —

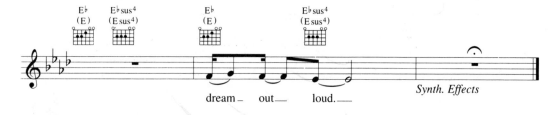

dream — out — loud. —   Synth. Effects

Verse 2:
Zooropa, a bluer kind of white
Zooropa, it could be yours tonight.
We're mild and green and squeaky clean.

Verse 3:
Zooropa, better by design
Zooropa, fly the friendly skies.
Through the appliance of science
We've got that ring of confidence.

Verse 5:
And I have no religion
And I don't know what's what
And I don't know the limit
The limit of what we got.

(Zooropa) Don't worry baby, *etc.*

Verse 6:
No particular place names
No particular song
I've been hiding
What am I hiding from?

(Zooropa) Don't worry, baby, it's gonna be alright
(Zooropa) Uncertainty can be a guiding light.
(Zooropa) I hear voices, ridiculous voices in the slipstream.
(Zooropa) Let's go, let's go overground.
(Zooropa) Take your head out of the mud, baby.